One Sacred Effort

One Sacred Effort
THE COOPERATIVE PROGRAM OF SOUTHERN BAPTISTS

CHAD OWEN BRAND AND DAVID E. HANKINS

BROADMAN
& HOLMAN
PUBLISHERS
NASHVILLE, TENNESSEE

ISBN: 978–0–8054–3163-6

Published by Broadman & Holman Publishers
Nashville, Tennessee

Dewey Decimal Classification: 286.132
Subject Heading: COOPERATIVE PROGRAM
SOUTHERN BAPTIST CONVENTION—MISSIONS
CHURCH FINANCE

6 7 8 9 10 11 12 13   12 11 10 09

We dedicate this volume to

the churches of the Southern Baptist Convention.

Contents

Foreword

It has been over twenty years since the Stewardship Commission of the Southern Baptist Convention published *Cooperation: The Baptist Way to a Lost World* by Cecil and Susan Ray. Simply the passing of time would justify another book about the Cooperative Program. Most things need updating every couple of decades. But the last twenty years have been unusually significant for Southern Baptists, making it even more critical for this subject to be addressed now. In these years Southern Baptists have reaffirmed their convictions about the truthfulness and trustworthiness of the Bible. The Convention has experienced the conservative resurgence, an almost unheard-of return to orthodoxy by a modern denomination. The SBC and its institutions are now at the forefront of conservative theology and historic Christianity in our culture.

The 1990s also saw the largest restructuring in Southern Baptist history. Guided by the Convention-adopted "Covenant for a New Century," the SBC was refitted for ministry in the twenty-first century. A part of that restructuring dissolved the Stewardship Commission and returned the assignment for Cooperative Program promotion to the SBC Executive Committee.

We have prepared ourselves theologically and organizationally for the new century. It is time for Southern Baptists to turn our attention once again to the cooperative missions methodology that has been so useful in the past. There are disturbing clouds on the horizon. Some of our brethren have begun to exhibit tendencies of "independents" that undervalue cooperation among Baptists. Others seem to be returning to the cumbersome and hapless "societal" methods of mission support from a century ago. Still others are redefining the Cooperative Program in ways that harm its basic unifying tenets.

I am convinced our Lord providentially gave the plan called "Co-Operative Program" to our Southern Baptist leaders in the 1920s. The mark of God's Spirit has been upon it. It has been used to propel Southern Baptists, by God's grace, into great kingdom advance. I am also convinced the Cooperative Program remains the most effective vehicle for carrying out our work.

Southern Baptists must be prepared to wage old battles on new battlefields. Will we who have recaptured theological soundness also recapture the spirit of cooperation? Are we not compelled to ask the question, "Shall we devote ourselves to cooperation as did our forefathers?" Conservative theology has triumphed in our day in our return to the biblical faith of our fathers. Shall we hold just as fiercely to the cooperative methodology instituted by those upon whose shoulders we stand? God has poured out his greatest blessings upon the Southern Baptist Convention when the churches, large and small, have cooperated for the sake of world missions and God's glory.

Chad Brand and David Hankins have prepared a book that tells who Southern Baptists are and how they get their work done. *One Sacred Effort* not only celebrates the Cooperative Program's great accomplishments of the past but champions its usefulness for the future. As you read, you will discover the pivotal role of the Cooperative Program. The Executive Committee's ministry assignment reads in part: "Assist churches through the promotion of cooperative giving." I am glad to have this informed study in our arsenal as we challenge a new generation of Baptist leaders to cooperate in the growth of the kingdom of God.

Sincerely in Jesus' name,

Morris H. Chapman
President and Chief Executive Officer
The Executive Committee of the Southern Baptist Convention
Nashville, Tennessee

Preface

The authors of this book are Baptists. We wish that to be clear at the outset, and we make no apology for it. It is not that we are arrogant about the fact, as if to say that only Baptists are genuine Christians or that the only churches in the world are Baptist churches. That is not it at all. We recognize that there are many Christians in the world who wear labels other than the "Baptist" one. At the same time it is our conviction that the Baptist understanding of the nature of the church is consistent with the teachings of Scripture, and, even more than that, we believe the Baptist interpretation is the understanding *most* consistent with the New Testament on this issue. That is, after all, why we are and remain Baptists! If we believed that, say, the Presbyterian or the Episcopal interpretations were closer to Scripture, we would be compelled to abandon the Baptist heritage in favor of one more biblical.

This book, then, is a book by Baptists, and it is primarily for Baptists as well, though we also believe non-Baptists will find helpful materials within these pages. At the very least, non-Baptists who read this book will be better informed (we hope) about the nature of Baptist hermeneutics and theology. Baptist people, though, will especially find this volume helpful, that is, if we (David and Chad) are able to present this material in the way we feel called to do. And, even more specifically, Southern Baptists will benefit most since the book is specifically a treatment of the way in which Southern Baptists have understood church and have attempted to implement a strategy for carrying out ministry together on a scale wider than that of the local congregation.

But we encourage Baptists from other traditions, such as American Baptists, Baptist General Conference, Freewill Baptists, even Two-Seed-in-the-Spirit Predestinarian Baptists (if there are still any of them around) to pick up this volume and find out whether there is any help in it for their understanding of their heritage and of the call of God on their churches for ministry.

The writing of this volume has been a shared task. Chad has concentrated on the biblical, theological, and historical backgrounds of Southern Baptists and the Cooperative Program (chapters 1–5 and most of 9). David has concentrated on the current practices and future possibilities for Southern Baptists and the Cooperative Program (chapters 6–8, 10–12, and part of chapter 9). Each has offered counsel to the other in all of the content. We have been aided by colleagues, assistants, and students in the preparation of the book, for which we are especially grateful. Debra Bledsoe, administrative assistant to the vice president for the Cooperative Program at the SBC Executive Committee, provided invaluable research and technical assistance for David. Carl Lee Bean, research assistant to Chad at The Southern Baptist Theological Seminary, provided invaluable aid in locating sources. We are also grateful to Travis Kerns, Ph.D. student at Southern Seminary, for preparing the index to this volume.

We are dedicating this volume to the churches of the Southern Baptist Convention. I (Chad) would like to give special thanks and consideration to those churches and pastors that influenced me during my formative years of childhood and early adulthood. Calvary Baptist Church, Nevada, Missouri; Commerce City Baptist Church, Commerce City, Colorado; and Central Baptist Church, Aurora, Colorado, were a major part of my life right through college graduation. Pastors Lon Brown, Jim Gerrish, Tom Pratt, and Carey Miller each put a stamp on me that will always be there. Those churches and pastors helped give me a passion for God and for the church that has never gone away, and I will always be grateful to them.

I (David) have been nourished, nurtured, called, and challenged by Baptist congregations. My childhood church, Grove Temple Baptist Church, Dallas, Texas, not only licensed and ordained me; it gave me my first opportunity to pastor. The people in that small congregation believed in me and helped prepare me for later service with Oak Crest Baptist Church in Dallas, First Baptist Church, Commerce, Texas, and Trinity Baptist Church, Lake Charles, Louisiana. Each of these churches made a difference in my life and, more importantly, have advanced the kingdom of God through their decades of faithful service.

We also would like to thank those we work with on our "day jobs." I (Chad) am thankful to the students, faculty, trustees, and administration of The Southern Baptist Theological Seminary. Each of those contributed in one way or another to this book. Pride of place goes to President R. Albert Mohler and deans Russell Moore and Jimmy Scroggins. They provided encouragement and advice at crucial moments in the production of this volume. Dr. Russell Moore and Dr. Gregory Wills also read parts of this manuscript and made helpful suggestions. The book is better for their suggestions and would be even better had I paid more attention to their recommendations.

I also want to thank the members of Mt. Zion Baptist Church in Elizabethtown, Kentucky, where I have served as interim pastor for the past two years. They are wonderful, mission-minded Baptist people, and they have blessed me immeasurably during the time I have been writing my part of this book. As always, my special thanks go to my lovely bride, Tina, for her patience and support during my absence at the computer.

I (David) have just transitioned from the SBC Executive Committee to the assignment of executive director, Louisiana Baptist Convention. I am thankful to Morris Chapman and the Executive Committee for the opportunity to launch some initiatives, such as this book, to remind Baptists of the great tool for missions that God has given us in the Cooperative Program. I am looking forward to a renewed sense of partnership among churches, associations, state conventions, and the Southern Baptist Convention as we seek to serve Jesus and his kingdom.

A Baptist from a prior generation said, "The Cooperative Program is the glue that holds Southern Baptists together and helps them stick to the Great Commission." May a new generation embrace the principles and practices of cooperative missions embodied in Southern Baptists' Cooperative Program!

Introduction

There was a crisis brewing in the 1920s. Resources were needed to get the work done. An inadequate collection and distribution system was impeding progress. Projects that had great potential were started, only to fail because supply could not keep pace with demand. People began to look for a solution. A visionary plan was suggested. Some said it was impossible—too much red tape, too many obstacles to overcome, and too much political resistance.

For sure, the plan was complicated and risky. It would involve setting aside regional differences. It would require a willingness to work together. Intensive strategic planning, financial sacrifice, and years of hard work would be necessary. But the struggle was worth it. It was a resounding success.

So it was that President Franklin D. Roosevelt spoke at the celebration of this great success—"the completion of the greatest dam in the world, rising 726 feet above the bed-rock of the river, and altering the geography of a whole region." The Hoover Dam was a reality. The president remarked on the problems that precipitated the construction of the dam:

> As an unregulated river, the Colorado added little of value
> to the region this dam serves. When in flood the river was a
> threatening torrent. In the dry months of the years it shrank to
> a trickling stream. For a generation the people of the Imperial
> Valley had lived in the shadow of disaster from this river which
> provided their livelihood, and which is the foundation of their
> hopes for themselves and their children. Every spring they
> awaited with dread the coming of a flood, and at the end of
> nearly every summer they feared a shortage of water would
> destroy their crops.[1]

He went on to remind the audience: "Ten years ago the place where we are gathered was an unpeopled, forbidding desert. In the bottom of a gloomy canyon, whose precipitous walls rose to a height of more than a thousand feet, flowed a turbulent, dangerous river. The mountains on either side of the canyon were difficult of access with neither road nor trail, and their rocks were protected by neither trees nor grass from the blazing heat of the sun."[2]

But then the work began. Through cooperation and sacrifice and labor, the vast unmanageable resources were harnessed for strategic and significant achievement:

What has been accomplished on the Colorado in working out
such a scheme of distribution is inspiring to the whole country.
Through the cooperation of the States whose people depend
upon this river, and of the Federal Government which is concerned in the general welfare, there is being constructed a system of distributive works and of laws and practices which will
insure to the millions of people who now dwell in this basin,
and the millions of others who will come to dwell here in future
generations, a just, safe, and permanent system of water rights.[3]

The construction of the Hoover Dam was a great solution to a great problem!

There was another crisis brewing in the 1920s. It, too, was a problem of inadequate support for critical endeavors. A people called Southern Baptists were seeking to fulfill the dream they had articulated eighty years before at the founding of the Southern Baptist Convention. In 1845, they had created their Convention for the purpose of "organizing a plan for eliciting, combining, and directing the energies of the whole denomination in one sacred effort, for the propagation of the Gospel."[4] Yet their effort was being hampered by lack of resources.

The number of denominational enterprises and institutions was growing. Each needed support. Each went about seeking the contributions of the congregations. Sunday by Sunday, fund-raisers from seminaries and colleges, orphanages and hospitals, mission boards and benevolent organizations fanned out among the churches asking the faithful for help. Some fared better than others. Some years were better than others. The gifts were distributed unevenly. The more popular, or perhaps the swifter, received a disproportionate share of the offerings. Other important ministries went begging. It was feast and famine . . . or, like the Colorado River, flood and drought!

Furthermore, the costs of raising the money sometimes approached 50 percent of the proceeds. The churches were beleaguered by an endless stream of denominational representatives needing "pulpit time" to make their appeals. On the whole the results were discouraging. No one was being adequately supported. Too much energy was being expended in the process by both the ministries and the churches. The growth of stewardship in the denomination was not keeping pace with the growth of obligation and opportunity. The Convention had a dream of "eliciting, combining, and directing the energies of the whole denomination," but they had no mechanism to make the dream come true.

Until 1925. Then the Southern Baptist Convention meeting in Memphis, Tennessee, adopted a recommendation from its Future Program Commission, chaired by Louisiana pastor M. E. Dodd, creating the "Co-Operative Program of Southern Baptists." What the Hoover Dam became to agriculture and industry in the southwestern United States, the Cooperative Program would become to Southern Baptists. The same superlative evaluation made by President Roosevelt concerning the Hoover Dam is fitting for the Cooperative Program. An undependable, uneven, inadequate support system of the past was fashioned into the Cooperative Program.

The Future Program Commission remarked at its inception: "The very difficulties which we have encountered and the testing time through which we have passed have revealed to the denomination its dependable financial resources and strength and have demonstrated beyond question the wisdom and the necessity of the co-operative plan of Southern Baptists."[5]

Decades later Albert McClellan, longtime Baptist leader with the Executive Committee (1949–1980) of the Southern Baptist Convention, would call the Cooperative Program "a significant fulfillment of the *one sacred effort* clause of the 1845 Constitution."[6] This ministry-support tool caused Southern Baptists to come of age as a denomination. It allowed them, by God's grace, to accomplish the world-changing mission they had embarked upon eight decades earlier.

This book attempts to tell the story of the Cooperative Program—its history, its functions, its accomplishments, and its future. To give appropriate context, the first two chapters go before and behind the Cooperative Program to examine the biblical, theological, and historical foundations that define Southern Baptists and differentiate them from other Christian and non-Christian religious groups. The next chapter examines "inter-congregational cooperation" from a theological perspective. Chapter 4 surveys united missionary endeavors throughout church history from the early church to the early days of the Southern Baptist Convention and is followed by a chapter on the creation of the Cooperative Program.

Turning from theology and history, chapters 6 and 7 describe the current organizational and decision-making processes of Southern Baptist life. The next three chapters outline the various convention structures, ministries, institutions, and relationships. Contemporary issues impacting the Cooperative Program are the subject of chapter 11. This leads to a discussion of the future of the Cooperative Program in the twelfth chapter. We conclude with a challenge to you, the reader, to advance the kingdom of God through cooperative missions.

For the first eighty years of their existence, Southern Baptists yearned for a way to make "one sacred effort" a reality. For the last eighty years, the Cooperative Program has served that role. If the Lord tarries, what will the next eighty years produce as Southern Baptists continue in "one sacred effort for the propagation of the gospel"?

Chapter One

The Baptist Vision

What is a Baptist church, and just what makes it different from other evangelical Christian bodies? That is a fair question, and in answering it, we would wish to make several things clear. One is that Baptists share many things in common with other Christian bodies or, to use the traditional terminology, other denominations. I want to say some things about that in a bit, but it also occurs to me that some who read this book may need to have another, more fundamental, matter clarified first. The various historically orthodox Christian denominations share many things in common, but it is important to distinguish them from other major religious traditions in the world.

RELIGIONS, DENOMINATIONS, AND CULTS

Sometimes you will hear a person say something like, "Well, there are many religions in the world, Baptist, Presbyterian, Mormon, Buddhist, Muslim, and so on, but they are all working at the same goal." I know that people say this because I have heard it myself. There is a terminological misunderstanding here—and probably a lot more than that! For one thing, we need to understand that Baptists and Presbyterians are not representative of different "religions," or at least we hope not. Historically orthodox Baptists and historically orthodox Presbyterians are members of the same religion—the Christian faith. They belong, rather, to different denominational traditions within the broader Christian heritage.

What about the reference to the "Mormon" in the quotation above? Here again, we must make a distinction. Though Mormons are connected to Christianity because they emphasize the importance of Jesus, they have not been part of what I call the "historically orthodox tradition." There is no space to go into that in detail here, but suffice it to say that the tradition which came from Joseph Smith and Brigham Young and which dominated Mormonism right into the twenty-first century held defective views on the doctrines of the Trinity, Christ, Scripture, creation, salvation, and the future life of believers. For this reason the Church of Jesus Christ of Latter-day Saints has generally been considered to be a Christian "cult." Some consider this language to be offensive, but in its original usage it was intended only to show that Mormonism is not part of the historic Christian faith, and for most of their history, Mormons were all too happy to agree with that assessment.[1]

That leaves the Buddhists and the Muslims. Guess what? Naming them different "religions" is correct. These are worldview and religious traditions that are outside the pale of Christianity, even though in the case of Islam there are some historical connections between the two. The important thing to keep in mind here is the difference between denomination, cult, and religion.

Let's return to the point I made earlier that the historically orthodox Christian denominations share certain things in common. I am going to make a case for Baptist distinctives through the rest of this chapter, but I want first to recognize our common commitments. One thing will become clear to the person who attempts to examine these shared beliefs and practices, and that is that we don't have the same amount in common with every single Christian denomination. Baptists are very close in ideology and practice to some Christian groups, but far—and sometimes very far—away from others.

It should come as no surprise, for instance, that Baptists stand at a distance from Roman Catholicism. This does not mean that there are no commonalities between the two. Roman Catholics affirm the Trinity, they hold an orthodox view of Christ, they believe in the inspiration of the Bible, and they look forward to the Second Coming of Jesus—at least those are their historic views. Historic Baptists would agree with all of this. The major differences between Baptists and Roman Catholics have to do with Catholic *additions* and *alterations*.

Roman Catholics have *added* to the faith in several ways. They have added to the biblical canon, that is, the list of accepted biblical books, by including the deuterocanonical writings in their Bible. The Catholic Bible officially includes material, sometimes known as the Apocrypha, which the Protestant Reformers rejected as having no place within the Bible itself. The Catholic heritage has also added doctrines which do not appear to have any substantial support from Scripture, such as the elaborate set of ideas related to the doctrine of Mary, the notion that the Pope is the heir of Peter, and that in certain circumstances he speaks infallibly, and the belief that there are seven sacraments rather than two New Testament ordinances. There are other examples, but these are the most significant additions.

Along with that the Catholic faith has *altered* biblical teaching at certain points. For instance, in direct contradiction to the teaching of Paul, the Catholic Church has argued against justification by faith alone and has contended instead for justification by faith plus works. An entailment of that doctrine is that no one can ever be assured of his or her salvation since the works might cease at some point and cause a person to lose the standing of righteousness before God. This is also a violation of the Bible's contention that true believers will never fall finally away.

The Catholic heritage has also altered the understanding of leadership in the church. As we will demonstrate later, the Bible teaches that there are two offices in a church—pastors (or elders, overseers) and deacons. But the Catholic Church has introduced a third office—that of the bishop, an office that is distinct from the pastoral office. These bishops became territorial governors of the church, ruled over by an increasingly complex hierarchy, and led from the top by a senior bishop, the "Vicar of Christ." As we will show, this understanding of church government stands in contrast with the biblical model.

The Roman Catholic view of the sacraments is also problematic. This church teaches that the sacraments become effective unto salvation in the lives of church members because the Catholic Church itself has been given the keys to the kingdom, and that kingdom door is opened up when the Catholic Church administers the sacraments. Though Rome has softened its general attitude toward Christians outside its fellowship since the 1960s, this doctrine of the keys essentially makes membership in the Roman Church a necessity for salvation.[2]

Roman Catholicism then represents a tradition within the Christian heritage but one which historically Baptists have found seriously problematic. Many early Baptists even considered the Roman Catholic Church and its earthly leader, the Pope, to be a representative of the "Harlot of

Babylon" from Revelation 18. Though such language is rare today, most conservative Baptists recognize the vast differences between many of their convictions and those of the Catholic Church. That is not to say that Roman Catholicism is just a bad apple all around. Many evangelicals were appreciative of Pope John Paul II and his stand for the value and the dignity of life and his passionate opposition to the evils of statist communism. In this respect they felt he was more of an ally than liberals or even moderates within their own denominations. But they also recognized that the theological and churchly differences were very large.

If Roman Catholicism differs from the Baptist heritage because it has added to and altered the faith at certain points, Baptist differences with, say, Presbyterianism, have more to do with varying *interpretations* of several important issues. Presbyterianism was born in the fires of the Reformation of the sixteenth century and was, thus, the offspring of the work of John Calvin, John Knox, and other men committed to the reform of the churches at this time. Presbyterians and continental Reformed Christians were committed to a high view of God's sovereignty in providence and in salvation, and they were also committed to a specific form of church government that became known as Presbyterianism.

When specific, self-conscious Baptist congregations began to sprout in Holland and England in the early 1600s, these Baptists identified theologically, in part, with various of the reforming groups of the time. By the late 1600s most of these Baptists held many views in common with the Presbyterians, including their belief in God's sovereignty in salvation.[3] Yet they differed with the Presbyterians at several points, most especially on their understanding of baptism and church government. These of course are important issues, and in many ways they define the Baptist heritage over against other Protestant theological systems, but the gap that separates Baptists from Presbyterians is not nearly as large as the gap that separates them from Catholics.[4]

IDENTIFYING THE BAPTIST IDENTITY

Just what is the "Baptist Vision"? In answering this question we must do more than simply address Baptist distinctives, but we can also do less than describe everything that is important to the Baptist heritage. We must do more than simply discuss those issues which are unique to Baptists, because in some cases the way in which Baptists articulate a point they have in common with other Christians takes on a whole new dimension of emphasis for Baptists due to some issues which are unique to them. This will become clear in just a bit when I talk about the authority of Scripture though that is not the only such issue. At the same time this discussion does not have to cover everything that is important to the Baptist theological/churchly heritage. To do that would require an entire volume itself, and that is simply outside our focus in this book.[5] It is possible, however, to sketch a brief outline of just what it is that has made and ought to continue to make Baptists tick.

Evangelicalism—Baptists under the Authority of Scripture

One major debate among Baptists today is over just which item ought to be first in a list such as this. Some Baptists contend that the fundamental Baptist principle is *soul liberty* or *freedom of conscience* and that one or the other of those items ought to have priority in any discussion of Baptist identity.[6] Those doctrines in some form are very important to a study of Baptist identity, and we will discuss them later in this chapter, but I am quite convinced that they ought not to stand in first place. There are several reasons the authority of Scripture should have pride of place in any discussion of the Baptist vision.

First, methodologically, Scripture needs to be considered since it is the interpretation of biblical texts that shapes our doctrinal convictions in the first place. We do not get our doctrines from our own experiences, culture, or our own intuitions but from the Bible. This is a Baptist conviction although it is not a Baptist distinctive. Most evangelical systematic theology texts begin, often after some introductory considerations, by examining, as the first doctrine for consideration, the doctrine of Scripture. This is one of those areas where Baptists share a common commitment with conservative Presbyterians, Methodists, and others.

This can be easily seen among Baptist systematic theologies by glancing briefly at the recent works of Millard Erickson, James Leo Garrett, Wayne Grudem, and Dale Moody.[7] These men represent different trends within Baptist life, but they all begin their studies of systematic theology with a discussion of introductory matters, sometimes called prolegomena, and then proceed immediately to an examination of the doctrine of Scripture. This is also the case with Baptist theologians of previous generations, such as J. L. Dagg, James P. Boyce, W. T. Conner, E. Y. Mullins, and even with an older, premodern systematic theology volume by John Gill.[8] They all discuss Scripture first.

Interestingly, though, this tendency is not unanimous. Recent Baptist theologian Stanley Grenz, in his 1994 volume, *Theology for the Community of God*, does not discuss the doctrine of Scripture until about halfway through the book.[9] One might not be surprised at that, though, once one learns that he was attempting to pioneer a new approach to systematic theology. Grenz did not ground himself exclusively on Scripture as the rock of truth but also incorporated history and culture as "sources" of theology.[10] So with the exception of the unusual approach of someone like Stanley Grenz, the general tendency among most Baptist writing theologians is to discuss Scripture first.[11]

A second reason for placing Scripture first is that when the early Baptists made a case for their own distinctive convictions on matters of baptism, the government of the church, the nature of the Lord's Supper, the importance of regenerate church membership, religious liberty, and other key Baptist ideas, they made their case from Scripture. In other words, everything else we will discuss in this chapter arises from biblical exegesis, and the early Baptists, especially, had to engage in such exegesis to articulate their distance from Anglican, Catholic, and non-Baptist Protestant doctrine. These ideas do not arise simply from the Christian observation of the nature of religious experience, modern culture, or the history of the church but rather from the Bible. It makes sense, then, to give pride of place to the doctrine of Scripture.

What is the *Baptist* view of Scripture? There is no one single such position since Baptists in recent decades have been all over the theological spectrum, from conservative to liberal, and it is in reference to this doctrine, perhaps more than any other, that one's position on the theological spectrum makes itself clear. Historically, though, Baptists have held that the Bible is God-breathed Scripture, the Word of God written, and that it is the sufficient rule of faith and practice.

As the God-breathed Word (2 Tim. 3:16), the Bible has God as its author. It comes to us by the instrumentality of human writers whose personalities are seen in the various stylistic peculiarities associated with each one. But this human mark has not marred the reliability or the divine authority of the text. Though the human writers have their own distinctives, their very language, though freely chosen by them, communicates exactly what God wanted us to have. This can be seen in such texts as Galatians 3:16, where Paul makes his theological case based on the fact that the word *offspring* (seed) used in Genesis 12:7 is in the singular, not the plural. Apparently the choice of words and, in this case, the fact that the term was singular and not plural makes his point.

Revelation is essentially verbal. Mystics and liberals have often argued that revelation bypasses the verbal and is at heart experiential and ineffable. But this is not a biblical notion. Historic, evangelical Baptists affirm that Paul's implicit trust in the words and even the form of these words from previous revelation is a lesson to us that we should give such implicit deference to the text as well.

This God-breathed Word is the very Word of God. This has become a disputed point. One will hear some people say that the Bible is not the Word of God since Jesus is the Word of God. Gordon Kaufman, well-known liberal theologian of our time, has stated, "Since it is Jesus Christ, and not the biblical words, that is God's revelation, it is misleading to refer to the text itself as inspired."[12] Similarly, Baptist writer Morris Ashcraft argued that we must make a significant distinction between Christ as authority on the one hand and the church and Scripture as mere "immediate authorities" on the other hand, with the role of Scripture being the preservation and communication "of the mighty acts of God."[13] He thus argues that the Bible is *only* the record of God's revelation, and that revelation is personal, not propositional or cognitive in nature. These are false distinctions.

Southern Baptist Seminary president E. Y. Mullins stated the matter clearly in 1923: "The Bible is God's revelation of himself through men moved by the Holy Spirit."[14] Mullins went on in this presentation to identify a number of doctrines which this "revelation" teaches, such as the deity of Christ, the bodily resurrection, the Second Coming, and so on, making clear that he did not mean that this "revelation" was merely personal, but that it was also cognitive. The real question of course is, What does the Bible itself teach about these questions? The answer is not hard to come by.

The Bible teaches that Christ is the very Word of God (John 1:1; Heb. 1:1–3). As such he is the conduit through whom God speaks to human beings and the great and final Word of revelation. Scripture is also the Word of God. We have already noted Paul's statement in 2 Timothy 3:16 that all Scripture is given by God's breath, this *Scripture* being a reference to all of the Old Testament revelation. It is all from God, all breathed by him, "the product of the creative breath of God."[15] Paul noted that the Old Testament Scriptures were given to Israel as the very Word of God (Rom. 3:2). God often spoke through the prophets (Jer. 37:2; Zech. 7:7, 12) so that what the prophet spoke, God spoke (Hag. 1:12). These are God's words. These words are not merely the *record* of revelation, though the Bible does record revelation. The point is that the Bible is not just a record of revelation. Too many biblical texts actually claim for themselves, or for other texts, that they constitute the very Word of God. Paul claims that his teachings are not from men but are in words taught by the Holy Spirit (1 Cor. 2:13). Peter endorses this claim when he refers to Paul's letters as "Scriptures" (2 Pet. 3:16). Christ is the Word of God, but we would have no reliable and infallibly trustworthy testimony to him without the New Testament text that is also God's Word.

This is not an either-or—either Christ being the Word of God or the Bible being such—but a both-and. Revelation, in other words, is *both* personal and propositional (or cognitive). Some moderate Baptists have attempted to drive a wedge between the relational teaching in Scripture and its cognitive or teaching function, but there is no sound reason to accept such distinctions.[16] Revelation "conveys both information and relationship."[17] Contrary to the position of Robison James, that the Bible is the Word of God *relationally* but not *descriptively*, we would argue that it is both of these things.[18] When the text tells us that God has established a day when he will judge the world, that is information (Acts 17:30–31). And in that very information we are told that this judgment will be through the appointed man, Christ, so that the intent of this message is to confront us with the person of Jesus. To say, then, that revelation is personal but not propositional is simply another false dichotomy. It is conceptual, personal, and spiritual.

Because the Bible is given by the very breath of God, it is a trustworthy word. We can approach it with confidence. Baptists have traditionally held that we can and ought to approach the Bible with a hermeneutic of trust, not a hermeneutic of suspicion. We give the Bible the benefit of the doubt. We do so because history has demonstrated that the Spirit of God has used the Word of God over the centuries to change people's lives. We also trust it because it has survived many attempts to prove it unworthy.

Even Baptists have joined in the attempt to criticize the trust-worthiness of Scripture. Baptist theologian William Rainey Harper published a lecture in 1894 in which he alleged that the apparent history of

Israel found in the Old Testament was not to be accepted as true. He still wanted to argue for the spiritual significance of the accounts, while denying their historicity. Southern Baptist Seminary Professor A. T. Robertson responded that such an argument was unacceptable. He asked, "Does it help matters to call the narratives inspired, after you have denied their historical reality?"[19]

A similar issue arose in 1961 with the publication of Ralph Elliott's book, *The Message of Genesis*. In that volume the Midwestern Seminary professor questioned the historicity of the accounts related to the creation of Adam and Eve and the fall of man, as well as narrative accounts throughout the book of Genesis. In his estimation these accounts were just parables, not historical records.[20] The ensuing events eventually led to his dismissal from Midwestern Baptist Seminary. This was one of the key issues that placed concerns in the minds of many Southern Baptists that their seminaries might have some faculty members whose theology was left of center.

In 1992 Elliott wrote a follow-up book which depicted his perspective on what had happened and continued to happen in SBC life in the following decades. He noted that a professor at another Southern Baptist seminary at the time had urged him to use "doublespeak." This professor apparently told Elliott that he held the same views as Elliott but that Elliott got into trouble because he would not resort to such subterfuge.[21] This has not been the historic view of Baptists, who have generally considered the Bible to be trustworthy, "from Genesis to maps."

This is also a *sufficient* word from God. In the passage we have cited several times, 2 Timothy 3:16–17, Paul noted that this God-breathed Word is given "so that the man of God may be complete, equipped for every good work." Believers must neither add to nor take away from God's Word (Rev. 22:18–19).[22] Claims to later cognitive revelations on the part of mystics, cult founders, and some in Pentecostal/charismatic circles are to be rejected.[23] This does not mean that God does not "speak" to his children in personal communion or that he does not make his presence known in their lives. What it does mean is that when someone states that God has given him some new teaching that is not found in the Bible, such as the claims made by Joseph Smith and other "prophets" in the Latter-day Saints movement, we are to reject such claims.

If an individual church or a teacher claims that he has the infallible and necessary interpretation of truth or of a set of texts, we are to steer clear of such persons. In the same way, if someone makes a prediction about some future event and states that all persons in the world are bound to accept his word as Scripture and order their lives accordingly, we are not to obey or fear such a person. The Word of God is sufficient as a guide for faith and practice—that is, for theology and life. As the psalmist said, "Great peace have those who love your law; nothing can make them stumble" (Ps. 119:165 NRSV).

Because the Bible is God's Word written, because it gives to us great truths about God and our salvation, because it communicates the person of our Savior to us, and because it is our sufficient guide, we can fly to it with intrinsic trust. Here is the gist of it. For most of Baptist history, Baptist preachers and teachers have gone to the Bible with absolutely implicit confidence in its truthfulness, its power to convey the truth about salvation, and its ability to change lives when preached or taught in the power of the Holy Spirit. Though Baptist scholars have examined the historical context, literary form, and textual history of Scripture with great thoroughness, the majority tradition of Baptists has been to bow before the teaching of God's Word, seeing it as the very teaching of God himself. They have refused to drive a wedge between Christ and the Bible, since Christ himself made clear that he did not come to question the Word of God in any fashion (Matt. 5:17–20) and since all we know objectively about Jesus we know from the Scriptures.

Voluntaryism—Baptists Affirming Individual Accountability Before God

Roman Catholic and early traditional Reformation churches (Presbyterian, Anglican, Lutheran) shared in common the notion that the church was in some sense the obverse of the state. The European political orders in the sixteenth century mandated all children to be baptized into the official church, and the confluence of church and state created enormous implications in such areas as religious freedom, theological integrity, and the importance and place of evangelism. Martin Luther had launched a theological revolution in 1517 with the posting of the Ninety-five Theses, thus inaugurating a public debate which would eventually lead to a political and churchly rift in Europe.

At the heart of Luther's reforms was his conviction that justification was by faith alone, not by faith plus works or by the sacraments of the church. This meant that one's personal salvation was no longer determined by one's relationship to the system of churches, priests, bishops, and rites connected ultimately to Rome, but was instead a personal matter between oneself and God. From this conviction, and from Scripture, Luther concluded that all believers were priests before God, and he further concluded that local churches ought to have a degree of autonomy from one another and not be ruled over by magisterial bishops or by a pope in a distant European city.

By the "priesthood of all believers," Luther did not mean that all Christians possess the "right of private judgment." Rather, what he meant was that "every Christian is someone else's priest, and we are all priests to one another."[24] In other words, God has made all believers into what Luther called "one cake" and made them all responsible for service to one another.

At this point Baptists ought to be getting a little excited and wondering why they have not heard of Luther the Baptist. Well, there are a lot of reasons, among which that Luther continued the practice of infant baptism, and that he saw no need to make church and state separate spheres of authority. In other words, Luther, though he seemed quite radical in 1517 when he started the debate, eventually proved to be something of a conservative reformer. He was conservative in the sense that he wanted to conserve much of what had been in place through the centuries of the Holy Roman Empire and much of traditional Catholic practice as well—such as the Mass—but he wanted to do so without Rome, without the Pope and the bishops, and without some of the worst theological aberrations introduced during the years of Catholic domination.

This is a case of conserving something that ought to have been eliminated. And Luther was called on the carpet for this by many of the younger reformers, men who once considered him their hero but who eventually called him names like "Dr. Pussyfoot" and "Professor Easychair."

Another tradition within the Reformation did see the need for a reformation more deep-rooted and radical; this collection of groups has been called the Radical Reformation by later historians. They were radical reformers in the sense that they wanted to take the Reformation right down to the very "root" of the problem as they saw it. That root was the linking of church and state in an organic fashion that resulted in the political order and the religious order being simply two sides of the same coin.

The other tradition in the Reformation, the so-called Magisterial Reformation, was magisterial in the sense that it linked the process of reform to a collaboration between the church and the magistracy. So, for instance, Luther pleaded the assistance of the German nobles in carrying out his work. Ulrich Zwingli worked hand-in-hand with the town council in Zurich to reform the churches in that city, and John Calvin was essentially hired by the Little Council of Geneva to reform church and city so they could effectively be free from Roman Catholic influence and taxation. The net result in all of these situations was that the authority of the two spheres, in one way or another, bled one over into the other. In Zurich this meant that the rising group of Anabaptists was liable to persecution since it constituted a separate faction within the church. If church and state are simply different ways of speaking of the same clientele, heresy or "schism" can easily be construed as treason or sedition. By 1527 Anabaptists in Zurich were being executed.

The Radical Reformers basically made two points: "We don't need the state's help in reforming the churches, and we don't appreciate the state's interference in the way we decide to do church." Menno Simons, a German Anabaptist, argued that he was actually completing the Reformation initiated by Luther. Luther's battle cry was, "Justification by faith alone!" In other words, a person's standing before God as righteous was occasioned by his belief in the gospel of Jesus Christ, not by virtue of his having been baptized as an infant into a church or by having had the sacraments administered to him. Menno asked the simple question to the Lutheran tradition, "If a person is justified in a personal act of faith, ought not that decision of faith be a prerequisite to one's being a member of Christ's body, the church?" In other words, only the justified are part of "the body of Christ." Why then is membership in a local body of believers something that is disconnected from the act of believing faith?

Menno was arguing for regenerate church membership and believer's baptism, and he was arguing for them based on the notion that justification by faith entailed a *voluntaryism*, and that this voluntaryism, if it is valid, ought to be applied to one's doctrine of the church. These Anabaptist congregations were "voluntary religious associations" gathered by a "freely and comprehensively conceived evangel, sealed by believer's baptism."[25]

It is important to understand this point, since one of the current disputes in Baptist thought lies right here in understanding the nature of freedom in the Baptist heritage. E. Glenn Hinson in his essay, "Baptists and 'Evangelicals'—There Is a Difference," makes this fundamental error, one which sets everything else in his argument askew. He contends that the principle of "voluntarism," which he identifies with soul competency, is the most important axiom of religion and the most important component of the free church (Baptistic) tradition: "E. Y. Mullins, for instance, correctly discerned that voluntarism or soul competency underlay the other axioms of religion despite the fact that Baptists may not often have alluded to it."[26]

The problem here, as James Leo Garrett pointed out in his response to Hinson, is that *voluntarism* is a philosophical concept which refers to "any theory that regards the will rather than the intellect as the fundamental agency or principle," whereas *voluntaryism* is "the principle or system of supporting churches, schools, etc., by voluntary contributions or aid, independently of the state."[27]

Is Hinson's understanding of the liberty principle in line with Scripture or with some philosophical notion of freedom that is at least in part alien to the Bible? Under the general heading of *voluntaryism*, a variety of key issues for Baptists must be addressed: soul competency, the priesthood of all Christians, religious liberty, believer's baptism, and regenerate church membership. The final two items are related to the notion of voluntaryism, but they are also connected to the distinct Baptist conception of the church as a congregational body and so will be considered under the next heading. We will examine these one by one.

Soul competency has become a banner issue in recent decades for some Baptists. They argue that conservatives, especially in the Southern Baptist Convention, have abandoned many of the convictions about freedom of the conscience that have been basic to Baptist belief since the earliest days of the English and American Baptist heritage. As we have already noted, some have argued that soul competency is the central Baptist distinctive. Among those who make this argument, at least some of them actually are making a case for a philosophical/theological understanding of freedom that is not the historic Baptist understanding of freedom of conscience.

James Dunn argues that soul competency, which he equates with the image of God in humans (*imago Dei*), has a further entailment. "Whatever else the classical teaching of *imago Dei* means, it means at least that persons, made by God, can respond to their Creator."[28] But this is not what Baptists have historically meant by soul competency. Garrett concludes that Glenn Hinson is doing much the same in his exposition of soul competency, that is, arguing that such an understanding of freedom is to be identified with the General (Arminian) Baptist understanding of free will. Garrett points out, though, that there is a difference between freedom as the capacity to choose between alternatives and freedom as the capacity to consistently choose the good or the righteous. One might have the former but not necessarily the latter.[29]

Since Particular Baptists such as John Bunyan and Baptists clearly opposed to Arminian beliefs such as Isaac Backus have also been at the forefront of defending freedom of conscience, soul competency has not historically been just the notion that all persons have the capacity in themselves to respond to grace. Those who so argue are probably revealing their own position on one major Baptist debate, but they are not helping the cause of clarification on this issue.

How then do we define soul competency? In light of the fact that Scripture teaches that unbelievers cannot understand the things of God and will not accept them (1 Cor. 2:14), it is important for us to reconsider the approach held by Dunn and Hinson. It seems that the notion of soul competency as they have described it is simply not a biblical notion. Perhaps instead, in some sense we should speak of soul "incompetence."[30] But if we understand the term in its historic usage, it can still be useful, even if it may not be the best phrase. Baptists have historically held that soul competency means that every individual is responsible to God, that each soul is alone before God, so that "neither parent nor government, nor church, may usurp the prerogative of God as the Lord of the conscience."[31]

In other words, this is the fundamental idea that all persons have an accountability to God and stand before him with a duty to repent of their sins and believe the gospel, since they will all stand before him in judgment to be judged according to the deeds done in the body. William Rone asserted that the New Testament teaches that "each soul is directly responsible to God and will eventually have to give an account to God."[32] This is what George W. Truett apparently had in mind in 1939 when he said, "For any person or institution to dare to come between the soul and God is a blasphemous impertinence."[33] Soul competency then is the conviction that each person will give an account to God and that no entity in this age has the right or the power to intervene between each person and God. The difficulty we face in using the term is that it has been co-opted for so many other purposes that it may have lost some of its value in clarifying the conversation. We might consider replacing the phrase with something like "soul accountability."

Related to but distinct from soul competency is the biblical teaching on the priesthood of all believers. This doctrine is taught specifically in passages such as 1 Peter 2:9 and Revelation 1:6. It is also a logical corollary of the truth that all persons are spiritually gifted and placed within congregations to serve and minister to the needs of one another. The doctrine of the priesthood of all Christians addresses a different issue than does soul competency. Some Baptist theologians, such as Fisher Humphreys, have sought to make these two issues identical.[34] But they are not. Soul competency pertains to all persons, not merely to Christians, but the priesthood concept refers only to Christians.[35]

The idea in the biblical texts we have referenced is that there is no hierarchy of priests who stand above individual Christians or who stand at the top of organizations or denominations to mediate effective ministry or who have the task of performing ministry exclusively to the exclusion of the others. The priesthood of all believers means that the church has an every-member ministry, with each Christian having an obligation to serve others within the church. Ministry is not to be consigned only into the hands of a relatively few "professionals."

This does not mean, of course, that churches ought not to have overseers; the Bible is clear that this is an important office in the church and that it carries a certain amount of authority (1 Tim. 3:1–7). That authority, though, does not mean that it is the overseers who exclusively do the work of ministry. At one level they are overseers, who ought to be obeyed (Heb. 13:7–17), while at another level they are fellow priests, joining with others in carrying out the work of ministry (Eph. 4:11–16). More on this later.

It is also important to note that the doctrine of priesthood does not imply that all persons can either do as they please or believe as they please. There was an elderly man in a church I pastored some years ago who came to me one day, complaining that someone had been taking verses out of the Bible. He said, "I remember my mother reading a verse to me as a child, but it is no longer in the Bible. The verse said, 'Every tub ought to sit on its own bottom.' What happened to that verse?"

Well, I can imagine a mother, wanting her son to do his chores like everyone else in the family, quoting such a "verse" with the authority of God behind it! But neither the notion nor the verse is there. The concept of priesthood has been used by some people to argue that doctrinal standards do not apply in Baptist life since everyone, as a priest, can make his own standards. Timothy George is again helpful here. "Among other things, [this doctrine] means rather, 'As a priest in a covenanted community of believers, I must be alert to keep my congregation from departing from the "faith once for all delivered to the saints'" (Jude 3)."[36] The doctrine of priesthood means that a community of believer-priests, in submission to the Word of God and under the authority of Jesus Christ, has the right to define for itself its interpretation of Scripture and its doctrinal perimeters, under the leadership of the Holy Spirit.[37]

This does not in any way negate the possibility that such communities might adopt confessions of faith. Baptists have been writing and adopting confessions of faith since their earliest days and using those confessions as both guidelines for belief and as tests for employment. Some of the same voices that have spoken loudly for the doctrine of the priesthood of all believers have also spoken loudly in favor of confessions of faith. James P. Boyce required subscription to the Abstract of Principles of all faculty who taught at Southern Seminary, writing, "It is no hardship to those who teach here, to be called upon to sign declaration of their principles, for there are fields of usefulness open elsewhere to every man, and none need accept your call who cannot conscientiously sign your formulary."[38] The priesthood of believers "has more to do with the Christian's service than with his status."[39]

Baptists have also been champions of religious liberty. In 1612 Thomas Helwys wrote *The Mystery of Iniquity*, calling upon the British crown to grant full religious freedom to dissidents, including the Baptists. Later in the century John Bunyan railed on the issue from prison, jailed because he refused to be quiet about his convictions. In America first Roger Williams and later Isaac Backus and John Leland called on colonial and state governments and eventually the new federal government to ensure the rights of those outside the state churches to be able to live their lives in peace and to abolish taxes which existed for the sake of established churches. Backus, writing in the 1770s in Massachusetts, used a brilliant strategy, by arguing that state taxes to support the Congregational Church constituted taxation without representation since many citizens were not members of that church and so had no say in its operations. You might imagine that such an argument would strike a chord in Boston, just freshly finished with a little party over some tea!

What is sometimes forgotten in this discussion is that these men did not argue for religious liberty based on Enlightenment principles of human dignity and the "rights of man." This was not even William Wallace crying out "Freedom!" from the gallows. Rather, these were men who argued for religious liberty from Scripture, from the doctrine of justification by faith, from their conviction that since the church ought to be a believers' church, no one's decision about membership in that church ought to be coerced. "There ought to be no union of church and state and no form of coercion in society in matters of faith. The union of church and state means either a coercion or discriminatory advantages. Either is an enemy of freedom and equality."[40]

Pastor and Baptist editor Curtis Lee Laws made the same point in his famous sermon, "The Fiery Furnace and Soul Liberty," when he called upon the visiting archbishop of Canterbury to cease his attempts to bring all British Christians under his rule by crushing nonconformity in 1902.[41]

Religious liberty ought to be guaranteed to all, but this does not necessarily entail a refusal to engage the state and political issues by Baptist people. As Philip Hamburger has shown in a recent study on this issue, the notion of absolute separation of church and state was not a view held by early Baptists and not even by many in the nineteenth century. They held, rather, to a more accommodationist perspective.[42] The sermons of Keach, Gill, and Spurgeon often called on the state to live up to the moral standards of the Bible. Isaac Backus supported prayers to be held by the Massachusetts legislature. Even liberal Harry Emerson Fosdick urged the federal government in the direction of prohibition based on the Bible's injunctions against drunkenness.

But in recent years Baptist moderates have attempted to argue that Baptists have historically not sought the aid of government to support moral causes or to have any engagement in religion at all. This is simply not the case historically. Baptists have supported the notion that there ought to be no coercion in matters of faith, that there should be no established church, and that people ought to be free to hold matters of faith conviction with no fear of government reprisal. But this does not mean the evacuation of the "public square" by Christians.

Congregationalism—Local Church Autonomy under Christ

There are two issues which are related to the Baptist belief that one's relationship to Christ and admission to the church are voluntaryistic that are also connected to the Baptist understanding of the church as a congregational entity, and so we will consider them (believer's baptism and regenerate church membership) under this heading of the local church under Christ. As the early church developed and spread across the Greco-Roman world, it took on several characteristics which in one way or another facilitated its development. Some of these were healthy and were in the tradition of biblical teaching, but others took early Christianity, to one degree or another, some distance from its roots in Scripture. Though the evidence from the New Testament seems clear that the role of overseer (bishop) and that of elder or pastor were identical roles, by the early second century those positions began to diverge in at least some locations in early Christianity.[43]

This development was not monolithic at first. The document known as the Didache, written somewhere between the end of the first century and the middle of the second, still pictures the position of bishop as identical to that of pastor. On the other hand, the Letters of Ignatius, probably written about AD 107, indicate that, at least in Antioch, the bishop had become a sort of pastor over the pastors.

Throughout the second century and beyond, the bishops took on an increasingly important and distinct role. In the empire-wide persecutions of the third century, the bishops became even more important since many pastors were martyred, and churches turned increasingly to the regional bishops to help them in such times of distress. In the middle of the third century, the Carthaginian bishop, Cyprian, began to develop a thorough-going theology of the role of the bishop in the church and of the role of the church in the salvation of its members. Bishops, in Cyprian's view, were rulers over the churches and pastors under their guidance and were themselves the representatives of the church. "The church is in the bishop and the bishop is in the church," he argued, indicating that bishops represent the whole church and that the bishops are to maintain their positions as those who direct and lead the church.

Cyprian also argued that "there is no salvation outside the church" and that "one cannot have God as his father who does not have the church as his mother." This then sealed the role of the bishops as those who ultimately were the dispensers of salvation to others who sought salvation within the church. As time went by, this trend deepened, until by the fifth century the church was dominated by a hierarchy of bishops that was ruled from the top by the bishop of Rome. Local congregations were led by elders/priests, but these persons were increasingly under the jurisdiction of others outside the local church itself. This Catholic "Episcopal" system was never completely universal, since dissident groups have always existed alongside the main tradition, but until the Reformation it dominated by far the vast majority of churches.[44]

The Reformation of the sixteenth century brought many changes to the churches of Europe, but these were not always changes in church order. The Anglican Church, for instance, retained rule by bishops though it rejected the bishop of Rome as its supreme head. But some reform groups moved away from Episcopacy. Lutherans retained bishops but altered their function and gave greater authority to local congregations.

In Geneva, Calvin, following the example of some other Continental Swiss and German Reformers, developed a rudimentary form of what would later be known as Presbyterianism. This style of polity probably harks back to second-century approaches that never quite developed fully, but under Calvin and later Knox, it consisted of each congregation being under the direction of a body of elders appointed by the church. Some of these elders then served on a "higher" body, known in Geneva as the "consistory," but in later developments generally called a "presbytery." That higher body had the responsibility to adopt confessions of faith, exercise discipline, settle disputes between churches, and ordain pastors and elders. These decisions then were mandated, with one level of authority or another, down to the churches.

Presbyterianism then is a system which is not just a top-down rule by bishops, since representation is sent up the line from the local congregations, but it is still a system in which final authority in some matters rests with a body outside of or higher than the local congregation. Both the Episcopal and the Presbyterial systems of polity practice the baptism of infants to bring them within the church's membership, though they tend to disagree among themselves about the exact significance of such baptism.

Baptists and other free-church Christians have objected to both of these systems of church governance. They have argued that the New Testament presents a picture of congregational polity, local church autonomy, and believers' church baptism and membership. Baptists believe that the Bible presents a clear, though not precisely detailed, picture of these issues, and they also argue that faithfulness to the text of Scripture requires us, as good disciples, to follow that model. Each local congregation in the New Testament is led by pastors (or elders, overseers), served by deacons, and exercises its own ministry functions within the congregation. Aside from the apostles, who died by the end of the first century, no other persons have authority over local churches that are not under their pastoral direction.

Baptists thus hold that local churches are congregationally led, autonomous bodies, under the direct headship and authority of Jesus

Christ. They reject the notion, often promoted by advocates of Episcopacy, that we ought to accept the evolutionary developments that took place in early church history since those developments brought about greater efficiency. Efficiency, Baptists have held, is no substitute for faithfulness to the text of Scripture. They have further argued that, while it may not be of the essence of true Christianity to have a New Testament ecclesiology, it is certainly to the well-being of the church that it strives to follow the biblical pattern.

Two key aspects to the following of this pattern are a belief in regenerate church membership and the practice of believer's baptism. These notions are found directly in Scripture and are also logical corollaries to the Reformation principle of justification by faith alone. There is no evidence in Scripture of any infant baptism, but Jesus did clearly teach that disciples, once made, are to be baptized (Matt. 28:19–20), and we have the clear testimony of the early church in Acts that new converts were to be baptized (Acts 2:38). Believer's baptism thus appears clearly to be the only New Testament model.

Also, since the early church only "added" (Acts 2:41) to its number those who were being converted and baptized, and since only those who have been Spirit-baptized are in the body of Christ (1 Cor. 12:13), Baptists have held that church membership is open only to those who have consciously placed faith in the Lord Jesus and who have followed him in baptism.

Missionism—the Great Commission as the Church's Great Task

Gospel proclamation has always been a central theme of Baptist life. Among the children and stepchildren of the Reformation tradition in the seventeenth century, Baptists, with their believers' church convictions, were in the vanguard of those who emphasized the necessity of hot-hearted evangelism. Not every one of them was fully evangelical, and not every one was heartily evangelistic, but with the Baptists who have been the most spiritually virile and theologically healthy, three tenets have fueled their passion for souls.

They were convinced, first, that God was mighty unto salvation and that he certainly could and would save a great multitude since he is sovereign in his providential guidance and in his saving authority. Second, they affirmed that evangelism entailed the articulation of doctrinal verities, "gospel truths," which sinners must understand and affirm if they are to be unbelievers no longer. Theological truth claims are not subordinate to the gospel but are integrally wedded to it. Third, their conviction about the believers' church fostered a doctrine of voluntaryism which impelled them to issue the unlimited call to all to repent and believe the gospel message. They were convinced that only that person who actually repents and believes will be saved, regardless of his relationship to a territorial or state church.

These advocates of the believers' church saw themselves, thus, finishing what Luther started with his ringing cry of *sola fide*. Later in this volume we will examine the efforts of Baptists to carry the gospel to the world, but at this point I would simply like to make a few observations about how Baptists have considered and have called for the passionate employment of the call to evangelism.

Baptists have certainly held differing views on the nature of salvation, with some holding to more of a conviction that God is sovereign in salvation while others gave greater emphasis to man's role in the process. But when they have been at their best, both sides have been deeply committed to gospel proclamation. God is sovereign, gospel truths must be proclaimed, and men and women must be urged to repent and believe the gospel.

For some, this might be a *non sequitur*. If God is sovereign, then why must we command sinners to repent and come to Christ in evangelism? Both Arminians, like Daniel Taylor, and hyper-Calvinists, like James Wells of London, concluded that the two ideas do not go together. Taylor contended with Andrew Fuller that his commitment to evangelism did not comport with his theology, while Wells lambasted Charles Spurgeon for not being faithful to the heritage of English Baptist preaching.

Both the Arminian and the hyper-Calvinist were out of their league, though. When Spurgeon was asked how he reconciled the sovereignty of God and the responsibility of man, he replied, "I never reconcile friends." Both men, and a host of others like them, were assured that their one task was to follow the Bible faithfully. If Scripture said that God is preeminent, powerful, and awesome in salvation, then they affirmed that. If it also said that men and women must repent and believe the gospel, then they affirmed that with the conviction that the two thoughts are not ultimately in conflict.

Andrew Fuller's great book, *The Gospel of Christ Worthy of All Acceptation*, constitutes his statement about the importance of hot-hearted evangelism. He argues from Scripture that faith in Christ is commanded in the Bible of the unconverted, that every person must approve of God's revelation, that lack of faith in Christ is a sin, that God punishes unbelief, and that faith is a duty even as other spiritual and moral dispositions are duties. "It is the duty of ministers not only to exhort their carnal auditors to believe in Jesus Christ for the salvation of their souls; but it is at our peril to exhort them to anything short of it."[45] Few were more passionate about evangelism than Keach: "Faithful ministers art willing to spend their Lives to win Souls to Christ, yea, to die upon the spot to save one poor Sinner."[46] God is sovereign, but sinners must repent. Preachers must command them to do so with passion and fervor.

Many of the best representatives of this tradition have been Baptists in America. Isaac Backus and Shubal Stearns were mighty evangelists, both influenced by the luminaries of the Great Awakening, such as Whitefield and Edwards. The same emphasis can be found in the preaching of the Baptist from the South, Basil Manly Sr. Manly was firmly convinced of the sovereign power of God to save: "My brethren, however mysterious and incomprehensible it may be, that God chose a poor sinner like me—freely chose me, loved me, redeemed me, called me, justified me, and will glorify me—I will rejoice in the truth, and thank him for his free grace! O, where is boasting then?"[47] This same preacher was also fervent and passionate in exhorting sinners to repent and believe the gospel. "Manly believed that in order to convict a sinner of his lost state, 'you must isolate him—you must make him feel alone'; the preacher must make each person feel that they [sic] were 'the person directly addressed, and concerned in what is said,' so that the message might be personalized and internalized."[48]

Adoniram Judson gave his life and so much more to carry the light of the world to the darkness of superstition and moral decadence in India and Burma two centuries ago. James P. Boyce invited D. L. Moody to erect his tabernacle on seminary property in Louisville in 1887, while seminary professors and students served as counselors for the Moody "crusade" in the river city that year. There were certainly doctrinal differences between Moody and Boyce but not on the matter of the free and passionate offer of the gospel to all who would hear it. On that they were of one heart and mind.

Many of us who have grown up Southern Baptist have spent the better part of our lives in the search for the lost and the proclamation of the gospel to them. This of course is not an end in itself; it is part of the larger task that lies before every true Christian—live your life every day to the glory of God! But the passionate proclamation of the gospel to a lost and dying world is one necessary component of the life that does glorify God. It is impossible to imagine that one could so glorify him without being evangelistic. It is our prayer that this commitment will never dim for the people who call themselves "Baptist."

In this chapter we have attempted to mark out some of the key issues that make Baptists who they are. Some of these are unique to the free-church tradition, some are not. But all of these are vital to the Baptist vision. In the next chapter we will attempt to spell out in more detail just what the New Testament perspective is on the nature of the local church.

Chapter Two

The New Testament Church:

Charismatic, Congregational, Centrifugal

W e Baptists have long held that we ought to do church in the same way the New Testament churches did, or at least as close as we can get. Perhaps I should rephrase that to say that we ought to do church the way the New Testament churches were *supposed* to do it. It is not hard to find churches right there in the Bible that were out of whack in a lot of different ways. We just have the conviction that whenever the Bible *prescribes* that the community of faith should act, believe, or behave in a certain way, we are mandated to do just that.

In addition, we recognize that sometimes the Bible *describes* patterns of action and belief that we are to follow, even when it does not actually command them. Of course, in these situations more care, discretion, and wisdom are needed to discern just when a description is also intended to be a prescription. We must do the best we can in such situations, while recognizing that we may not always agree about which is which. The point I am making, though, is that Baptists believe the Bible contains specific teachings about how we ought to organize and govern the church and also about how we ought to effect its mission and ministries.

THE NEW TESTAMENT CHURCH AS CHARISMATIC

Even before his ascension to the Father, the Lord Jesus told his disciples that their witness would extend to the ends of the earth (Acts 1:8). The rest of the book of Acts and indeed the entire rest of the New Testament spell out the remarkable way in which this process was begun by the first generation of Christians. Jesus intended his followers to do ministry in a centrifugal manner—they were to be a whirlwind of power and activity, energized by the Holy Spirit, sending the gospel message out as far as possible as quickly as possible. He also instructed them by his Spirit to gather together as communities of faith in order fully to carry out the mission he left them to do. In this chapter we will examine these issues so that we can have a clear idea about just what the task is that lies before us.

The Holy Spirit and the Church

The first stage in the process for the early disciples, of course, was to receive power for the great task. "Wait in Jerusalem," the Lord told his disciples, "until you receive power from on high." This was not some kind of psychological maneuver on Jesus' part, as if to say that power only comes upon those who sit and wait for it. No. God had purposed to give the gift of the Holy Spirit to his people as the confirmation and fulfillment of the New Covenant. Old Testament saints had received empowerment by the Spirit for carrying out certain tasks of ministry, but the Spirit was not given to them as a permanent possession. For Jesus and the New Covenant disciples it would be very different.

In the opening pages of the Gospels, we find that Jesus has received the gift of the Spirit without measure.[1] Jesus was conceived in the womb of his mother by the activity of the Holy Spirit (Luke 1:35). He was anointed with the Spirit at his baptism (Matt. 3:16). He was led by the Spirit in the wilderness and was successful in resisting Satan and in not succumbing to despair at the lack of food, in total contrast to both Adam in the garden and Israel under Moses (Luke 4:1). By the power of the Spirit, he succeeded where they failed. In his inaugural message at the synagogue in Nazareth, he read from the place in Isaiah where the prophet predicted the coming of one who would be able truly to say, "The Spirit of the Lord is on Me, because he has anointed Me to preach" (Luke 4:18–19; Isa. 61:1).

In the power of the Spirit, Jesus cast out demons and did mighty works (Matt. 12:28–29). Through the Spirit he offered himself to death that he might atone for the sins of those who had always lived by the flesh and not by the Spirit (Heb. 9:14). And by the Spirit he was raised from the dead to demonstrate to any who still doubted that this was the Spirit-anointed divine Messiah of Old Testament expectation (Rom. 1:4; Heb. 1:3–8).[2]

One thing is abundantly clear from these texts: The divine Messiah was the one on whom the Spirit was poured out without measure. Another truth is about to become clear: This new age would see this same Holy Spirit poured out on "all flesh." In Acts chapter 2 we find the disciples gathered in an upper room waiting for the "promise of the Father." On the day of Pentecost that promise is fulfilled as God pours out the Holy Spirit on the disciples of Jesus. Peter makes the point clearly that the risen and exalted Lord Jesus is the one who has poured out his Spirit on those who repent and believe this gospel (Acts 2:33–38).[3]

Why Pentecost? Pentecost is the New Testament name for the Old Testament Feast of Firstfruits (or Weeks; see Lev. 23:15–17). That feast took place fifty days after Passover, and it was a celebration of the first gift of the harvest. Israelites were to take the first of the harvest, bring it to the temple in Jerusalem, and offer it there to the priests. This was an act of faith. It was Israel saying to God, "We trust you that you will grant to us the full harvest of our crops. We are so confident in you that we are willing to take the first items we harvest and give them to you rather than horde them up for ourselves, 'just in case.'"

By the time of Jesus, the Feast of Pentecost had taken on another significance. The rabbis had calculated that the Feast of Weeks fell on the day that Israel arrived at Mt. Sinai to receive the law from God. Pentecost, then, held a twofold significance—as a testimony to God's faithfulness in giving the law to his people and as a reaffirmation on the part of the people of the importance of covenant faithfulness *to* and trust *in* God. After receiving the baptism in the Spirit, Peter preached to the gathered crowd. He made the major claim that Jesus is the Lord who has now poured out his Spirit on all flesh, and Peter then offered three other observations.

First, this gift of the Spirit is the sign of the second climax of God's covenant with his people (Jer. 31:31–33). Once God wrote his law on tablets of stone with his own finger; now he is writing his law on the hearts of his people.

Second, whereas the original Feast of Firstfruits consisted of Israel giving gifts to God, this new covenant celebration consists of God giving the gracious gift of his Spirit to all mankind, the Spirit who is himself the "firstfruits" of salvation for all who believe (Rom. 8:23). In other words, the concept of the law as *merely* an external guide has been replaced by the new teaching and the new reality that the Spirit writes the law permanently on the hearts of God's people. This does not mean that the law has been abolished (Matt. 5:17–20). Rather, it means that the law has come full circle since Paul informs us that Christ condemned sin in the flesh "in order that the law's requirement would be accomplished in us who do not walk according to the flesh but according to the Spirit" (Rom. 8:4). It might be better to state that the gift of the Spirit on this occasion shows both the continuity with God's purposes in giving the law and at the same time the contrast with the misunderstanding of the law as the essential means of salvation.

Third, as Moses had ascended the mountain and received the law from God, so Christ has ascended on high and poured out his Spirit on his church (John 16:5–11; Acts 1:8). The ascent is followed by the gift.[4] The result is that all those who repent and believe the gospel from this time on receive the gift of the Holy Spirit—a Spirit who empowers his church to carry out the commission of the Lord Jesus.

This *baptism in the Spirit* on the day of Pentecost is of monumental significance for our understanding of the mission of the church.[5] The presence of the Spirit with the church is, in effect, the presence of Jesus. This is an important principle for Baptist people since Baptists have historically focused their major attention on Jesus. Some churches have focused especially on the Father and others on the Spirit, but we are, truly, "Jesus people"! What we need to see here is that the gift of the Spirit to us enables us even more to be focused on Jesus. Jesus had told his followers that he would not be able to send the "Comforter" unless he himself left but that this Comforter would carry out the mission which the Lord himself had begun (John 16:7–16). This Spirit is the Spirit of Christ (Rom. 8:9).

That does not mean that the Holy Spirit is simply the "spirit" (or the inner man) or the force of Jesus. This Spirit is himself an individuated person in the Trinity and so is identifiably distinct from, though never divided from, the Father and the Son. This is seen in that he is called the Spirit of Christ and the Spirit of God (Rom. 8:9). These are difficult ideas to formulate and grasp, but it is important that we see Father, Son, and

Spirit as distinct from but never divided from one another and also that each "person" of the Trinity is involved in the work of the other members. Jesus' claim that he would pour out the Spirit is one of the most important evidences that he himself is the divine Messiah.[6] It is in this way that the Spirit continues the work of Jesus in the New Testament church. Because of the presence of the Spirit within Spirit-baptized persons, it is truly the case that Jesus is with us and that he is continuing his ministry. He could say to his disciples, "Lo, I am with you always," because the Holy Spirit conveys the presence of Jesus to us.[7]

So who are the Spirit-baptized persons in the church today? Before 1901 this question was only rarely posed. But a movement arose in the midwestern United States that year, a movement that by the end of the decade will literally have spread around the world, which would make this question the centerpiece of a new spiritual and theological tradition—the Pentecostal tradition.

In January 1901, at a small holiness Bible college in Topeka, Kansas, Charles Parham, principal of the college, led his students to study the Bible in an attempt to answer the question, What is the sign of Spirit baptism? They concluded that the sign was speaking in tongues, and within a few weeks several of the students had the experience of speaking words they had not learned. Parham later influenced an African-American student named William Seymour. In the spring of 1906, Seymour moved to Los Angeles to help a small, racially integrated mission work. Within days people in the mission church meetings were speaking in tongues and interpreting it as the sign of Spirit baptism, or the gift of the Spirit.

This Azusa Street Revival (named for the eventual location of the mission church) would capture the attention of Christians from across America and around the world, as they came, witnessed what was happening, often had the same experience, and then transported it back to their home churches.[8]

The early Pentecostal movement was committed to several key doctrinal and experiential realities, but one of the most important was "Spirit baptism with the evidence of tongues." These pioneers of the Pentecostal movement contended that, though the Spirit is active in bringing people to salvation, they do not receive the Spirit as an empowering presence at salvation. Instead, this reception generally occurs at a later time, and the evidence that a person has been so Spirit baptized is that he speaks in tongues. "Tongues," in this context, is not necessarily the gift of tongues that Paul describes in 1 Corinthians 12 but is, rather, tongues as "initial evidence of Spirit baptism."[9] But is this the correct understanding of Spirit baptism?

Baptism in the Spirit is mentioned seven times in the New Testament though most of the references are simply parallel repetitions or later quotations of a single statement by John the Baptist. "I baptize you with [or, in] water for repentance, but the One who is coming after me is more powerful than I. I am not worthy to take off His sandals. He Himself will baptize you with [or, in] the Holy Spirit and fire" (Matt. 3:11; cf. Mark 1:8; Luke 3:16; John 1:33; Acts 1:5; 11:16). Paul also refers to Spirit baptism in 1 Corinthians 12:13. "For we were all baptized by [or, in] one Spirit into one body—whether Jews or Greeks, whether slaves or free—and we were all made to drink of one Spirit."

The first five of these texts point to the fulfillment at Pentecost, as is clear from Jesus' quotation of John the Baptist's statement in Acts 1:5—a clear reference to what was going to happen in Jerusalem, "not many days from now." This was the moment when these Jewish disciples received, or were baptized in, the Spirit. John had predicted that the Messiah would baptize in the Spirit and fire, and in Acts 2:3 we are told that when the Spirit came, tongues of fire rested on the disciples.[10] The other reference to Spirit baptism in Acts (11:16) comes after the conversion of the Gentile, Cornelius. Peter, now back in Jerusalem and explaining why he entered the house of a Gentile, notes that God had given to the Gentiles the same gift he gave to Jewish disciples at Pentecost, and he cited tongues as the evidence.

What then was the purpose of tongues in Acts 2 and Acts 10? In Acts 2 the Spirit came upon those gathered, likely in the "upper room" (Acts 1:13; 2:1 refers to "in one place"), and they "began to speak in different languages, as the Spirit gave them ability for speech" (Acts 2:4). Why? What was the purpose of speaking in languages? In Jerusalem, gathered for the Feast of Pentecost, were Jews from "every nation under heaven" (Acts 2:5). The Jews had been scattered in a series of dispersions that dated back to at least the fall of the north to Assyria in 722 BC and continued with the Babylonian captivity in 587 BC and other defeats to foreign powers in the years since then.

By the first century AD Jews were, as the text states, found in every nation under heaven. Some of these sons of Abraham were from families that had been living outside the Holy Land for centuries. Many of them had lost the mother tongue and could only read the Bible from the Greek translation, the Septuagint. But many of them had maintained faithfulness to the Lord and would return as often as possible to the great Jewish feasts.

Now, with Christ risen and pouring out the gift of the Holy Spirit on his disciples, the new age had truly come, and full gospel proclamation could and must be made to all the earth. Because many of these visitors could not speak in Aramaic, and not all of them would even have been well versed in Greek, it was important for them to hear the message of the gospel in a language which they knew very well—their own language. The gift of languages, then, was partly for the purpose of effective evangelism.

God gave this gift of languages for another purpose as well. God was pouring out his Spirit in a display that marked, in a very real sense, the birth of the New Testament church. When the nation of Israel was born in the Exodus and the giving of the Old Covenant, those events were accompanied by the miraculous work of God in rescuing his people from Pharaoh. As Paul stated, those fathers were "baptized into Moses in the cloud and in the sea" (1 Cor. 10:2). Now at the birth of the New Covenant community, the new humanity was baptized in the Spirit of Christ, and this baptism was accompanied by its own baptismal miracle—the miracle of speaking a language these people had never learned. Even those present who could speak Greek and Aramaic were dumbfounded by this remarkable act of God.

Parallels and contrasts with Old Testament events are striking. In Genesis 11 God cursed the peoples of the world by dividing them into different languages so they would find it more difficult to conspire in rebellion against him. Now, at least symbolically (or, eschatologically), he has removed that curse and has brought all persons together into a new humanity, a church not divided by national, racial, ethnic, or even linguistic distinctions.[11] In the Old Testament, the Spirit is given only to some persons for extraordinary tasks.[12] But according to Peter's Pentecost sermon, quoting from Joel 2:28–32, the Spirit will now be poured out on all flesh, so that sons, daughters, old men, and even servants (who would have been Gentiles in the days of Joel) will now receive the Spirit.

It is also curious to compare the results of Peter's preaching with what happened at Sinai. At the giving of the law under Moses, the people rebelled against God. God judged them, killing three thousand (Exod. 32:28). But at the giving of the Spirit at Pentecost, people repented of sins and received the gift of the Spirit, and three thousand were saved (Acts 2:41). These parallels and contrasts are too obvious to be coincidental.

Pentecost, then, is as defining a moment as the inauguration of the Old Covenant under Moses. The first Spirit baptism at Pentecost immersed the new community in the Spirit, thus empowering them for obedience and for service. The Gentile Spirit baptism in Acts 10 made clear that Gentiles had received the same gift of salvation as had the Jews, and in the same way—by grace through faith and not by keeping the Mosaic code.

What about us? The answer lies in the Spirit baptism text we have not yet examined—Paul's statement in 1 Corinthians 12:13. Look at what he says. "For we were all baptized by [or, in] one Spirit into one body— whether Jews or Greeks, whether slaves or free—and we were all made to drink of one Spirit." If one compares this statement with the John the Baptist prophecy, one will notice real parallels. John said that he (John) baptized "in water unto repentance," but that one is coming who will baptize people "in the Holy Spirit." Since he uses the preposition "in" (*en* in Greek) and it is water in which he baptizes, it is most natural to translate that as "in water," not "by water." In the second phrase, speaking of the baptism Jesus will bring about, he says that Jesus will baptize people "in [*en*] the Holy Spirit."

In keeping with the parallel, we ought then to understand that in the former baptism, John is the baptizer, water is the element into which people are baptized, and the end (goal) of that baptism is repentance. In the latter baptism Jesus is the baptizer, and the Spirit is the element. But something is missing. What is the end of this baptism? John's prophecy does not tell us.[13] Paul, however, in his comment in 1 Corinthians fleshes this out in more detail.

Paul at first seems to be talking about something different from John the Baptist.[14] He writes in the past tense, "we were baptized," and at first flush it seems as though, here, that the Spirit is the baptizer, since most translations read "by one Spirit [we were baptized]." But these differences disappear on closer examination. As for the past-tense verb, one would expect that persons who have already been Spirit baptized would speak about it in the past rather than the future or even the present. Paul writes to the Corinthians as those who have already gone through this. Is this a different kind of baptism from the one John predicted?

John prophesied a baptism in which Jesus would be the baptizer, but the common translations of 1 Corinthians 12:13 seem to make the Spirit

out to be the one doing the baptizing, "by one Spirit." This is in effect a bad translation. The same preposition, "in" (*en*), is used as was used by John. This should read, "In one Spirit we were all baptized into one body and were made to drink of the one Spirit."[15] If it is read this way, it is consistent with the other texts that mention Spirit baptism. Of course, the context is different since now we are dealing with a state of affairs that is post-Pentecost and even post-Gentile-Pentecost. Paul answers for us two questions in this text: first, do Christians who were saved after the time of the early book of Acts receive a Spirit baptism as well, and second, what exactly does Spirit baptism bring about in the believer?

The answer to the first is a resounding *yes!* All believers receive the Spirit and are Spirit baptized (compare with Rom. 8:9). "It is 'having the Spirit' which defines and determines someone as being 'of Christ'; it was by receiving the Spirit that one became a Christian."[16] When does that happen and what does it do? It happens at the moment of conversion, and it is the mechanism by which we are placed into the body of Christ, as Paul makes clear in this text.

In other words, all persons who are in the body of Christ are Spirit baptized and all Spirit-baptized persons are in the body of Christ. Furthermore, not only were we baptized, "immersed" (not sprinkled—a point this Baptist theologian would like to make quite strongly!) in the Spirit, but the Spirit has also been poured into us, "and made to drink of one Spirit." We are in the Spirit, and the Spirit is in us. This is not a novel idea in Paul's writings. We are "in Christ Jesus" (Rom. 8:1), and Christ is in us (Rom. 8:10). We are in the Spirit, and the Spirit is in us (Rom. 8:9–11). We are totally engulfed by the Holy Spirit of God, inside and out.

We must raise another question at this point. Is there some kind of "initial evidence" that a person has been Spirit baptized? The standard Pentecostal tradition dating back to Parham's Bible college in Topeka answers that question with a yes. The Pentecostal position has been that Spirit baptism is subsequent to conversion/initiation, with the initial evidence being speaking in tongues.[17] Increasingly, many scholars, even some within the Pentecostal tradition, have rejected this approach.[18]

The issues are too complex to analyze here, but I will make one or two points. We have already seen in our analysis of the "Pentecosts" of the book of Acts that tongues speech there was evidential but not individually evidential; rather, the tongues speech was for the purpose of validating the first miraculous gift of the Spirit and then the subsequent outpouring on

the Gentiles. Further, with the exception of Acts
tured a corporate group of people, there are no mc
in the New Testament. Finally, if Spirit baptism ha
we have tried to establish in this discussion, and i
pretation of initial evidence is correct, then every
at that moment to speak in tongues, no matter what his denominational
or theological background. Clearly this does not happen, even in the more
pneumatically (Spirit) centered churches. The doctrine of Spirit baptism
as subsequent to conversion with the initial evidence of tongues is, thus,
to be rejected.[19]

How then is the Holy Spirit God's eschatological agent of redemption?
God intended his church to carry out its mission in the power of the Holy
Spirit. From many texts early in the book of Acts, it is clear that this very
thing happened. The Spirit is the Spirit of power and of holiness. The
Holy Spirit's primary work is to engender faith in those whom God will
save.[20] He does this by conquering our resistance to his work in our lives
and bringing us to the place of repentance and faith. This is accomplished
through the preaching of the Word.

Jonathan Edwards once said that the words of a preacher who is prepared and Spirit filled are like hammers in the hand of the Spirit. The
Reformation (Protestant and Free Church) tradition has often emphasized
the importance of the link between Spirit and the Word. This is partly
because some of the radicals during the Reformation wanted to separate
the Spirit from the Word and emphasize Spirit only. Luther's former col-
league Karlstadt, for instance, proposed the notion that the Spirit was not
even subject to teachings found in the Scriptures but was free to violate
Bible teaching.[21] This led the Reformers to focus on the literal meaning of
the text as a check against raw subjectivism in religious matters. For them
Spirit cannot be separated from Word since it was the Spirit himself who
gave the Word.

An emphasis on the actual, specific teachings of Scripture, then,
encouraged the Reformers to believe that the Holy Spirit would quicken
those truths to the hearts of men and make them into different persons
by virtue of union with Christ.[22] Ours must be a theology of both Word
and Spirit.

If you look at the disciples of Jesus before the day of Pentecost, you
will find a group of men who were inconsistent, weak, indecisive, and not
entirely faithful. If you look at the same group after Pentecost, you will

a different group of men. Now they are men of faith, men of courage, undaunted in their proclamation of the truth about Jesus Christ. That is not to say that they were perfected or that they were no longer subject to sin, defeat, or indiscretion.

Certainly Peter did not quit himself well in the Antioch event Paul discusses in Galatians 2. One might also ask some serious questions about the Jerusalem church and its failure to stand up for Paul when he was arrested in Acts 21–23. Receiving the gift of the Spirit does not automatically make one into a spiritual dynamo with no possibility for future failure. What it does do is to enable the people of God to carry out the mission to which he has called them and to do so with the confidence that they do not have to rely on their own ingenuity or wits. It means that Christian people have hope for the transformation of character that comes about through the new birth.

We are new creatures in Christ, and though our new-creature-ly-ness is not yet complete, it is certainly the case that we are not what we once were, and this is due to the gift *of*, birth *through*, and baptism *in* the Holy Spirit. Even more importantly, this is a corporate gift, given by God to his church so that he might fill it with his power.

Gifts for Ministry

The presence of the Spirit in the church means also that the church has received gifts of the Spirit for the express purpose of ministry. Several passages of Scripture outline the nature and purposes of these gifts (1 Cor. 12; 14; Rom. 12:3–8; Eph. 4:11; 1 Pet. 4:7–11). Several specific texts also make clear that *each and every* Christian is spiritually gifted (1 Cor. 12:7; Rom. 12:3, 6; Eph. 4:7). While we cannot offer any detailed discussion of these gifts in this treatment, we will make a few pertinent comments about theological and historical issues related to their use in the Baptist context.

Spiritual gifts were clearly employed in ministry in the New Testament churches. This is obvious from the fact that several New Testament writers treat this subject and at least one, Paul, does so in multiple writings. What is also clear is that to a large degree the widespread use of gifts for service in the church faded from the scene at least by the period of late antiquity (about 600 BC). As the Roman Catholic system of bishops developed, the doctrine of the keys took on greater prominence, and since only duly ordained persons possess the "keys," others were relegated largely to being just the recipients of ministry. This placement of all ministry in the hands of a few is known as sacerdotalism. With this procedure firmly in place, there was little room for most laypersons to make significant contributions to the spiritual lives of others.

The Reformation helped to bring about the beginnings of change. Luther's doctrine of the priesthood of all Christians and his doctrine of vocation—that all callings and vocations are from God—were steps in the right direction. Still the Lutheran and Reformed churches kept a fairly large barrier standing between clergy and laity. The evangelical Anabaptists made a few more inroads into what we might call an "every-member ministry" but still maintained distinctions, even to the point in some circles of keeping the office of bishop.

The Great Awakening in America and the Evangelical Revival in England, along with German Pietism, opened doors for the laity to teach the Bible in small groups, to preach as "laypreachers" in open-air services, and to serve in other capacities once held exclusively for the clergy. In America the spiritual needs of the expanding frontier caused Baptists to employ the use of farmer-preachers, especially among the Separate Baptists. So people with gifts for service but without formal training or even ordination became important components in the westward expansion of ministry and the spread of revival across America.

The Pentecostal movement would provide its own contribution to the rediscovery of spiritual giftedness. Non-Pentecostals (for want of a better term) have often struggled with how to understand, define, and assess Pentecostalism. Some treatments have rejected the Pentecostal tradition outright. Alma White, head of the Pillar of Fire holiness denomination in the early twentieth century, registered her conviction with the title of the book she wrote about the movement: *Demons and Tongues.* G. Campbell Morgan referred to it as "the last vomit of Satan," while R. A. Torrey expostulated that it was "emphatically not of God, and founded by a Sodomite."[23] Harry Ironside, later pastor of the Moody Church, opined in 1912 that both the Pentecostal and holiness theologies were "disgusting . . . delusions and insanities."[24]

Many Baptists of the early twentieth century were no less severe in their assessment, in spite of the fact that early Pentecostalism featured not a few Baptists. The first large group of Baptists who received the Pentecostal experience was the Free Will Baptist group in the Carolinas. In 1908 they organized the Pentecostal Free Will Baptist Church, which now has about 150 churches in the Atlantic states.[25] The Assemblies of God leadership in the early days owed more to Southern Baptists than to any other single denomination. Eudorus N. Bell was a graduate of the Baptist Stetson University in DeLand, Florida, and of The Southern Baptist Theological Seminary in Louisville, Kentucky.[26] He went on to pastor a Baptist congregation in Fort Worth, Texas. After receiving the "Pentecostal experience" in 1908, he offered to resign his church, but the church leaders prevailed on him to stay. A year later, however, he parted company with the Baptists when his new teaching instigated great controversy in the congregation.[27] Bell went on to become the first general chairman (later called general superintendent) of the Assemblies.

Other Baptists who played a strong role in early Pentecostalism included Warren Fisher, Frank Bartleman, William Branham, Tommy Hicks, and Arch Collins. J. Roswell Flower noted that "it was the Baptist influence which brought about the change in the doctrinal position on sanctification" in the Assemblies that moved them from the fivefold tradition to the fourfold, that is, away from their roots in the holiness church tradition.[28] In the twentieth century the Pentecostal churches have probably received more new members from Baptists than from any other denomination.[29]

These facts alone are probably sufficient to understand the negative Baptist reaction to Pentecostalism expressed by one scholar. Historian Claude Howe speaks for most Southern Baptists when he notes, "Southern Baptists have been molded by the Reformed tradition modified by revivalism and evangelicalism."[30] In specific reference to the charismatic movements of the late twentieth century, he adds, "In many respects, a charismatic experience is foreign to Southern Baptist life, stressing a second blessing where Baptists prize the first."[31] It does seem that some Baptists in the South might be termed "radical evangelicals," but for the most part "enthusiasm," and "Pentecostalism" have not been characteristic of the Baptist heritage.

Time, though, sometimes lends at least a slightly different perspective. What put many evangelicals off from the Pentecostal churches, theological differences aside for the moment, was their tendency to move to emotional excess, and their frequent expressions of superiority over those who had not received the "baptism with which they had been baptized." I, for one, believe it is possible to give a somewhat more positive assessment of Pentecostalism, without at the same time concluding that the Pentecostal/

Charismatic movements are the last great outbreak of revival for the end of the ages, which many Pentecostals have believed.

I would argue that the Pentecostal movement is part of a larger group of awakenings that have impacted some parts of the world for Christ in the last century. Other examples of this series of "awakenings" would be the Welsh Revival, the college revivals of the 1930s and 1970s, the impact of crusade evangelism begun by Moody and carried on by Billy Graham, the various spiritual inroads brought about by Keswick spirituality, the Third-World revivals in Korea and Africa, the explosive growth of several conservative denominations (such as the SBC), and the return of attention to Puritan spirituality due to the work of J. I. Packer and D. Martyn Lloyd-Jones. Others could be mentioned.

Anyone with a little knowledge of these movements will recognize that they are theologically and culturally disparate. Some would be offended that one might mention Puritanism and D. L. Moody in the same breath. Such persons will have forgotten that Charles Spurgeon invited Moody to the Metropolitan Tabernacle to preach on more than one occasion.

Two points here are important.

First, a movement does not have to be theologically pure in order for it to be a work prompted by the Spirit.[32] It is often the case that there is a level at which an awakening is the product of the work of the Spirit, while at other levels things are happening which actually bring appropriate criticism to the movement. This happened in the Great Awakening with some frequency, as it did in the camp meetings of the Second Great Awakening, where even Baptists rolled, danced in the Spirit, got the "holy laughter," barked, and "treed the devil."[33] We should reject such extravagances as being real signs of revival, but their presence is not a definite indicator that no revival is present.

Second, it is important to recognize that in an awakening or revivalistic situation, our individual responses to the revival are, well, *our* responses. The fact that someone has some kind of enthusiastic experience is no indication that the Holy Spirit causes that specific phenomenon to happen. A lot of what we experience is governed by our own interior makeup. If one concludes, then, that an awakening does not have to be theologically pure and that our responses to the Spirit are *our* responses, one could then conclude that the Holy Spirit has been involved in movements in history which are suspect in certain ways. Let me boil it down in this way. My pastor in college used to say that speaking in tongues was either of the Lord, of the flesh, or of the devil. I am saying there is another option. I am also saying that even we non-Pentecostals can appreciate some contributions of the Pentecostal movement, while being critical of others.

The Pentecostals emphasized the importance of spiritual gifts. Baptists in the early twentieth century were wary of such language and ideas. I would argue, though, that in a sense, we were right up there with Pentecostalism in this. As I indicated earlier, Baptists have long known the value of "lay ministries." Baptists have also long been committed to involving church members in various ministries of the church. My experience growing up in a Baptist home was probably common. It seemed that we were always at the church. My mother would be teaching VBS, working with the Girls Auxiliaries, putting together food baskets for the indigent, serving on committees. My dad would be church treasurer, would go out on church visitation, and would help out a widow in the church whose car had broken down. These are acts of ministry one and all. They involve service, and some of them involve skills and inclinations to be gifted at certain tasks. We did not talk about "spiritual gifts" in my church where I was a teenager in 1969, but people exercised such gifts nonetheless.

What we need to get down to is this—spiritual gifts enable us to serve the Lord and one another in Christian service. They enable us to be engaged in an every-member ministry. This is a ministry where laity (to use a word which has limited usefulness but which apparently can't just be eliminated) stand alongside pastors and other vocational ministers to carry out the work of ministry. Paul says in Ephesians 4:11–12 that God gave the leadership gifts to the church, including the gift of pastor-teacher, to "equip the saints for the work of ministry" (NRSV). It is *all* the saints who do "the work of ministry," and it is the task of pastors to equip them for just this service.

Remember that every Christian is spiritually gifted (1 Cor. 12:7) and that every one has some ministry tasks to carry out. We believe this. This means that Baptists are, in reality, "charismatics." We are not among those engaged in and committed to what has become the worldwide charismatic renewal movement. But we are known as charismatic nonetheless in our commitment to the conviction that every member of the church has a calling, a ministry, and spiritual enablement from the Holy Spirit of God to carry out that ministry. In fact, we were charismatic when charismatic wasn't cool! We were involved in every-member-ministry 250 years ago, and we are still at it today.

THE NEW TESTAMENT CHURCH AS CONGREGATIONAL

From what we have just been discussing—the fact that all Christians are called and gifted to serve—it ought to come as no surprise that the New Testament pictures individual churches as congregational entities in which all members can share a part in making decisions that impact the ministries of those local churches. This approach has historically gone under the name Congregationalism, and we introduced it in the last chapter as part of the Baptist vision. What we want to do in this chapter is to look at the biblical data to see if they support such a model and then to examine what the Scripture teaches about governance in general and the structure of such governance. One point ought to be obvious but is nonetheless worth mentioning. The term *church* in the New Testament refers primarily to local congregations of believers.[34] It is never used of the place where such believers gather to meet, which is why early Baptists referred to those places as "meetinghouses," and not as "churches."

"Congregationalism locates the authority of the church in each local body of believers. No person or organization is above or over it except the Lord Jesus Christ alone as its head."[35] There are several strands of evidence in Scripture that support this claim, many of them in the Acts of the Apostles. In Acts 6:1–7 the Twelve urge the disciples to "seek out from among you seven men of good reputation" (NKJV) who could be appointed to care for the Hellenistic widows. Whether these were the first deacons or not is not the most important question here. What is important is that the apostles told the members of the Jerusalem church to select these who would serve, thus involving the congregation in the decision.

Acts 11:22 states that the Jerusalem church sent Barnabas to Antioch. When Paul and Barnabas returned to Antioch from their missionary journey, they gathered "the church" together and reported to the members all they had done. Presbyterians often appeal to Acts 15 as the first presbyterial meeting in Scripture, but this is a misunderstanding. Acts 15 features the Jerusalem elders, the apostles, and members of the Jerusalem church making an important decision. "Then it seemed good to the apostles and the elders, with the whole church, to choose men from among them to send to Antioch with Paul and Barnabas" (Acts 15:22 NNAS). "Then it seemed good" was a political term in that world for "voting" or passing something in the public assembly.[36]

This does not constitute a hierarchy of some body of elders gathered in another location, instructing local churches about how to handle their affairs.[37] The letter from the Jerusalem church imposes no heavy burden upon Gentile Christians but "asks" that they recognize certain issues as important in relating to their Jewish Christian brethren.[38] For this to be a "presbytery" there would have had to be representatives from all of the churches, but the Galatian churches had no representation at all, nor apparently did other Judean churches.

In 1 Corinthians 5:2 Paul rebukes the Corinthian church for not disciplining the man who was living in sin. It is clear that Paul anticipated that the church should have done so and that it had the authority to do so. The right of discipline "belongs to each particular church or congregation. . . . The bishop or pastor was not reproved for neglect of discipline; but the church itself, in its organized capacity."[39] In 2 Corinthians 2:6 we have the account of a man whom the Corinthian church had disciplined and who had apparently repented. Paul praised them for what they had done and encouraged them to restore the man. It is obvious that the "congregation as a local body of believers took part in the process."[40] Other texts could also be brought to bear,[41] but it ought to be clear from this discussion that the New Testament depicts the churches as congregational bodies in which the membership takes an active role in decision making.

A church has the right and responsibility to call and ordain its own elders or pastors and deacons. Paul reminded Timothy that he had been called to the ministry by the "laying on of hands by the presbytery" (1 Tim. 4:14 NNAS). "Presbytery" here means the collection of elders (or pastors) in a congregation, not some board or body of individuals "higher" than the local church. In congregational polity there is nothing "higher" than the local church, and a local congregation does not need outside "authorities" from a denominational office or from a larger church in the area to legitimize ordinations, though it might invite such persons to participate in such proceedings if it wishes.[42] "Since each local church is directly subject to Christ, there is no jurisdiction of one church over another, but all are on equal footing, and all are independent of interference or control by the civil power."[43]

A congregation has the authority to administer its ordinances, baptism and the Lord's Supper (1 Cor. 1:14–17; 11:17–34). It has the responsibility to proclaim the gospel to the community surrounding the church and the authority under Christ to do so (Matt. 28:19–20; 1 Tim. 4:1–5). It also has the right and the responsibility to exercise church discipline upon members who have violated covenant with the body (Matt. 18:15–20; 1 Cor. 5:1–13).

Local churches also have the responsibility to discern true teaching from false and to reject heretics and those whose teachings are in contrast to the Word of God. Paul wrote to Timothy that in the last days false teachers would infiltrate the church in order to lead astray the people of God (2 Tim. 3:1–9). He urged Timothy, "But you, continue in what you have learned and have firmly believed, knowing from whom you learned it" (2 Tim. 3:14 ESV). John also wrote of false teachers who had attempted to corrupt the church to which he penned his first epistle, referring to them as antichrists, and stated that they had finally left the congregation "because they were not of us" (1 John 2:19 KJV).

Congregations generally adopt a confession of faith as a touchstone by which to evaluate the beliefs and teachings of church members and church leaders, in order to ensure that false doctrine is not allowed to penetrate the teaching offices in the church. It is perfectly right and appropriate for a church to do so, and individual congregations have the authority to determine just which confessional documents will guide and guard their own concerns.[44]

All of this adds up to what those who hold to congregational church polity refer to as the autonomy of local congregations under the lordship of Jesus Christ. In other words, there is no corporate spiritual entity higher than the local church, and each local church is therefore self-governed under the Christocracy of the Savior. Each church is thus accountable to Christ alone for how it carries out its mandates of worship, evangelism, service, and missions. This does not mean that its relationship with sister churches is irrelevant or unimportant. Autonomy does not necessarily involve independence; one can be congregational and still cooperative.

But it does mean that no other church or entity has the authority to interdict its decisions. No denominational body can dictate policy or procedure to a local congregation. Associational directors of missions are not bishops who have the right to tell local pastors what their churches can and cannot do. Associations and denominational bodies may themselves establish criteria for membership in those organizations, and in so doing may exclude some congregations from being able to join them or to maintain a relationship of good standing. But they may not invade the congregational life of a local church and demand conformity or change. A denominational or associational body may *exclude*, but it may not *invade* a local church.

We have labored to make the point that churches have an every-member ministry, that all saved persons in a congregation possess spiritual gifts and therefore ministries for the building up of the church in love, and that each congregation is self-governing under the direction of Scripture, the lordship of Jesus Christ, and the guidance of the Holy Spirit. Does that then negate the need for order and governance within the church structure? Does it mean that there are no delegated positions of direction and leadership within the congregation? The answer is, absolutely not.[45]

Remember, Baptists are duty-bound to follow Scripture in every way, and one of those ways is in the manner in which we determine to order and govern our churches. Though it may seem contradictory to some people, the New Testament teaches both that all persons are spiritually gifted and have a say in congregational life and at the same time that local churches are to be led by pastors. Since it is in Scripture, we have no option other than to follow that Word.

First, Scripture teaches that God places persons in the church who have the responsibility to *lead*. Paul lists "leading" as one of the spiritual gifts in Romans 12:8. This ought to make clear that there is no disjunction between the conviction that all people are gifted while some take a more public and leading position. Scripture also teaches that church members are to "obey" their leaders and to "submit to them" (Heb. 13:17). This is strong language. Of course, such leaders are not to be autocrats, but rather, they ought to lead with a servant's heart (1 Pet. 5:1–5). But lead they must if they are to follow the biblical mandate. The Bible often depicts such leaders as strong, Spirit-filled men who are not afraid to make decisions or take strong stands, as one would see especially in the early chapters of Acts. That is entirely warranted in our day as well.

The primary leadership position in church life is that of the *pastor*. It is common for many contemporary Baptists to use this nomenclature, and then to make it more specific by adding adjectives—senior pastor, associate pastor, youth pastor, and so on. I have even heard of one large church that has a "mints pastor," a person who places mints on the windshields of the cars in the church parking lot during the service. (Perhaps we would wish to have some limitation, then, about just which adjectives can be legitimately added to the term.) The New Testament uses this term, *pastor*, to refer to the role of the leader who preaches the Sunday service and who carries primary pastoral responsibilities in the life of the church. Interestingly, though, it only uses the term one time in that capacity, in

Ephesians 4:11. There are other terms, however, which describe the same office.

One very frequently used designation is "overseer." The word in the Greek New Testament is *episkopos* and is translated in the older English versions as "bishop." That is an unfortunate translation, actually a transliteration of the Greek word, and probably employed by the KJV translators since there already existed an office of bishop in the Anglican Church. The problem is that Anglican bishops, like those in the Catholic Church and other "episcopal" bodies, governed large groups of churches and their pastors. The term *overseer* in the New Testament is not used of such an office, as we will see.

One of the best-known texts that uses this term is 1 Timothy 3:1–7, a passage which gives a list of the qualifications and some of the duties of overseers. Among the duties of overseers in this passage, two stand out as prominent—an overseer is to be "apt to teach" (1 Tim. 3:2 KJV), and he must be one who knows how to govern well (1 Tim. 3:4–5) since governance is one of the responsibilities of "overseers," as the term itself implies. Another example is found in Philippians 1:1 as Paul addresses the letter to the saints in Philippi, "including the overseers and deacons," a text which identifies the two offices in the early churches, the office of overseer and that of deacon. Paul also reminded the Ephesian church leaders that God had given them the task of oversight in their own church (Acts 20:28).

The other common term is the word, elder, *presbyteros* in the Greek New Testament. This term is used quite often to refer to the primary leadership office in the church. We are told, for instance, that during the return trip of Paul's first missionary journey, he and Barnabas "appointed elders in every church and prayed with fasting," and then commended them to the Lord for their new leadership responsibilities (Acts 14:23). Peter wrote to a first-century congregation, and before he was finished, he addressed the elders of that church, identifying himself as a fellow elder, and urging them to care for God's flock (1 Pet. 5:1–5). In Acts 20 Paul is on what he perceives to be his final journey to Jerusalem. Landing on the coast of Asia, he sends for "the elders of the church" of Ephesus (Acts 20:17) and gives them a series of instructions.

Paul also gave Titus instructions to appoint elders in each of the churches in Crete (Titus 1:5–9), while James instructed the sick of the church to call on the elders to pray and anoint them (James 5:14).

These are only a sampling of the texts, but they give a fairly clear picture of elders as leaders and teachers in the congregations.

What is the relationship between the role of elder and that of overseer? What is the relationship between these roles and that of pastor (Eph. 4:11)? One who reads these texts carefully will discover that there is no distinction. These are simply interchangeable terms for the same office. This is clear from several passages, the first being the text in Acts 20:17, where Paul addressed the Ephesian "elders" (*presbyteroi*). After reminding them of his ministry there, the apostle exhorted them, "Be on guard for yourselves and for all the flock, among whom the Holy Spirit has appointed you as overseers (*episkopoi*), to shepherd (pastor) the church of God, which He purchased with His own blood" (Acts 20:28). In this one paragraph, in reference to the same group of men, Paul called them *elders* and *overseers*, and then told them to *pastor* (verb form) the flock of God that he purchased with his blood.

Similarly, in 1 Peter 5, in a text we have already looked at, Peter addressed the "elders" of this church and challenged them in this way: "Shepherd [pastor] God's flock among you, not overseeing [form of the *episkopos* term] out of compulsion but freely, according to God's will" (1 Pet. 5:2). What begins to come clear is that the office of elder, overseer (bishop), or pastor is the same office.[46] Three terms are used, of course, each of which gives a slightly different and nuanced understanding of the task to be performed. The leaders who are called to this task must be men who can lead wisely (elders), who can lead effectively (overseers), and who lead spiritually (pastoring or shepherding the flock).[47] The point is that in reference to Scripture, the pastor can also be legitimately called elder, or even bishop!

Many questions may come to mind at this point, but the limitations of this treatment allow us time only to address one or two. How many pastors, or elders, ought a church to have? Can a church have one pastor, or ought all churches to move in the direction of a plural-elder model? The issues are complex, and it is not likely that all will ever agree. So be it. When you boil down the conversation on this matter, it comes basically to this—some contend that all churches ought to have a plurality of elders, some argue that the Bible teaches a single-pastor model of leadership, while still others propose that either of these models might be biblically appropriate, depending on the situation. A further subset of debate within the plural-elder model has to do with whether there is a distinction between ruling elders and teaching elders. We will briefly suggest some lines of discussion in sorting out these issues.

The New Testament certainly does describe churches appointing more than one person to the position of elder. We noted earlier that at the end of the first missionary journey, Paul appointed "elders" to lead each church. We also saw that Paul addressed the letter to the Philippians to the "overseers and deacons." Both are in the plural. The church at Ephesus also had "elders" (Acts 20:17). Paul instructed Timothy to entrust what he had been taught to "faithful men," who then could also teach others (2 Tim. 2:2). This may very well be a reference to elders. It is this evidence that led James White to conclude, "God intends the church to possess a plurality of elders."[48] But is that the only viable option?

Several passages might point in the direction of single eldership, at least in some situations. In 1 Timothy 3:2 Paul wrote that the "overseer" must be above reproach. The term is singular, not plural, as is also the case in Titus 1:7. A few verses later in 1 Timothy, Paul turned his attention to the other office, that of deacon, but there he used the plural, "Deacons likewise must be grave" (1 Tim. 3:8 KJV). The one is singular, the other plural. One overseer is implied, but a church has multiple deacons. In addition, Jesus sent the letters to the seven churches in Revelation, in each case to the "angel" of each church. While scholars dispute the exact identity of these "angels," it is probably best to see them as the messengers, or "pastors" of the churches.[49] In each case, the letter is addressed to the "angel" of the church.

Strong notes, "In certain N. T. churches there appears to have been a plurality of elders. . . . There is, however, no evidence that the number of elders was uniform, or that the plurality which frequently existed was due to any other cause than the size of the churches for which these elders cared. . . . The N. T. example . . . does not require a plural eldership in every case. . . . There are indications, moreover, that at least in certain churches, the pastor was one, while the deacons were more than one, in number."[50] Even in situations where there were multiple elders, it is likely that one of them would have been the leading elder or senior pastor.[51] The evidence seems to indicate that there were varying models for this in the early churches.

Related to the question of the number of elders is the question, Is there a difference between ruling elders and teaching elders? Based on his interpretation of 1 Timothy 5:17, John Calvin answered in the affirmative.

Historically, Baptists have been on all sides of these questions. William Kiffin in the seventeenth century argued for a plurality of elders but made no distinction between ruling and teaching elders.[52] On the other hand, Benjamin Griffith in 1743 contended that ruling elders had the task to "assist the pastor in governing the church."[53] Augustus Strong, as we have seen, wrote in 1907 in defense of the single-pastor model, but also argued that plural elders fit some situations better. On the distinction between teaching and ruling elders, Strong wrote, "The gifts of teaching and ruling belonged to the same individual."[54] Daniel Akin has a very similar approach.[55]

Mark Dever and James White, on the other hand, contend that the plural-elder model is the one most consistent with Scripture, with White clearly arguing also that there is a distinction between teaching and ruling elders.[56] These men are Baptists one and all. People equally committed to following Scripture and to a congregational form of church government can still differ from one another about just how they work that out in the details of their polity. In the end this is probably not a hill on which to die, one way or the other.

Granted that we have an every-member ministry and that our churches are governed and led in a manner that is consistent with Scripture, what are we now to do with all that? It is to this question that we will turn as we bring this discussion to a close.

THE NEW TESTAMENT CHURCH AS CENTRIFUGAL

Evidence from Scripture is abundant that the early church saw its task as nothing less than the evangelization of the entire world. Jesus told his disciples to go into "all nations," making disciples (Matt. 28:19–20). Paul contended that this very thing was happening during his lifetime (Col. 1:6; Rom. 16:26), though he also recognized that the task was far from being completed (Rom. 15:24). All persons need this salvation since all are lost in sin, and there is no reason to hope that people will be saved simply by inferring the true God from the natural world around them (Rom. 3:23; 1:18–32). That means then that mission must proceed from Jerusalem to the uttermost parts of the earth (Acts 1:8).

The only hope that sinners have is that they find redemption through Jesus Christ (Acts 4:12; John 14:6). It is not enough simply that Jesus died for lost sinners; those lost sinners must confess with their mouths Jesus as

Lord and believe in their hearts that God has raised him from the dead in order to be saved (Rom. 10:9–14). There is, thus, a volitional element to salvation, something that Baptists have long held to be crucial. Further, we can be confident that those who do believe the gospel message will certainly be saved, since it is the power of God for salvation for all who believe (Rom. 1:16).

Even as Peter went to the house of Cornelius, a Gentile, to proclaim to him the word of the cross, so we must continue to extend the boundaries of proclamation until the entire world has opportunity to hear. The early church was centrifugal—spinning out missionaries with all possible speed, and so the church in our day must be centrifugal as well. God has empowered us for ministry, as we discussed early in this chapter. That empowerment ought to send us constantly out and beyond ourselves.

The biblical model for ministry is never one in which we are constantly bringing resources in for our own work without at the same time constantly working to disseminate resources for the larger work. We are organized into Christ-honoring congregations which have resources for service, and it is crucial for us to use those resources to expand ministry beyond the walls of our own churches, from our own communities and across the globe to people whose languages we do not know and whose customs will appear strange to us. That is our mandate, a mandate we have followed since the day the SBC was born in 1845.

All of this is to be done so that God may be glorified in his church and so that the world may have gospel proclamation that is clear, forthright, and uncompromising. "The sole object of the local church is the glory of God, in the complete establishment of his kingdom, both in the hearts of believers and in the world."[57]

The purpose of this chapter has not been to detail a complete doctrine of the church for our time. That task requires a complete study of its own. All we have sought to do in these pages is to examine the task before us and to recognize that God has equipped us, has given us the tools and organizational focus that we need to carry out the task of glorifying him through the proclamation of the gospel to the ends of the earth. Just how well have we done with that over the centuries? Just how centrifugal has the church actually been? How have Baptists fared in their involvement? We will address those questions in chapters 4 and 5.

Before we do that, it is important for us to ask some serious questions about the viability of linking arms with other churches in carrying out this "larger work." Does Scripture teach that each congregation is responsible for mission and that it ought to pursue that call by itself? Or does the New Testament indicate that individual congregations can gather in cooperative ministry to do together what might be difficult or impossible for them to do alone? We will take up those questions in the next chapter.

Chapter Three

Toward a Theology of Cooperation

S ince the earliest days of the faith, churches have engaged in cooperative efforts in carrying out their mission.[1] In some cases these structures of cooperation have been architectonic and have dominated the individual churches within the system, while in other cases the structure has been barely perceivable to outsiders. Systems of cooperation have emerged in a variety of ways, sometimes evolving with no apparent intention by the early fathers of the movement, but seeing the grandchildren eventually taking on large and grandiose obligations which the founders may not have foreseen or appreciated had they had such foresight. In other cases the founders may have envisioned a scale of cooperation that then never really deviated throughout the development of the tradition. In yet other situations a standard for cooperative ministry was established which developed more complexity over time but remained committed to the original vision.

If a tradition of churches is going to engage in cooperative ministry, it ought to do so self-consciously, with attention being given to the key intellectual and spiritual elements of such a venture. The most important intellectual task in this reflection is an examination of Scripture and what it says about the nature of the church and ministry and whether it endorses or at least makes room for such cooperation. Before we examine Scripture for such texts, we must first raise some questions about the hermeneutics or interpretive principles that underlie such a task. We will do this by looking at some historical examples of how different thinkers and groups have approached this issue. After taking that look, we will see if the Bible does support cooperative ministry and in what ways. Then, after looking at the Bible, we will consider some potential pitfalls and advantages of a cooperative method in ministry.

THE BIBLICAL BASIS FOR COOPERATION

It is commonplace to note that Baptists as a people have made their most important contributions in the general field of ecclesiology, the doctrine of the church. This is generally true. One of the abiding convictions that has driven Baptist ecclesiology is the conviction that the church of today ought to emulate as much as possible the patterns of life, governance, worship, and ministry of the ideal church explained in and, to one degree or another, depicted by the New Testament.

When I was a youth growing up in a small Baptist church in Denver—a part of the country where we Southern Baptists were in the distinct minority—I asked my pastor what it was that made us different from other Christians. Denver may be short on Baptists, but it is long on Roman Catholics, and most of my school friends went to Mass regularly, though perhaps not to confession as often as they should have. His answer was the tried-and-true (accurate, though incomplete), "Baptists base their church practices on the New Testament church example."

That was good enough for me at the time, but I eventually discovered that lots of churches made the same claim, and their approaches to church governance, ministry, and practice were often very different from ours. So we have to ask the further question, "Just what does it mean when Baptists and others make the claim that their approach to church is to follow the biblical pattern?"

The Regulative Principle in Baptist Hermeneutics

We Baptists claim to follow the New Testament in the way we structure our church and churchly institutions. Baptists believe that the Bible lays out a model for church order, ministry, and polity and that we must discern and follow that order to the best of our ability. Among Baptists, however, there is a point of contention as to just how detailed that set of policies is in Scripture and whether there is any room to use strategies proaches to ministry which are not directly found in the Bible but are also not forbidden. Some Baptists hold, somewhat strictly, that the New Testament lays out a very clear guideline for virtually everything related to church order, that this guideline is inflexible, and that we are duty bound to imitate it. Historically, this idea is known as the Regulative Principle of Church Order.

Other Baptists take a slightly different approach. They agree with those who maintain the stricter view that our polity and approach to ministry must never deviate from biblical injunctions or from clear narrative depictions of what ought to be standard, but they go on to argue that beyond such standards there ought to be some latitude. This difference of opinion might be designated as the difference between a strict and a loose appropriation of the Regulative Principle.

It might be helpful to give a couple of examples from other denominations first in order to understand this difference. Baptists are not the only ones who have held to the Regulative Principle. Campbellites[2] and Presbyterians also contend that church must be structured on New Testament principles, and Presbyterians, at least, come to quite different conclusions about the nature of that polity than do Baptists. Anglicans rejected this notion altogether, as have many other episcopal bodies. J. I. Packer, for instance, rejects the Regulative Principle, calling it a "Puritan innovation."[3]

In the Campbellite tradition one can easily see the difference between a traditional Church of Christ congregation on the one hand and many contemporary "Christian" churches on the other.[4] Traditional Church of Christ congregations allow no musical instruments in corporate worship. The reason? In the narrative parts of the New Testament, we have no descriptions of the use of instruments in worship but only "as part of everyday life (Matt. 9:23; 11:17) and as illustrations (1 Cor. 13:1; 14:7–8), but they are never mentioned as part of the assemblies of the church or accompanying Christian religious music."[5] Out of a strict commitment to the Regulative Principle, therefore, the Churches of Christ will not use them.

I happen to live in Louisville, Kentucky, just about a mile from the largest "Christian" church in America, Southeast Christian Church. Every Sunday they worship with a large instrumental ensemble. Somewhere along the way this branch of the Campbell tradition adopted a looser usage of the Regulative Principle and came to believe that since instruments are not forbidden in the New Testament, their use ought to be allowed.

Presbyterians likewise affirm the Regulative Principle. The concept has deep roots in Presbyterianism, forged in passionate religious controversy in the seventeenth century. King Charles I of England decided to enforce the Church of England's episcopal system of church government on the Scots, and since he was also their king, he had the authority to do so. Scotland had established the Presbyterian "kirk" as the state church in 1574, but in 1634 King Charles abolished the kirk and authorized Archbishop William Laud to appoint bishops to enforce Anglican standards in Scotland. Bad decision! Less than four years later Scottish nobles formed the National Covenant, cast out the hated bishops, declared Presbyterianism alive and well, and two years later marched in war against the king. This set in motion a series of events that cost Charles I his head, but in 1660 when his son was crowned to a restored monarchy, he set out to punish these "Covenanters." Many Scots were killed.

The root issue here was the right of Scotland to organize its churches along what it considered to be biblical guidelines as opposed to the imposition of a form of church order by the English crown. The Covenanters died over the Regulative Principle; more precisely they were willing to give their lives for the right to order their church in the way they believed the Bible taught.

Conservative Presbyterians today are still very committed to this. "Moreover, he [Christ] has ordained for his church, in order that all things might be done decently and in order, a system of government, the details of church are either expressly set forth in Scripture or deducible from it by good and necessary inference."[6] The word *necessary*, in that quote from Presbyterian theologian Robert Reymond, is key. His position represents a very strong kind of Presbyterianism, though perhaps not exactly "divine-right" Presbyterianism.

It is interesting, though, that there are various levels of understanding and enforcement. Early Presbyterians often sanctioned only the singing of psalms in public worship, but many today, even among conservative Presbyterians, do approve of hymns. I have several Presbyterian friends, though, who not only reject the singing of hymns but constantly debate with one another over how many psalms ought to be sung in each service and just how often churches ought to sing the imprecatory psalms in worship![7] Even conservative Presbyterians are not in full agreement on the extent of and consistent application of the Regulative Principle, and they were among the first to articulate it.

Most Baptists have held to some version of the Regulative Principle as the basis for structuring church order. This can be demonstrated by examining Baptist confessions of faith. The First London Confession, for instance, states it thus:

> The Rule of this Knowledge, Faith, and Obedience, concerning the worship and service of God, and all other Christian duties, is not man's inventions, opinions, devices, laws, constitutions, or traditions, unwritten whatsoever but only the word of God contained in the Canonical Scriptures.[8]

The Second London Confession offers this:

> The Light of Nature shews that there is a God who hath Lordship, and Soveraigntye (Sovereignty) over all; is just, good, and doth good unto all; and is therefore, to be feared, loved, praised, called upon, trusted in, and served with all the Heart, and all the Soul, and with all the Might. But the acceptable way of Worshipping the true God, is instituted by himself; and so limited by his own revealed will, that he may not be worshipped according to the imaginations, and devices of Men, or the suggestions of Satan, under any visible representations, or any other way, not prescribed in the Holy Scriptures.[9]

The Abstract of Principles, written in the nineteenth century, enjoins a similar concern:

> The Lord Jesus is the Head of the Church, which is composed of all his true disciples, and in him is invested supremely all power for government. According to his commandment, Christians are to associate themselves into particular societies or churches; and to each of these churches he hath given needful authority for administering that order, discipline and worship which he hath appointed.[10]

Other confessions have similar kinds of affirmations.

Historic Baptist figures similarly have defended the Regulative Principle, though with differing degrees of specificity. John Gill propounded his view of the Regulative Principle most clearly in a pamphlet entitled "The Dissenter's Reasons for Separating from the Church of England." Gill penned it in 1751 in response to a Welsh Anglican who sought to have all dissenting children in Wales catechized according to the Thirty-Nine Articles of the Church of England. Gill critiqued the Anglican Church on several points he viewed as unscriptural, including its unbiblical system of church polity. "We like it not better for its being constituted by men: a Church of Christ ought to be constituted as those we read of in the *Acts of the Apostles*, and not established by *Acts of Parliament*."[11] He also pointed to the Anglican use of ceremonies—bowing to the east, bowing to the altar, and bowing at the mention of Jesus' name—as being "pagan, Jewish, or Catholic" inventions without warrant from Scripture.[12]

Benjamin Keach, another seventeenth-century Baptist, had much to say about public worship, one aspect of the Regulative Principle. As proof that he was a proponent of the Regulative Principle, the English separatist signed the Baptist Confession of 1689, which included a clear article on the scriptural governance of worship. Born in Stokeham, England, in 1640, Keach was converted at age fifteen and was baptized by immersion, having become convinced through study of the Bible of the truthfulness of believer's baptism.[13] Keach labored repeatedly against the state church, spent much time in prison for preaching, and lived under the constant threat of imprisonment at the hands of those who, on behalf of the Church of England, sought to suppress religious dissent. On one occasion in 1664 Keach was nearly killed when troopers arrested him at a dissenting meeting, almost trampling him to death under their horses' hooves.[14]

Keach was "the first to introduce the regular singing of hymns into the normal worship of the English congregation,"[15] adding them at the conclusion of the Lord's Supper at his Southwark church sometime between 1673 and 1675. Most General Baptists at this time did not practice any kind of group singing. One pastor of an older General Baptist church objected to all public singing, saying that not all persons have "tuneable voices." He also argued that public singing allowed the unconverted to participate and that singing set songs was as bad as praying prayers that were printed out. He also said that congregational singing would allow women to participate and that this would be a violation of Paul's prohibition, not allowing women to speak in the church service.[16]

Particular Baptist pastors generally disagreed with the General Baptists about this and affirmed together the importance of public singing but debated the issue of psalm singing as opposed to hymn singing, passionately, with some contending that Keach was violating sound hermeneutics.[17]

Keach responded in 1691 by publishing "The Breach Repaired in God's Worship; or Singing of Psalms, Hymns, and Spiritual Songs, proved to be an Holy Ordinance of Jesus Christ." Keach supported the practice of hymn singing, arguing from such texts as Ephesians 5:19; Colossians

3:16; and James 5:13. He argued that hymn singing was consistent with the Regulative Principle and was permissible so long as those sung were "absolutely congruous to God's Word."[18] He also argued from Job 38 that if the angels sang at creation, then it was the duty of worshippers to sing.[19] By the middle of the eighteenth century, hymn singing had become a common feature of Particular Baptist worship, and in the later New Connection churches, it would be so also for General Baptists.[20]

Faithfulness to the Bible's teachings on ordinances and on the nature of the church itself also is relevant to this discussion. In the mid-nineteenth century a major debate erupted among Southern Baptists on these matters. J. R. Graves argued that both Catholic and Protestant churches had corrupted themselves by their failure to follow the biblical standards. Graves concluded that churches which failed to follow the Bible on ordinances, offices in the church, regenerate church membership, and several other doctrinal concerns were not churches at all. Even groups such as Presbyterians and Methodists, which were close to Baptist principles on many doctrines, were merely religious organizations, not churches, and their members were not in the kingdom of God.[21]

Graves also denied the existence of any kind of "universal church" and contended, rather, that the word *church* is used in the New Testament solely of individual local congregations.[22] The "Landmark Movement" that Graves founded would provoke a significant controversy that divided Baptist from Baptist, especially across the Southwest. At the heart of Graves's approach was his conviction that every detail of church order, mission, and identity was spelled out in Scripture; that he, Graves, had identified just what those details were; and that any deviation from that pattern rendered a "church" to be not a church.

Historically most Baptists had believed in the notion of the "universal church," though they recognized that the primary usage of the term *church* in the New Testament was of local assemblies of believers. Some early General Baptists, such as Thomas Helwys, held positions that were similar to those of Graves, but they were the exception.[23] J. L. Dagg, writing in 1858, agreed with part of Graves's argument, that "one of the earliest corruptions of Christianity consisted in magnifying the importance of its ceremonies, and ascribing to them a saving efficacy."[24] He believed that a restoring of the true ordinances, believer's baptism and the Lord's Supper, to their original purity was "a service to which God has specially called the Baptists."[25] He was also convinced that Scripture provided a clear and

straightforward picture of how a church should order itself and carry out
its mission.

> Church order and the ceremonials of religion are less important
> than a new heart; and in the view of some, any laborious inves-
> tigation of questions respecting them may appear to be needless
> and unprofitable. But we know, from the Holy Scriptures, that
> Christ gave commands on these subjects, and we cannot refuse
> to obey. Love prompts our obedience; and love prompts also the
> search which may be necessary to ascertain his will.[26]

Prior to Graves, Baptists were not entirely sure how to classify non-Baptist
churches, but they generally did classify at least pedobaptist Protestant
churches as that—churches.[27] Dagg, writing at the outset of the Landmark
controversy, argued that the word *church* in the New Testament referred
exclusively to congregations of immersed persons, but he went on to say,
"We are bound to admit the application of it to an assembly of unbaptized
persons solemnly united in the worship of God."[28] He did not question
the genuineness of pedobaptist churches, only their degree of faithfulness
to the Word of God rightly interpreted. Dagg, while holding firmly to
the belief that we must follow the biblical pattern in organizing church
life and polity, nonetheless held to a less strict interpretation of that than
did Graves in his willingness to recognize other churches as being truly
churches.

It ought to be evident from this brief survey that Baptists have generally held to the Regulative Principle. It ought also to be clear that they
have not always agreed as to the means of its employment or the extent
and specificity of its application. They have also not always agreed about
interpretations of specific texts that were relevant to its application. But
they have generally agreed that Baptist churches ought to follow the biblical pattern to the best of their knowledge and ability when it comes to
the order, worship, polity, internal life, and mission of the church. If we
are to argue that cooperative ministry between local churches, then, is
appropriate, we will have to establish that from Scripture. First, though,
we need briefly to recap two or three important points from the previous
chapters.

The Nature of the Church

Let us briefly review several points we have already established.
Baptists have held historically that individual churches are autonomous

bodies of believers with pastors (elders, overseers) and deacons gathered as the body of Christ and under his headship. These bodies do not need to gain permission from or authorization from other such bodies to carry out the work of ministry. When the church at Antioch determined to send out Paul and Barnabas to the Gentile regions, for instance, it did not consult with the Jerusalem church or other Judean, Samaritan, or Gentile congregations. The leaders of that church noted that it was the Holy Spirit that led the church to so act. When Paul gave instructions to the Ephesian elders in Acts 20, he made it clear that the elders of that congregation had the responsibility to teach, exercise authority, and root out potential heresy from their own congregation. They were not ordered periodically to submit themselves to a college of bishops or a local presbytery.

Each congregation to which Paul wrote letters was likewise treated as a fully functioning, internally governed, self-policing congregation. Though Ignatius a half century later would instruct local churches to follow the bishop, Paul told them to pay heed to his inspired instruction but not to appeal to any outside body or individuals. In Revelation 2–3 each local church to which Jesus dictates letters is treated as an independent congregation, not part of some collective Asian presbytery or synod.

The autonomy of local congregations under the lordship of Christ entails several convictions. One, no one outside that church can instruct it as to its duties or its internal structure. Two, autonomy means that a congregation has the great responsibility of policing itself of heresy and of taking the responsibility of carrying out its task of evangelism, missions, worship, discipleship, and of instructing the next generation in the faith. If it fails, it is the fault of that congregation, not of some larger ecclesial body. This also means that each church is fully a church. Each congregation is a microcosm of Christ's body or, better yet, is Christ's body, and as such it must follow the leadership of its head.

This autonomy also means that each congregation must determine under God who are to be its pastors and deacons. These persons may not be appointed by some outside entity. Though apostles sometimes did appoint elders/pastors in churches in the New Testament, there is no continuation of the office of apostleship in that manner in the church of subsequent generations. Congregations, under the direction of Scripture (the apostolic gift to later generations) and the guidance of the Holy Spirit therefore have the right and responsibility to call and ordain their officers.

These are the basic components of New Testament church order. If each congregation is autonomous, then, does that also involve the notion that each is completely independent of the other? It is to that question that we now turn.

Baptists and Cooperative Association

Cooperative ministry requires some kind of structure to be in place in order to carry out that cooperation. In the early days of the modern Baptist movement, that structure came to be known as the "association." We simply do not know the exact date and location for the first Baptist association.[29] But we do have enough general information about early associational life in England and America to draw some conclusions.

While English Separatists and Baptists both were convicted that churches are comprised of local assemblies of believers with their own leaders gathered under the lordship of Christ, they also recognized that there was need for some form of extraecclesial formal relationships. One factor that drove this centripetal concern was the need for fellowship, a need that was partly due to the persecution early Baptists faced. Evangelism was another factor. Gathering in larger groups than merely the local assembly provided Baptists an opportunity to cast the net wider. The existence of churches that were scattered, though still part of one local church, also compelled early Baptists to form associations, along with the need to identify with some kind of group which would have more or less acceptability.

Regular Baptists in America, most of whom were committed to the Regulative Principle, also made use of associations and viewed them as autonomous organizations that served in an advisory role. This was certainly the case with the Philadelphia Association, the one that set the model pattern for Baptist cooperation for most that would follow.

Baptists as we know them today—that is, the Baptist groups that formed in Holland and England around the turn of the seventeenth century—faced the question of cooperative ministry from early on. The Second London Confession recognized the importance of interdepen-

urches.

ae particular congregations be distinct and
very one a compact and knit city in itself; yet
alk by one and the same rule and by all means
ave the counsel and help of one another in all

needful affairs of the Church, as members of one body in the
common faith under Christ their only head.

The men who drafted and affirmed this document formed in 1689 the
General Assembly of Particular Baptists. They were wary, though, of
making too much of the union, for they feared damage to local church
autonomy might result if local churches came under the jurisdiction of a
body which might eventually take on presbyterial functions.

English General Baptists were not so wary of denominational authority, and so they tended both in the seventeenth and eighteenth centuries
to form strong denominational (or associational) structures that held sway
over local churches. They required young people to be married within
the General Baptist communion and in general monitored the moral
and church life of the congregations and their members.[30] Curiously, the
notion of complete independence of a local church did not seem to hold
much attraction to these early General Baptists; rather, the question was
as to just how much authority an association might have.

In America, the first association of Baptists was formed in Philadelphia
in 1707, largely as a result of the tireless work of Elias Keach, son of the
British Baptist pastor we discussed earlier. In 1742 this association formally
adopted a confession of faith based on the Second London Confession.[31]
Shubal Stearns and Daniel Marshall founded the Sandy Creek Baptist
Church as the first Separate Baptist church in North Carolina in 1755.
Three years later nine Separate churches in the region formed the Sandy
Creek Baptist Association.[32] The proliferation of associations in the late
eighteenth century is a demonstration that Baptists generally saw great
value in association, though certainly the relationship between individual
congregations and associations varied greatly from place to place.

We have already noted the Landmark notion of the nature of the
church and that only Baptist churches are truly churches. The Landmark
leaders of the nineteenth century also taught the complete independence
of local congregations. J. R. Graves emphasized that the New Testament
church was "a single congregation, complete in itself, independent of all
other bodies, civil or religious, . . . amenable only to Christ."[33] He also generally opposed the Southern Baptist Foreign Mission Board and contended
that missions ought to be done only through the local church. In 1900,
Samuel Hayden, a Texas pastor, led a secession of churches from the state
convention and formed the Baptist Missionary Association, an association

committed to virtually no denominational structure and to the belief that missions should be done through the local church alone.[34]

J. L. Dagg argued for the notion of "independence" but also contended that a "happy intercourse might subsist between the churches, if they were all walking in the Spirit, sound in faith, correct in order, and careful in discipline."[35] Dagg, as a Southern Baptist theologian, supported the denominational structure but also warned against the dangers of granting authority to structures outside the local church.

In the early twentieth century many American churches were torn by the conflict that accompanied the advent of liberal theology imported from Europe. Presbyterians, Methodists, and Baptists, especially Northern Baptists, waged internecine warfare within their own denominational structures beginning about 1910 and on through the decade of the 1920s and even beyond.

Southern Baptist fundamentalist leader J. Frank Norris began in 1920 to rail against certain Southern Baptist leaders, such as J. M. Dawson and George W. Truett.[36] That same year he attacked the SBC's Seventy-five Million Campaign on the grounds that it violated local church autonomy.[37] He was angry because he believed that the campaign represented an attempt on the part of the denomination to get into the wallets of his church members. By 1923 Norris had branded the Baptist General Convention of Texas and Baylor University as hotbeds of liberalism. That same year he formed the Baptist Bible Union, a loose association of "independent" Baptist churches. The independent Baptist movement was underway in spades.

Independent and Landmark Baptists in this century have often rejected denominationalism in favor of virtually total independence. Landmark Baptist I. K. Cross contends, "Our churches . . . simply refuse the convention system because they believe it is an innovation of the nineteenth century."[38] He argues, in the typical fashion of those who rejected the missionary emphasis of the nineteenth century, that Luther Rice's approach to building support for missions through the Triennial Convention was nothing more than Congregationalism (the denomination, that is) copied for a new group.[39]

T. T. Shields, first president of the Baptist Bible Union, argued that one of the reasons for his break with the Northern Baptist Convention was its "ecclesiasticism" and "overlordship."[40] The new union, said he, was only for the purpose of fellowship, not of organization or domination.[41]

The independent Baptist movement constituted a rejection of the kind of associational ideology that Baptists had enjoyed since the seventeenth century.

Cooperation as a Scriptural Reality

The real question, of course, is not whether Baptists have "always done it that way" but whether it is scriptural. While it is true that in the New Testament churches were understood to be local autonomous bodies under the lordship of Christ, it is also the case that New Testament churches engaged in joint efforts for both fellowship and mission. In Acts 8 Peter and John traveled to Samaria. Philip the evangelist had been engaged in a great ministry there. When the apostles in Jerusalem heard of this work, they dispatched Peter and John to the city (Acts 8:14). We ought not to see this as a presumptuous act on the part of the Jerusalem apostles but rather as their glad participation in and assistance to the new Samaritan Christian experience. The new work "was endorsed, received, and enthusiastically participated in by the whole church."[42]

Upon arriving, Peter and John prayed for them, and they then were given the gift of the Holy Spirit (Acts 8:17). After the Spirit fell upon the Samaritans, Peter and John returned to Jerusalem after first preaching in other Samaritan villages (Acts 8:25), and even Philip was led by an angel to leave in order to witness to the Ethiopian eunuch (Acts 8:26–39). The Jerusalem church did not attempt to govern the Samaritans from afar but rather joined in the work in this new location, not to "supervise" it but only to share with it what it had to give.

A second example of cooperative ministry concerns a church that proved itself later also to be committed to cooperative work. The stoning of Stephen sparked a wave of persecution of the Jerusalem Christians (Acts 8:1–3). That wave of animosity sent many Christians packing out of Jerusalem to other places. Fear of reprisal, however, did not cause them to be silent about their faith. Instead, they became powerful evangelists for the cause of Christ in places such as Phoenicia, Cyprus, and Antioch, "speaking the message to no one except Jews" (Acts 11:19).

Some daring men of Cyprus and Cyrene took a different approach in Antioch and preached the gospel to Gentiles. This was not an innovation since Peter had already done the same thing at the house of Cornelius, it is still the case that evangelism of the Gentiles was uncommon this experiment. Luke writes that "the Lord's hand was with th large number who believed turned to the Lord" (Acts 11:21). Again, the Jerusalem church heard about this evangelistic effort and sent a favored son, Barnabas, to visit.

Sending Barnabas was an important decision. Had the Jerusalem Christians sent someone who might have been more questioning about Gentile conversions (and we know from later texts that there were such persons), this new work might have been damaged in its infancy.[43] There might have developed two versions of Christianity from the very start due to polarizing attitudes about the first "Gentile church." But they made the right choice. Barnabas was already known as an "encourager," and in addition, he was a Cypriote Jew, so he would likely be sensitive to such a situation (Acts 4:36–37). After arriving and being encouraged about this new fellowship, Barnabas exhorted them "to remain true to the Lord with a firm resolve of heart" (Acts 11:23). Barnabas then traveled to Tarsus and fetched Saul to return with him to Antioch, and the two of them "met with the church and taught large numbers" for a year.

Certainly it is the case that Barnabas was sent by Jerusalem to check out this novel situation—a truly Gentile church. It was "only natural" for the Jerusalem church to show such an interest.[44] Barnabas was sent to advise the Antiochenes and undoubtedly to report back to Jerusalem. But it is clear that Jerusalem did not micromanage the situation. Barnabas was not an apostle, and it is likely that Jerusalem did not believe an apostle had to go since an apostle had already inaugurated Gentile Christianity with Cornelius. Further, Barnabas took it upon himself to bring Saul (Paul) to Antioch to help him. Perhaps he had already heard of Paul's growing interest in Gentile evangelism.[45]

That itself may have raised some eyebrows in Jerusalem since earlier they had eyed him with suspicion (Acts 9:26), but again, they did not interfere in the situation. They had sent someone to help the new church, thus demonstrating their desire to help any way they could, but those helpers stayed as the "teachers" only for a year and did not represent a permanent interfer____ ___ _____ Jerusalem in the Antioch church. It also appears that _____ "moved their membership" to Antioch. They were _____ ermanent pastors there, but it was to this church that _____ missionary endeavors, making this their base of opera-

_____ erusalem Council" constitutes a third time in which _____ made a contribution to other churches. Some "men from Judea" came to Antioch and were causing trouble. There is no evidence that the Jerusalem church had sent them. The church at Antioch sent Paul and Barnabas to Jerusalem to consult with the Christians there about the matter (Acts 15:2–3). This conference was initiated by Antioch, not by Jerusalem, so that this was not a matter of the "home church" dictating policy unsolicited.[46] The Jerusalem church met, with elders, apostles, and the other members of the church all participating (Acts 15:4, 12, 22).

The church in Jerusalem decided to send a letter to Antioch, answering their questions and making minimalist suggestions to them ("to put no greater burden on you than these necessary things"). They sent the letter "to the brothers" of the churches in question, not to the pastors (Acts 15:23). When the church at Antioch received the letter, they received it with joy because of its encouragement (Acts 15:31).

Several things are clear from this passage. One, this was not an episcopal mandate since it arose from questions raised by the church at Antioch and was sent by messenger to Jerusalem. The apostles, of course, had multichurch authority, but they only used that authority in situations where it was necessary. Their general tendency was to allow local churches to work out their own issues. Two, this was not the first "presbytery" meeting, in the sense meant by Presbyterians.[47] The only persons present were Paul and Barnabas from Antioch and the brothers, elders, and apostles of the Jerusalem church. For this to be a meeting of the presbytery, the churches of Syria, Cilicia, and Galatia would have needed representation. "In all that took place congregational involvement and action are present at every turn."[48] Yet at the same time the Jerusalem church was involved in assisting the churches of Syria and Cilicia in solving a problem.

The New Testament demonstrates other kinds of cooperative ministry as well. Financial support for other churches factors highly in several of Paul's letters (Rom. 15:26; 1 Cor. 16:1; 2 Cor. 8–9) and in Acts (Acts 11:27–30). In Acts 11 Paul and Barnabas took the collection gathered by the believers in Antioch and brought it to Jerusalem. This was probably the year AD 46, because Josephus relates that a famine hit Judea especially hard that year, and this visit probably corresponds to Paul's statement in Galatians 2:1–10 about his going to Jerusalem "because of a revelation" (see Acts 11:28).[49] The church at Antioch would later (Acts 15) seek help from the Jerusalem church in solving a dispute, but here, earlier on, the Antioch believers contributed to the physical needs of their brethren to the south.

Later, on Paul's third missionary journey, he was deeply concerned again about financial needs among the Jerusalem Christians. Each letter he wrote on that journey mentions the problem (Rom. 15:26; 1 Cor. 16:1; 2 Cor. 8–9). In Romans 15:26 Paul referred to the gift already given by the Macedonian and Achaian Christians as a *koinonia*, literally, a "fellowship." The word can be translated as "contribution," but there is "certainly an allusion to the word's common use in Paul to denote the loving intimacy of the Christian community."[50] Paul solicited the help of every Christian church he could in coming to the aid of their brothers and sisters in Jerusalem. Churches are to take opportunity to help other churches when the need arises.

In Romans 16:1–2 Paul commended Phoebe, who was from Cenchrea, to the church in Rome and encouraged them to receive her and assist her in any way they could. Paul referred to her as a "servant" (*diakonon*), which could either mean that she was a great worker from Cenchrea or that she was a "deaconess."[51] If Paul meant that she was in some sense a female deacon, it is important to remember what the role of deacons was in the New Testament. They were "servants" who assisted in practical areas of ministry. They had no governing role whatsoever. That is clear from a comparison of the qualifications and duties of overseers and deacons in 1 Timothy 3:1–13. The qualifications and duties listed are very similar, with the exception that overseers were to be apt to teach and that they must govern well; no mention of teaching or governing is listed for deacons. Though deacons in later times often have had governing or semigoverning roles, no such capacity is mentioned in the New Testament.

If Phoebe was a "deacon," it is likely that she engaged in the kind of ministries that Paul listed in 1 Timothy 5:9–16—ministries to other women. In this writer's opinion Paul was not listing her as a female deacon, but that does nothing to detract from his high praise of her service to her home church.

Paul commended Phoebe to the Roman church. It is likely that Phoebe carried this letter to the Roman church, so Paul was giving her an introduction to them. He commended her to them and encouraged them to receive what she had to give in terms of service for ministry. He also urged them to "assist" her in any way possible. We simply do not know the reasons why Paul selected her to carry the letter. She may have been making the journey to Rome for other reasons, business or otherwise, and so Paul simply asked her to do him this service.

What is apparent is that she would have some opportunity to serve the Roman church while she was there, and they would have an opportunity to minister to her. This is an example of someone from one church going to another church to do works of service.[52] Christians are not limited to doing service only in the churches of which they are members but can serve other congregations as well.

In a similar way Timothy assisted Paul with his work in Derbe and Lystra (Acts 16:1–5). Timothy was from Lystra, was probably converted during Paul's first missionary journey, and had been ministering in both Lystra and the nearby town of Iconium, as is clear from the statement in the text that the brothers from both Lystra and Iconium "spoke highly of him" (Acts 16:2).[53] This already shows that this man, though he was likely a member of the church at Lystra, had also been serving in another church which was not his own. Now Paul enlisted his aid in ministry "from town to town," so they engaged in a ministry together through which "the churches were strengthened" (Acts 16:5). Here again is a man who was not an apostle but who would have an extremely active ministry through the coming years, serving churches all over the region.

Paul enlisted others as well to his ministry cause, including Luke. In Acts 16 Paul reached the city of Troas. Here, for the first time since Luke joined Paul at Troas, the author of the book uses the first person plural ("we") in recounting the narrative.[54] Troas was likely Luke's "home church," and now he became another traveling companion with Paul and a member of the "ministry team."

A careful reading of the account makes clear that Luke accompanied the missionaries to the city of Philippi but then appears to have been left by Paul in Philippi since the "we" section ends as the others headed on to Thessalonica (Acts 17:1) and only resumes when Paul returned to Philippi (20:6). Paul likely left Luke there so he could help the church—which now included Lydia, the Philippian jailer, and others—grow and achieve stability. Paul himself could not remain since he had already been arrested there and imprisoned by the authorities.

That the church achieved stability is clear from the opening lines of Paul's letter to the Philippian church, in which he greeted the church, together with its "overseers and deacons" (Phil. 1:1). Once again we see that a person who was a member of one church, Luke from Troas, could engage in ministry outside of his own congregation and yet still not supplant the ministry or leadership of that local congregation.

In 2 Timothy 2:2 Paul ordered Timothy to "commit to faithful men who will be able to teach others also" the truths he had heard from Paul. Since "teaching" is featured as one of the two primary duties of pastors in the two letters Paul wrote to him, Paul was likely commending Timothy to educate men for pastoral ministry, what Robertson calls, "an endless chain of teacher training and gospel propaganda."[55] The verb *commit* (*paratithemi*) is used in Acts 14:23 where Paul and Barnabas appointed elders and committed them to the Lord. Paul also used it in Acts 20:32 in committing the Ephesian elders to the Lord, so the word has high prominence in the context of preparing and commissioning men for ministry.[56] Timothy of course was serving the church in Ephesus when Paul wrote this last of his letters to him.

We do not have a great deal of information about the size or constitution of the Ephesian church, but several hints give us some data. In 1 Corinthians 16:19 Paul sent greetings to the Corinthians from the "churches in Asia." He then sent a further greeting from the church that met in the house of Priscilla and Aquila. That "house church" was of course in Ephesus, and it was, then, from this church that Paul sent the letter to Corinth. The fact that Paul specified the church in their house leads some interpreters to conclude that Paul was implying that there were other such "house churches" in Ephesus and not simply a single congregation in that city.[57] This would be consistent with what scholars now know about the early churches.[58] It might also explain Paul's comment to the Ephesian elders in Acts 20:20 that he declared the truth in Ephesus both publicly, perhaps in open-air preaching, and "from house to house," that is, from house church to house church. Of course he might only mean that he visited individuals in their homes to instruct them.

Regardless of how one resolves the interpretation of that passage, by the middle of the decade of the sixties, Ephesus likely had a number of congregations, and in the near vicinity other congregations also were springing up. Paul's injunction to Timothy to commit truths to faithful men who would in due time teach others was probably his admonition to create something like the first Bible college. This "college" would affect more than just the future pastors of the church in which Timothy was currently serving; it would offer training to elders from other churches as well. This is consistent with Timothy's many years of serving with Paul and the many churches his life would impact.

I could adduce more examples from the New Testament, but this ought to be enough to establish the point. The early churches were autonomous bodies under the lordship of Christ, but they were not independent entities. Instead, they assisted one another in ministry, they sought advice from one another when faced with difficult situations, and they sent money to help one another when there was a need. They sent and received ministries from individuals from other churches, assisted in pastoral training of one another, and in general were interdependent congregations which, though they stood on their own feet on most occasions, were always willing to give and receive ministry and assistance when it was agreeable to both the sending and receiving churches.

In chapter 9 we will examine the entities of the Southern Baptist Convention and the way in which they enable individual Southern Baptist congregations to be involved in ministries at the larger levels beyond the walls of their churches and even the boundaries of their cities. The kinds of services offered to Southern Baptist churches through the work of these entities fits into one or more of the categories we have seen at work in this survey of the New Testament's emphasis on cooperative ministry.

If you keep in mind that these entities are funded by local congregations for service to congregations and to the "larger work," it ought also to be clear that what the SBC has done is simply to take a biblical model for cooperative service, ramp it up to work on a global scale, and then to streamline it to make it more financially viable. In so doing, it can make use of the resources given by Baptist people and utilize them with the highest level of accountability and stewardship possible for ministry. This is not efficiency for efficiency's sake. I will argue that efficiency for efficiency's sake can lead one away from the biblical model for church. But if we can maintain a biblical model and at the same time make it efficient, then that is the best of both worlds. The question we do have to ask before concluding this analysis, though, concerns the possible dangers inherent in cooperative ministry.

COOPERATION AND THE DANGER OF COMPROMISE

If you take a look at church history, you will find plenty of examples of cooperative ministry ventures that went awry. It is important to learn from those mistakes, so we need to take a little time to see just what might go wrong.

Encroaching Episcopalism and Presbyterialism

All through the history of baptistic-type churches, they have constantly been tempted to abandon congregational polity for some kind of unbiblical form of connectionalism. Menno Simons was made a bishop among the South German Anabaptists. It is likely that the Radical Reformation was enough in infancy that this did not immediately appear to be incongruous to the brethren, but it does seem odd to us today. More problematic was the tendency among New Connection Baptists in England to see their founder, Daniel Taylor, as a virtual patriarch of the movement, bringing all the other pastors "under his spell."[59]

Equally troubling were the developments in the British Baptist Union in the early twentieth century, under John Shakespeare, whereby superintendents were appointed with regions of churches over which they governed. This brought about an amalgam of Congregationalism and Episcopacy into a denomination that had been once proud of its purely congregational status.[60] Though not as rigid or invasive, the SCODS initiative in the American Baptist churches in the 1970s produced a situation in which a governing body of some two hundred persons made decisions that were passed down the denominational line.[61] Today ordination is basically a regional matter in the ABC, not a local church responsibility. These flirtations with Presbyterial and Episcopal styles of association ought to be troubling to those who hold to historic Baptist principles.

It is also possible to create a kind of inchoate Episcopalism out of a single local church. Church growth strategies today are often market driven, with little or no attention paid to what the Bible has to say about church. Several new groups are popping up across the country which are essentially franchises of a "mother church" in another city. But the "franchises" have little or no semblance of self-government. Similarly, in some cities individual congregations are developing several satellite churches. This does not necessarily entail a violation of Baptist principles. Many seventeenth-century Baptist churches existed in two or more locations at the same time for various reasons, but they retained a commitment to Baptist integrity.[62] The key here would be to establish just who are the pastors or elders and deacons and just what constitutes church membership.

Another potential danger for polity, though it does not necessarily rift to Presbyterial or Episcopal governance, is the emerging ovement. It is increasingly difficult to understand just what the conception of church actually is in this movement, but it is obvious that it constitutes a deviation from the biblical model and that, like some of the others we have discussed, it is market and culture driven. The current leaders play fast and loose with Scripture, especially as regards the nature of the church, and it is likely that the next generation of leadership will be even less committed to biblical fidelity.[63] Absent from this movement's theological orientation is any real biblical notion of what the church is supposed to be. If we can just make it up as we go, does it not seem likely that we will make it into the image of the surrounding culture rather than attempting to transform the people in that culture into the image of Christ (Rom. 12:1–2)?

It is often the desire for efficiency that drives these models. But efficiency must always take a backseat to biblical fidelity. As I noted earlier in this chapter, efficiency is a good thing but not when it causes us to compromise the truth.

Theological Minimalism

It is crucial that cooperation be based on a commitment to truth. When Peter and John learned of Philip's ministry in Samaria in Acts 8, they went there for two reasons. One, they went to see whether the work was genuine, and two, to impart the gift of the Holy Spirit to this second stage of the expanding church. In 1 Corinthians 11:16 Paul gave instructions to the Corinthian church about its patterns of worship and leadership and added, in effect, "This is what all the churches believe and practice." In 1 Timothy 3:15 Paul referred to the church as the pillar and ground of truth. If the church is to continue to be the church, it must base its existence, order, polity, mission, and inner workings on the teachings found in the Word of God.

One of the dangers of cooperation is that a sort of lowest common denominator concept of truth might develop. Some in our own denomination have held that this is what ought to be the case. Historian Bill Leonard argued that in the years before 1979 there was a sort of tacit recognition that we would not debate any but the most crucial theological issues lest it hurt the cause of missions and baptisms. He referred to it as the "grand compromise."[64] The fact is that no such tacit compromise ever existed among the heart and soul of Southern Baptist people. Moderates and liberals may want such minimum coverage, and it certainly would be possible to make the requirements too stringent, but the fact is that without ideological unity in the main we cannot walk together as a common body of churches, since truth is at the heart of the gospel itself.

As many biblical texts make clear, cooperation is based on obedience to God and affirmation of the truth. When someone preaches another gospel, wrote Paul, it is time to tell him so, and if he does not repent, it may be time to end cooperation. That is not to beg the question, "Just what is 'another gospel'?" It might be helpful, then, to give some attention to the kind of compromises that could threaten the purity of gospel preaching.

As we have seen in other parts of this study, Baptists have traditionally held the Bible in high regard and have not questioned its trustworthiness in recording the great historical events found in its pages. Even Robison James, a critic of the doctrine of biblical inerrancy, admits that "a good many rank-and-file Christians, if asked whether there are errors in the Bible, will say no."[65] James then goes on to argue that such claims cannot be defended in the world of modern critical scholarship, but he does acknowledge that conservatives have "the rank-and-file" with them.

Baptists have held orthodox views on the nature of Christ, the triune being of God, the fatherliness of God the Father, the truthfulness of Scripture, and many other doctrinal concerns. It comes as a surprise to some, then, that a Baptist scholar such as Glenn Hinson would say about the Gospel sources that "however objective they claim to be, they have biases. At the same time, most possess, in varying degrees, some element of fact."[66] He goes on, "In the case of the Gospels, one can safely conclude that a kernel of historical fact underlies the early church's handling of the material."[67] Are we supposed to be encouraged? Does it not seem odd that a theologian in the tradition of Gill, Spurgeon, and Boyce can find only a "kernel" of truth in the Gospel accounts?

In a similar vein another former Southern Baptist seminary professor wrote, "The Bible is errant with many self-contradictions. The Bible has errors in the field of science. The Bible is not historically accurate."[68] Baylor's C. W. Christian, in his 1973 volume, *Shaping Your Faith*, made this comment on the trustworthiness of Genesis: "This disparity between Genesis and Darwin, if it comes down to it, has really been decided for all of us in Darwin's favor."[69] In the estimate of these scholars, the Bible, as it

)wn to us, is not historically reliable.

ave taken their criticisms beyond simply rejecting the trust-
of the Bible and have critiqued the church's historic under-
God and of Christ. Speaking at a Unitarian church in 1977,

University of Richmond professor Robert Alley said, "I see Jesus as really a Jew. I don't imagine for a moment that he would have had the audacity to claim deity for himself. I think the passages where he talks about the Son of God are later additions—what the church said about him."[70] This again is a rejection of biblical inerrancy, but in this rejection Alley stabs at the very heart of the faith.

Jeff Pool, former Southern Baptist seminary professor, claims that the name for God, "El Shaddai," means "mother," or "breasted one."[71] He uses this interpretation to call for a feminization of our understanding of God. But a survey of the commentaries on texts such as Genesis 17:1–2 and Exodus 6:3, classic texts where that designation for God is found, do not support his claim.[72] Only one or two obscure essays on the topic agree with his contention, with most, even of the less conservative, commentaries simply stating that the term means "powerful," or "Almighty."[73] One wonders why Pool decides to agree with such a minority report interpretation such as this when even world-class scholars like Westermann reject it. Why take this as a "hill on which to die"?

A theologian from Stetson, Kandy Queen-Sutherland, gave the annual presidential address to the National Association of Baptist Professors of Religion in 1996. She critiqued the patriarchalism of the Old Testament and called for a new feminization of the faith. She found especially appalling the notion of war in the Hebrew Bible, when "Yahweh," the bad god of the Israelites, "their warrior god, led the attack to take the land, considered their gift by divine promise."[74] Queen-Sutherland finds much in the God of the Old Testament to reject. One assumes that Professor Queen-Sutherland will give us a more appealing interpretation of God at some future point.

At the height of the controversy over whether there truly were liberals in Southern Baptist institutions, Kirby Godsey, president of Mercer University, released a book about theological parameters entitled *When We Talk about God . . . Let's Be Honest.*[75] The book calls into question key doctrines such as the virgin birth of Christ, the deity of Christ, the truthfulness of the doctrine of the Trinity, the doctrine of substitutionary atonement, and the exclusivity of the gospel. Even some moderates in the SBC were troubled by the book. Russell Dilday commended much in the volume but also noted, "I think his views in large part fall out parameters of what most Baptists would hold theologicall Mohler was more direct, claiming that Godsey "remade th spiritual search fully compatible with modern secularism."[77]

Robison James, in the essay we have cited several times, argues that Southern Baptist pulpits have been missing what he calls a "nourishing" employment "of the proven, critical approaches to the Bible."[78] One wonders if he has in mind the kinds of biblical criticism noted in these last few paragraphs. Certainly these scholars have utilized "critical approaches to the Bible," but their usage led them to reject major portions of the Gospels and of the Old Testament to reinterpret traditional views about God in light of modern theories of human relationships and to reject significant doctrines in light of modern thought. How is this "nourishing"?

Earlier Baptists were aware that this danger lurked within the halls of modernism. The editors of the Virginia Baptist *Religious Herald* offered this opinion about liberal Baptist theologians in 1884:

As soon as he found out he was not a Baptist, the one thing for him to do was to hand on his credentials, wish his brethren well and quietly walk out of their ranks. . . . But not so. About the last thing that one of these unhinged and noisy men who have an attack of omniscient liberalism will do is quit on us. He holds to his place, draws his salary, and makes a brilliant effort to "reform" the Baptists. . . . He goes only when it becomes impossible for him to stay. His staying may upheave and disrupt the school which employed him under the mistaken notion that he was a Baptist; but what cares he for that?[79]

Sentiments like this could be multiplied hundreds of times over from denominational and theological leaders in the 1880s, but by the second quarter of the twentieth century, the tune in many Baptist academic circles began to change.

What most Southern Baptists would like to see is some form of accountability. It is not likely that most of these theologians offer their real opinions at the little country church in the vale, but they do air them in scholarly journals and at professional societies—and in the classroom. Most Baptist people would like to know that their missionaries and the professors of theology at their seminaries do believe that the Bible is trustworthy, that Christ is who the Bible says he is, and that we affirm God as he is presented to us in Scripture—wise, holy, righteous, benevolent, just, and truthful, whether from the Old Testament or the New.

This is the reason the entities of the Southern Baptist Convention expect their employees to affirm the confession that we as a Convention adopted—in 1925, 1963, and 2000: The Baptist Faith and Message. That affirmation assures the members of Southern Baptist churches that our cooperation together is a cooperation in common theological convictions and that we pledge, as servants of the entities that serve the churches, to teach in accordance with and not contrary to that statement of faith.

COOPERATION AND FULFILLING GOD'S MANDATE TO THE CHURCHES

What is it that cooperation can enable us to do in the service of Christ as the SBC today? If the New Testament churches cooperated with one another to provide relief in times of financial hardship and in the expression of love, so can we for those who stand in need of help in our day. If the New Testament churches cooperated together in carrying out ministry beyond their local congregations, as stewards of a larger work, so can we in missions at home and abroad. If the New Testament churches sometimes sought guidance and direction from sources outside their own church, voluntarily seeking from those who would voluntarily provide it, so can we seek and assist with guidance and direction today. If the New Testament churches sometimes in their infancy needed someone from another church to provide leadership at least in their early days, then when young churches today need leadership from the outside and they willingly seek that help, we can provide it in our time as well. If those churches could band together in the cause of training teachers and pastors for the ministry, so can we in our time.

As we attempt to work together in cooperative ministry, we must keep several key principles in mind. We must always keep in mind that we must follow Scripture and avoid unbiblical methods in pursuit of accomplishing spiritual goals. We must always keep in mind that there are limits to our authority in the several spheres of ministry and influence—the local church is autonomous from other outside bodies, under the lordship of Jesus Christ. We must keep in mind that the fields are white unto harvest and that the greatest advantage of cooperative ministry is that we can thereby do the best job of reaping that harvest. And we must always keep in mind that the task before us is to glorify God through the building up of the body of Christ.

In the next two chapters we will survey the ways in which churches through history have found ways to carry out the Great Commission—often in cooperative ventures with other churches.

Chapter Four

Churches on Mission:
Following and Funding the Great Commission

Passion for the gospel and commitment to the centrifugal vision for the church did not abate at the death of the apostles. Missionary fires continued to burn for a long time and in a sense never died out though the universal commitment to continued mission would often become a secondary issue for the churches. Great stories abound from the earliest years of Christian mission, and it would be exciting simply to retell some of the inspiring accounts, but that would have to be another chapter or another book entirely.

In this chapter we will explore some examples of the churches at the task of taking the gospel to unknown regions, but our main focus will be on how the churches found ways not only to do missions but also to finance the task. We will also investigate whether only individual churches did missions, or whether churches worked together to do that which individual congregations might not be able to do. That will enable us before we are finished to compare and contrast approaches to the evangelization of the world and also to appraise the various ways in which the gospel proclamation has been supported financially.

THE EARLY CHURCH

Money is a common theme in the writers of the early and medieval church, including discussions of tithing, giving alms, and giving to support the church and ministry. The *Didache* actually mentions tithes being given to prophets. It notes:

> Every genuine prophet who wishes to settle with you "has a right to support." Similarly, a genuine teacher himself, just like a "workman, has a right to his support." Hence take all the first fruits of vintage and harvest, and of cattle and sheep, and give these first fruits to the prophets. For they are your high priests. If, however, you have no prophet, give then to the poor.[1]

The author of *Constitutions of the Holy Apostles* wrote that Christians should bring their firstfruits to the church to care for the priests. These are to be given to the bishop who is a father and a lord. The text goes on to distinguish which offerings should be given to the priest and which should be given as alms to the poor.[2] This early writing also asserted that the bishops of its day stand in the place of the high priest of Israel, while the presbyters (pastors) have assumed the role of the Old Testament priests, and the deacons and other officers are parallel to the Levites.[3]

Cyprian in the third century encouraged support for the church leadership.

> Formerly the Levites occupied this position under the law; for as the land was divided and the eleven tribes received their property, the Levites, who were set aside for service in the temple and at the altar and for other services, received no portion. While the others busied themselves with the cultivation of the land, the Levites were to concern themselves with the worship of God and to receive a tithe of the agricultural production of the eleven tribes for their support.[4]

Cyprian's point is that the clergy have succeeded the Levites in the new dispensation. The Cappadocian fathers urged parishioners to tithe to the church but did not specify how extensively such tithes were to be exacted. That is, there was not at this point any inflexible mandate of tithes or, likely, any system of record keeping concerning who actually did give.[5] It is also not entirely clear just how these tithes were to be used, though certainly one use was for the care of buildings and the support of pastors.

DEVELOPING CATHOLICISM

The earliest church was apparently supported almost entirely by tithes and freewill offerings. Often the wealthy gave funds directly for the support of various missions endeavors. Constantine's mother, for example, built several clinics for the care of the ill in places far away from Rome itself.[6] In the aftermath of the Constantinian settlement, the church began to grow even more in wealth. This, however, brought on a new financial crisis. "The ardor of voluntary giving abated when lands and possessions were settled upon the church."[7] Augustine complained of this and called on Christians to return to the practice of tithing.[8] He also urged, "Cut off then and prune off some fixed sum (for Christ's treasury) either from thy yearly profits or thy daily gains."[9]

Though tithes were often intended for the poor in the early church, by the seventh century this was less likely to be the case. Gregory the Great called for the tithe to be used for the bishop, the clergy, the poor, and the repairs of churches.[10] Saint Severinus, who died in 482, had implored his people to tithe, assuring them both an eternal and a temporal reward: "If you had offered tithes for the poor, not only would you enjoy an eternal reward, but you would also abound in worldly comforts."[11] In the Carolingian Empire, tithes were enforced, even on slaves.[12] The tithes were to be given to the priests, some of whom even identified a connection between tithes and the sacraments. One priest in 835 refused to give communion to persons who did not tithe.[13]

What did the clergy do with these tithes after receiving them? In some regions as early as 345, the priest was expected to turn over at least some of the money to the bishop. From around the eighth century it became common for bishops to collect one-third or one-fourth of the total tithes.[14] The Synod of Trosly in 909 urged that tithes be taken "under the authority and supervision of the bishops."[15] This led to the practice of tripartition and quadripartition, because in some bishoprics the funds were to be divided four ways: priest, buildings, poor, and bishop, and in others only three ways.

Beginning in the twelfth century bishops and monasteries were mandated to contribute to the papacy by means of annates, annual fees paid in exchange for the right to hold ecclesiastical office. This was increased and codified during the Avignon papacy (1309–1377). Bishops were also charged fees when bulls were issued.[16] Such funds were in turn collected from the people. So the work of the larger "denomination" was carried on by tithes, though indirectly. In addition, the lay investiture controversies of the Middle Ages concerned whether tithes would be assessed by the church or by the civil government. Similarly, some kings, such as Francis I of France, levied taxes against the clergy—taxes which could only be paid by extracting the funds from parishioners through increased expectations for tithing.[17]

One other form of revenue was the gift given (or paid), whether at a shrine or to a "seller," in anticipation of an indulgence, which would procure a diminution of the amount of time spent in purgatorial suffering. Such funds were supposed to go to Rome but were sometimes parlayed to a variety of beneficiaries.

Some popes, such as Leo X (1514–1521), put offices up for sale in order to raise revenue for the church. In order to keep up with the demand for money, he created over two thousand new salable offices, including an order of four hundred Knights of St. Peter, who paid one thousand ducats each for the title and privilege, plus an annual interest of 10 percent. The annual budget went up to one-half million ducats during his rule, but that still was not enough to satisfy Leo's expenditures. Sixtus IV (1471–1484) placed heavy burdens on those required to pay annates. He hired one hundred lawyers to oversee the financial affairs of the papacy and to sue any recalcitrant bishops. When Archbishop Zamometic of Basle accused him of simony and licentiousness, he promptly excommunicated the city of Basle and had the archbishop thrown into prison where he died two years later of suicide. Always considered immoral by reforming Catholics, these practices, together with the sale of indulgences, became a key catalyst which ignited the continental Reformation.[18]

The Roman Catholic Church in its evolved form in the high Middle Ages expected that congregants would be faithful in paying tithes to the priests, generally tithes of goods but also of liquid assets. They were also to give alms to the poor, even as some of the income of the church was to be given to the needy. Beyond that funds were collected from bishops and other high church officials in the forms of annates and taxes on bulls. Bishops, of course, collected such resources from the collections of tithes made by parish priests. Other, often less savory methods included simony, exorbitant taxes, and unholy political alliances for financial gain. Of course, some of the money procured through these means was used for financing the work of missionaries, monasteries, and even theological education. But such methods for funding the kingdom, even at best, are seriously problematic.

When the New World began to open up to exploration and conquest, the Catholic Church also saw a new avenue for mission, but one that might be more expensive than mission work, say, in far northern Europe. In the late fifteenth century the church issued a series of bulls and declarations which called upon monarchs to help in the support of mission work.[19] The bull *Inter Caetera*, for instance, authorized Ferdinand and Isabella of Spain to send missionaries to the New World and to take charge of the evangelization of the Indies. *Eximiae Devotionis* in 1501 allowed monarchs to tax the colonies for the mission work that was being sent to them. That is in effect to say, "We are here to save your souls, but you must pay the freight." Julius II in 1508 allowed the Spanish crown to appoint its own bishops in the Indies so long as the crown took care of all expenses in the mission endeavor. This was in contrast to the historic policies of the church that did not allow for lay investiture under any circumstances. Another downside to this policy was that it did not allow for any indigenous leadership to develop in these colonies so that later, when the Spanish fortunes fell in the Indies, the churches fell with them.[20]

THE REFORMERS

Luther, Calvin, and the other Reformers proposed new ways for sponsoring kingdom ministry. Luther's views on this were closely related to his doctrine of the two kingdoms. He argued that both state and church were ordained by God, the state having the authority to preserve peace and restrain evildoers. The Saxon Reformer taught both that the spiritual realm ought to be independent of the temporal realm and is superior to it and also that the prince had a "custodial role" in the establishment of the territorial church.[21] The work of the state, God's "left hand," as Luther understood it, "enabled the gospel to do its proper work even in the midst of sinful society."[22]

Luther's understanding of the tithe was different from the other Reformers. He argued that tithes ought to be taken from interest earned from money loaned out for profit. This would have the dual function of combating usury and also of supporting the work of ministry.[23] He also contended that tithes should be given in coordination with the work of ministry, but that they should be paid not to the church but to the magistrates and princes for safe management.[24] They would then distribute to the church what it needed to remunerate pastors and bishops, care for the upkeep of the churches, extend the gospel to new regions, and care for the poor.[25] Luther urged, then, that the state had the obligation to finance the work of mission through tithes obtained from both "secular" and "sacred" offerings.

Calvin marks a departure in many ways on the use of money by Christians. Calvin, for instance, was the first to give a full-blown endorsement of restricted usury on the part of Christians.[26] Calvin also did not believe that the Old Testament law concerning the tithe had been superseded by the New Covenant. In his commentary on the Gospels, the Geneva Reformer wrote concerning the tithe, "Hence we conclude that all the commandments are so interwoven with each other that we have no right to detach one of them from the rest."[27] In Calvin's scheme in Geneva, elders from each local congregation also served on the Consistory, a body that was the prototype for the later "Presbytery."[28] Offerings were received at the local church level (and some funds were channeled through city taxes), but it was in reality the Consistory that determined how funds were to be used. The funds collected were channeled through the deacons appointed by the Consistory, but the deacons also came under the authority of the city council. They then served as the treasurers for the churches of the city, paying salaries, purchasing commodities, and providing for benevolence.

Calvin's ecclesiology gave to the Consistory a certain amount of authority over the local churches. Through the Consistory, the Genevan churches carried out ministries of theological education, benevolence, and mission. The mission commitment of Geneva was profound, because Calvin regularly sent preachers out to serve in hostile France. He was also influential in the Huguenot mission in Brazil in 1555 led by Gaspard de Coligny.[29] Some said that one's graduation diploma from the academy was also one's death certificate.

RISE OF THE BAPTISTS

Modern Baptists, who arose out of English Separatism around the turn of the seventeenth century, crusaded for a very different understanding of the church than all the groups we have examined thus far. Against the Magisterial Reformers' notion of a state church which encompassed all persons residing in a specific geographical locale, Baptists maintained, in the words of a General Baptist confession of the time, "That the church of Christ is a company of faithful people . . . separated from the world by the word and Spirit of God . . . being knit unto the Lord, and unto one another, by Baptism . . . upon their own confession of faith."[30] Baptists confessed that a person is saved by grace through faith alone, that only the saved ought to be baptized, and that only the baptized can be members of the church. Therefore, enrollment in a state church is inconsistent with the biblical doctrine of salvation, and coercion in matters of faith is a violation of God's Word.

Several implications sprouted from this understanding of the church. First, these Baptists mandated that hot-hearted evangelism was necessary in order to bring persons into the kingdom. No one is a disciple by virtue of birth or of having been christened as an infant but only out of an individual profession of faith. Second, the church and its ministries are not to be supported by state funds since the state is not coessential with the church but by freewill offerings of church members. Then, third, since believers are linked together by their common profession as members of a local church under the authority of Christ alone, all forms of "top-down" ecclesiology, whether Presbyterian or Episcopal, are inconsistent with the biblical model for the church. There is no human authority structure above that of the local congregation.

Baptists in England and America increased exponentially beginning in the last half of the seventeenth century. Their rapid growth forced them to consider just how they, as autonomous local congregations, might still be able to work in concert with other Baptist congregations. There were differences of opinion in this matter. General Baptists tended to view "local congregations as in some sense branches, or local units, of a larger church. They had no difficulty speaking of the 'General Baptist Church,' which was composed of the local churches or congregations."[31] Particular Baptists, though, "regarded each local congregation as complete and independent within itself. They did not speak of the 'Particular Baptist Church,' but only of Particular Baptist Churches."[32]

Both General and Particular Baptist churches in England and America developed associations, and these associations banded together to carry out certain kinds of common ministries, such as funds for assisting impecunious pastors or widows of pastors. But just how might they fund ministry together on a larger scale? That question would be asked pointedly as the eighteenth century drew to a close.

MODERN MISSIONARY MOVEMENT

In 1792 William Carey insisted that British Baptists heed the Great Commission. Here was a call for a united effort to expend Baptist energies in the *larger field* of ministry—more than "Jerusalem and Judea." In order to do this, Carey knew he needed support from Baptist churches and individuals in England who were likewise committed to the evangelization of the world. He would need their prayers, but he would also need their financial support. Together with Andrew Fuller, Carey organized the Baptist Missionary Society.

Carey had early on pled with the association of which he was a part to support a mission to India. It was tough going. In May of 1792, Carey was asked to preach at the annual meeting of the Northamptonshire Baptist Association. Ministers from twenty-four churches were there. Carey took Isaiah 54:2–3 as his text, a text that spoke of enlarging the tent and of inheriting the Gentiles. The sermon climaxed with six words spoken by Carey: "Expect great things. Attempt great things."[33] This "deathless sermon," as it came to be called, served as the watchword for a new generation of British and American Baptists who were passionate about the mission field and seeing lost people saved.

Carey became one of the first to go to the foreign field, departing for India in 1793. His church did not want him to go, and at first his wife determined that she would remain behind. But she later changed her mind, and on June 13, 1793, the family set sail for India. The trip took five months, and it would be seven years before the first convert, Krishna Pal, would come to Christ through Carey's efforts. But Carey considered it all worth the cost, even though part of the cost would be the loss of his own wife.

Carey and Andrew Fuller had an agreement. "I will go down it if you will hold the rope," Carey said to Fuller. Fuller held the rope, spending endless hours traveling England, raising support for the mission work. This was a new idea for many, and not a few Baptists were reluctant to give to a cause so far away. Eventually Carey and the other missionaries were forced to go into business to support the publishing, staffing, and other needs of the mission. This would eventually result in hard feelings and a breaking of fellowship after the death of Fuller. But the Baptist Missionary Society learned lessons from that tragedy as well and committed itself to a more dedicated process of fund-raising so that its missionaries' needs would be fully met on the field.

Baptists in America also supported the work of the English missionaries. "The transfer of funds from individual Baptists in America to foreign mission fields began as early as 1793 when a Dr. Rogers of Philadelphia was appointed to receive gifts for the English Baptist

Mission [sic] Society 'and was able from time to time to transfer considerable sums.'"[34] Before long, though, Baptists in America would have
their own missionary work to support.

BAPTISTS IN AMERICA UNITED FOR MISSION

In 1814 Baptists in America joined together to form a union for the
sake of foreign missions. It was called the General Missionary Convention
of the Baptist Denomination in the United States for Foreign Missions
(also known as the General Missionary Convention or the Triennial
Convention). The catalyst behind the formation of this convention was the
need to provide support for such missionaries as Adoniram Judson. While
it was referred to as a *convention*, its approach to doing its work had more
in common with the *society* method.

Two methods have been used by Baptists for carrying on interdependent work in America, both of which have been in use since before 1814.
In 1766 the Philadelphia Association established a permanent missionary
fund, "the interest whereof to be by them laid out every year in support
of ministers traveling on the errand of the churches, or otherwise, as the
necessities of said churches shall require."[35] This fund was gathered in
quarterly collections from the churches and was administered by the association.[36] Other associations, such as the Charleston and the Sandy Creek,
followed suit. In 1802 the Shaftesbury Association in Vermont appointed a
committee to handle mission contributions, examine candidates, consider
time and place of appointment, and administer salaries.[37] This approach is
virtually a mirror of the later approach of the SBC.

But another method could also be found in America at this time. This
style was modeled after the mission work of Carey and others through
the Baptist Missionary Society of England. In America this society
method caught on as a viable way to support mission work both at home
and abroad, as can be seen in the founding of the Massachusetts Baptist
Missionary Society in 1802.[38]

One of the key questions facing the new organization in 1814 concerned just what direction this new church body would follow. Would
it take the associational path or the society road?[39] Would it be a strong
denominational body, or would it rather be an instrument for effecting
foreign missions and that alone? In the earliest days, under the leadership
of Southerner Richard Furman, the Convention moved in a denomina-

tional, associational direction. Furman was passionate about missions but was heartbroken that there was no real mechanism for filling the need. He offered this question to the Charleston Association in 1802:

> Is it not in our power at this time to send out a missionary or
> missionaries, well qualified for the work, to preach the gospel to
> the many destitute people in various parts of our land; and do
> not zeal for the cause of God and love to the souls of men,
> require of us strenuous exertions in such an undertaking?[40]

This was not the first time he would raise such a question, nor would it be the last. He envisioned a cooperative effort for both home and foreign missions that would be based in an association or denomination that would operate mission work and ministerial education out of the common association, a "general denominational body to promote ministerial education and domestic missions in addition to foreign missions."[41]

When the Triennial Convention formed in 1814, there was some common consent that the convention would move in that direction. But by 1826 this had all changed. Francis Wayland and other key northern leaders eventually determined that they would have no centralized denominational structure, and so they moved back to an order in which each benevolence had its own completely autonomous structure. This rejection of the associational model would be one of the sparks that would ignite the separation between Baptists North and South less than two decades later.[42]

By the mid-1820s many leaders grew more and more dissatisfied with the organizational direction of the Triennial Convention. Southerners especially did not like the society method for missions. To them it lacked focus and so was not an efficient way of carrying out the Great Commission. Among American Baptists in the years from 1802 till 1919 there were at least eleven different general foreign missions societies and twenty-two more which women's groups conducted.[43] This fact served to highlight the dissatisfaction of men such as William Bullein Johnson and Richard Furman.[44]

The problem was that the society method was intrinsically anti-denominational since the representatives of each benevolent society were more committed to the society than to the cohesive denominational structure as such. In addition, there was no sense of true denominational representation. The societies were overlapped but not united.[45] Baptists in the South were content to tolerate the societal method for supporting the larger vision for a while. By the mid-1840s, however, the gap between Northerners and Southerners had widened to a chasm.

On May 8, 1845, 293 delegates from various Baptist bodies in the South met in Augusta, Georgia. This meeting, known as the Consultative Convention, was set to determine whether they would go their own way and form a separate organization from the Triennial Convention. The major architect was William Bullein Johnson of South Carolina. Johnson proposed a denomination model for doing the work of the Convention. He came to the convention with a draft for a new constitution in his pocket that featured both foreign and home mission societies under one governing organization. "Thus, in contrast to the Triennial structure with separate, autonomous, and independent societies for each benevolence, the Southern Baptist Convention provided for one body that would promote all benevolences that commended themselves to it, with an emphasis on denominational unity rather than any single benevolence."[46]

The Southern Baptist Convention would be "one Convention, embodying the whole Denomination, together with separate and distinct Boards, for each object of benevolent enterprise, located at different places, and all amenable to the Convention."[47] The first official convention of the newly formed body met in Richmond, Virginia, the following year. At its founding the SBC numbered 4,126 churches, 351,951 members, with baptisms of 23,222 that year.

This new Baptist body reverted to the associational model which had been in use in Philadelphia over eighty years previously, though at a multistate level and incorporating more churches and members than any association heretofore. Article V of its constitution made clear that this was to be a departure from the approach of the Triennial Convention:

The Convention shall elect at each triennial meeting as many Boards of Managers, as in its judgment will be necessary for carrying out the benevolent objects it may determine to promote, all which Boards shall continue in office until a new election. . . . To each Board shall be committed, during the recess of the Convention, the entire management of all affairs relating to the object with whose interest it shall be charged.[48]

In some sense the associational structure of the new SBC was similar to the original order of the Triennial Convention in the years 1817–1820.[49] However, what this early SBC constituted was actually a mixing of the two types of structures, for though it was organized as an association or convention, it still handled support as designated giving to specific causes, and not as a giving to the association as such for its distribution to the various benevolence causes.

This then was an attempt to put new wine into old wineskins, importing the society method of funding into an associational method of organization. There was apparently an inability to think through all of the implications of this at the time; it would take another seventy-five years before a solution would be offered. Johnson himself probably did not recognize that retaining some elements of the society method in the structure of the new body would hinder its ability to set in motion the new vision he had articulated. The biggest hurdle was that support for the benevolences of the Convention came through designated giving.

In the next chapter we will chart the early successes and difficulties faced by this new approach. We will then show how Southern Baptists found a solution to the difficulties through a method that was both biblical and efficient.

Chapter Five

The Southern Baptist Convention:

Stewards of a Larger Work

The new Convention started its work immediately. J. B. Jeter was selected to head the Foreign Mission Board, and Basil Manly was chosen for the Domestic Mission Board. Both boards had meetings within a few months of the Consultative Convention to set strategies in place for leading the churches of the new Southern Convention to make an impact in the larger work beyond the boundaries of their own congregations and towns. Meanwhile, W. B. Johnson worked feverishly to promote the new Convention across the South. The SBC was off to a good start, but challenges lay ahead.

GROWING PAINS OF THE NEW DENOMINATION

In the early days of the Convention, there was definite apprehension about the manner in which the larger work would be funded. In June 1846, at the end of the sessions of the first Southern Baptist Convention, an offering was taken for foreign missions and another for domestic missions. The boards of managers then assumed leadership in this matter. They appointed agents "who would spend varying amounts of time in designated areas, promoting foreign missions and soliciting funds for the work."[1] Some assumed these posts as employees of the agencies, while others acted as volunteers in collecting funds. The financing of foreign (and home) missions during these years was "largely dependent upon agents for both publicizing the work of the board and raising the financial support necessary for sustaining its work."[2]

Though it seems foreign to modern Southern Baptists, the work of these agents was the lifeblood of the mission boards. Yet there were many problems with this process. Agents were allowed to keep about 20 percent of what they collected, and after expenses that amounted to about 25 percent.[3] It was a costly approach to raising money. The Domestic Mission Board (called Home Mission Board after 1874) also had its struggles employing agents, especially in the depression-hit years after the Civil War. In 1876 the Board collected over $19,000, but 44 percent of that was spent on administration, the largest amount of which went to pay agents.

Protests about the use of agents soon followed, which further led to the Convention prohibiting their employment for home missions. The next year, as a result, the board witnessed a serious decline in resources. But the Home Mission Board persisted and in 1882 appointed I. T. Tichenor to be its secretary. He rescued the board from the possibility of oblivion and along the way made several important contributions to the SBC at large, including laying the foundation for the later Cooperative Program by his philosophy of planned, systematic giving to home mission work.[4]

Further, there were problems with the frequency of visits by agents. Many smaller churches would receive a visit from a representative of one of the agencies only once or twice a year. The whims of people and of nature could interfere with the ability of a church to make contribution to that benevolence. A storm might cause the agent not to show up or the congregation to remain largely at home that Sunday. Churches might go for two or three years and make no contribution to missions at all due to the haphazard way that such collections were taken. So the board was "at the mercy of an uncertain income."[5]

In other situations, especially with larger or urban churches, the problem was *too many* visits by agents. In 1851 the general agent of the General Association of Baptists in Kentucky noted in his annual report, "Wherever I went, I found that other Agents of other Societies had preceded me, and done what could be done; and that the Pastors and Churches were complaining of the number and expense of agents, while many of the ablest churches either had, or were talking of, adopting some plan by which they might keep agents out."[6]

Agents were not the only way in which funds were raised for the larger work. The SBC used a series of strategies to raise funds from 1845 to 1919:

(1) Annual appeals were made at the meetings of the Convention, including occasional special rallies or mass meetings; (2) following the tradition of Luther Rice, representatives were appointed to visit the churches for some of the causes; (3) appeals were made at the annual associations, often by special committees appointed to report on the SBC agencies; (4) a Vice-Presidents Committee was appointed annually by the Convention and consisted of the vice-presidents of the various boards, one for each cooperating state to represent the boards in their states; and (5) beginning in 1908, an annual Apportionment Committee was approved by the Convention to set state goals for the two mission boards.[7]

As early as 1859 there was discontent with the way funds were collected and allocated. The minutes of the Convention that year noted, "A general dissatisfaction with the agency system was indicated, but no better plan was yet formulated."[8]

The new century saw Southern Baptists searching for and slowly coming to a better way to carry on their kingdom work. In 1908 the Convention appointed the Apportionment Committee for setting state goals for church contributions to home and foreign missions. It lasted until the Seventy-five Million Campaign was begun in 1919. "This committee was suggestive of the dawn breaking for the Cooperative Program and the Executive Committee."[9] In 1913 the Convention appointed a commission to study the structure and plans of Southern Baptist organizational life to determine whether they were best adapted for "soliciting, combining, and directing the energies of Southern Baptists and for securing the highest efficiency of our forces and the fullest possible enlistment of our people for the work of the Kingdom."[10]

The catalyst for this action may have been the Laymen's Missionary Movement. This group, begun in 1907, was made up of businessmen who were appalled at the lack of efficiency in the SBC and called for "more business in religion."[11] In another sense it was the Sunday School Board that drove the Convention toward better efficiency since it had to show a profit each year.[12] Better days were ahead for Southern Baptists and their commitment to the Great Commission, but things would grow worse before they improved.

A MAN WITH A PLAN: J. B. GAMBRELL AND THE SEVENTY-FIVE MILLION CAMPAIGN

During the first seventy-two years of its existence, the SBC had no central denominational bureaucracy. Each agency had its own board, executive, and minimal clerical staff by the beginning of the twentieth century, but there was no "central office" which tied these entities together. The glue of the SBC was its annual meeting in May or June, and an elected nonsalaried president chosen year by year to preside over the meetings. Beyond that the Convention was simply a large, loosely knit collocation of churches all committed to the Baptist vision and the Great Commission. Except for their (voluntary) support of the mission boards and the Sunday School Board and their (not mandatory) involvement in associational life, Southern Baptists at that time resembled some of the associations we now know as independent Baptists.

The first Executive Committee, established in 1917, brought about a huge, though somewhat gradual, change in all of that, as well as in the way the SBC did its work. The first Executive Committee was composed of only seven members, but a year later it was enlarged to twenty-four. The Convention that had been sensitive to centralization in the latter half of the nineteenth century began to lose that concern in the 1920s.[13] The Executive Committee would soon have its first test.

On the opening morning of the 1919 convention, President J. B. Gambrell proclaimed, "It is my deep conviction that this Convention ought to adopt a program for work commensurate with the reasonable demands on us and summon ourselves and our people to a new demonstration of the value of orthodoxy in free action."[14] In his Home Mission report at the convention that same year, J. M. Dawson claimed, "America is in fact God's new Israel for the races of men. . . . A Christianized world waits on a Christianized America. The South is America's best hope."[15] Heady words, indeed!

A Committee on the Financial Aspect of the Enlarged Program recommended that the Convention raise $75,000,000 during the next five years. The Financial Campaign Committee was appointed, headed by George Truett, with one member from each state (fourteen). This committee met with the Executive Committee and the executive secretaries from each state and from the general boards. The Sunday School Board in Nashville gave the committee a meeting place with an office and secretarial help. L. R. Scarborough, president of Southwestern Seminary, became general director and I. J. Van Ness was appointed treasurer. Quotas were established for each state, and the proceeds were budgeted out for each SBC board, as well as for state concerns, such as colleges, orphanages, and hospitals.

The rest of 1919 was scheduled for promotion, and an every-church-member canvass was to take place November 30–December 7, named "Victory Week." Information, inspiration, and enlistment went hand in hand in this project, and there was truly a unified effort on state and national levels to make it work. The total amount pledged was over ninety-two and one-half million dollars. By the time of the next convention in May 1920, over twelve million had actually been given, and this was taken as a harbinger of good things to come. Church people, college students, seminarians, and pastors all gathered the last weekend of October to pray for the campaign and to commit themselves to do their part. But at the May 1925 session of the Convention, Scarborough reported that only a little over fifty-eight and one-half million dollars had been collected.

One of the factors in the failure to make the goal was a depression that hit the United States in 1920. Farmers were hardest hit, and at this time over 23,000 out of less than 26,000 SBC churches were rural or in small towns. As the campaign wound down in the middle months of 1924, the state papers issued urgent calls from well-known SBC and state convention leaders, calling on Southern Baptists to fulfill their pledges. Frank Burkhalter, Baptist journalist and publicity director for the campaign, claimed that Southern Baptists' tobacco bill would pay their pledges. He called upon Baptists to practice self-denial in order to complete the task.[16] L. R. Scarborough offered several challenges in the latter half of 1924.

> Now we face a double task as Baptists: the finishing of the old
> Campaign in a worthy way and the inauguration of the new in
> an aggressive, effective manner. This is difficult to do, but a
> united, aggressive, evangelistic, spiritual democracy can do it.[17]

He went on to call for "a revival of old-time, Pentecostal, spirit-filled revival in every church in the South and in every destitute place in reach of Baptists. . . . Denominational programs are like eggs. If you put them on ice they will not hatch."[18] There was a sense about the Seventy-five Million Campaign that failure was unacceptable.

> Failure is not always a disgrace. But in this case it would be. . . .
> Failure would be inexcusable and mortifying. Through all time
> to come we would have to bear the reproach of failure—failure

to do what God called us to do, failure to do what we were able
to do and failure to do what we pledged ourselves to do. It must
not be. That cost would be too great. It would weaken the
morale of our denomination. . . . It is inconceivable that we
should fail. If Baptists fail, what then? Who is to do the work
we are called to do? Who is to teach the world a whole gospel?[19]
The prospect that the campaign would end in failure was a devastating
thought.[20] Yet fail it did, despite some heroic efforts by individuals and
groups to bring in the final "sheaves."[21]

The net effect of the failure to reach the goal was deep debt for
the boards of the Convention, which had borrowed money for capital
improvements based on large pledges and early returns in the giving.[22]
The pledged commitment was seventeen million dollars over the goal.
The boards figured that the "shrinkage" on that pledge would result in
coming out still at the seventy-five million mark.[23] Because of the debt,
basic functions of the boards were dramatically impacted. The Foreign
Mission Board was unable to provide three million dollars for drastically
needed improvements on the foreign fields. In June of 1924 that board
turned down applications of ninety-five young men and women to serve
overseas in mission work because of its indebtedness.[24] There was a debt of
$882,000, which constituted an increase of $107,000 over the debt of just
one year earlier.

The sense of general malaise in the Convention was patent. A cur-
sory survey of the state papers in late 1924 almost leads one to a state of
depression even now, as one sees numerous editorials, advertisements, and
news pieces, all with the same theme—the failure of the campaign and its
consequences.

This episode needs, however, to be set in perspective. In some ways the
Seventy-five Million Campaign was a remarkable success. Southern Baptists
had raised nearly sixty million dollars for extending the larger work. This
was more than the total of all gifts to the denomination in the previous
seventy-four years combined. Additionally, nine thousand churches that
contributed to the campaign had never given to denominational causes
before. The campaign also introduced the churches to "a prototype for the
Cooperative Program, the unified church budget, and the Every Member
Canvass for contributions, a trio that revolutionized Southern Baptist
life."[25] They had truly entered the twentieth century with a new focus on

world evangelization and had demonstrated that they could carry out a massive effort to raise resources to engage in that worldwide vision.

The Southern Baptist Convention proved during this financial effort that it had a heart as big as the world and that it just might make a huge impact on that world in the decades ahead. That does not mean that the key leaders saw it that way in 1924. But all was not hopeless even then. As early as 1923 leaders in the Convention had begun to anticipate a shortfall in the Seventy-five Million Campaign.[26] That year, while the previous campaign still had a year and a half of life left in it, plans were set in motion for a new campaign, one with no time limit attached.

THE COOPERATIVE PROGRAM: THE LAST, BEST HOPE

In 1924 the SBC met in Atlanta. That convention in 1924 called for churches to do two things: to finish off the collection of the Seventy-five Million Campaign, and to conduct an every-member canvass of individual pledges for state- and Convention-wide causes for the year 1925.[27] This survey would then form the basis for the state convention budgets for the year, as well as the budget that the SBC would set for its various Convention programs.

M. E. Dodd was chairman of the Committee on Future Program, first appointed in 1923, then reappointed in 1924. In the fall of 1924 he wrote a series of articles, which were featured in the state papers, on the new method. These articles were an exposition of the eleven recommendations approved by the 1924 convention for the 1925 funding program. The first included an every-member canvass of the churches, to be taken November 30–December 7, 1924. This gave the state conventions time to have their fall meetings so that they might have a part in the process and yet did not conflict with the ending of the Seventy-five Million Campaign, which would wind down in the final weeks of December.

The purpose of the Future Program was to "put our denominational work on a substantial, permanent, and continuous basis."[28] There was a need for pledges of $15,000,000 during this canvass period in order for the unified budget to be met. Dodd and other Convention leaders believed that this new approach provided the answer to the various SBC financial woes. "Not only is the New Program a kingdom necessity, it is also our Program. We made it. It is the result of the best thinking of our denomination, led as we believe by the Spirit of God. It is Scriptural."[29]

The Cooperative Program was remarkably simple in principle. Churches were to canvass members for pledged giving for the following year in the fall. Based on those commitments, churches set their own annual budgets. Out of those budgets they would commit a percentage of their total revenue to give to the new Cooperative Program. This financial commitment would stand in the stead of previous special offerings made to individual causes every time an agent showed up at the church with his plea for funds for state or national convention concerns.[30] There would be no more such visits. That percentage of revenue would be sent on to the state convention office, preferably on a monthly basis. Each state convention would also formulate a budget for its programs, based on expectations of revenues from the churches and would live within those financial boundaries.

State conventions each sent a percentage of Cooperative Program receipts on to the SBC. The goal was for a fifty-fifty split, with the state convention keeping half and the SBC receiving the other half.[31] The SBC, based on its expectation of annual receipts, would then set its own budget. The Executive Committee of the Convention would determine just how the total amount was to be apportioned to the various agencies, with the lion's share of the resources always to go to missions, especially foreign missions.[32]

This was a move to a unified budget for the Convention, something new not only for the SBC but also for many churches.[33] The program that was being discussed at the 1924 convention brought churches ever more into an understanding of the need for a budgeted approach to Convention giving.[34] The commitment to a unified budget for the Convention was central.

> At this point our Unified Program will either break or be saved. If it should break at this point, by an under-emphasis upon the whole program and an over-emphasis upon the individual object, then we will find ourselves back where we were five years ago, with every object contending for all it can obtain, to the exclusion of other equally worthy commitments.[35]

This was in essence a return to the original vision of W. B. Johnson, a vision which had been partly short-circuited by the shortsightedness of Baptists for the previous seventy-five years. It was too much to expect that the SBC leaders in 1845 would have adopted an approach to financial support fully consistent with their commitment to the associational model. They would have had to abandon designated giving to particular benevolences and committed themselves to undesignated support of the Convention itself, a move which was counter-intuitive to those men at that time. It would have constituted a radical break with tradition. So they continued to follow a society pattern of funding within an associational structure, which created certain weaknesses.[36] Those weaknesses were now, potentially at least, no longer part of the equation.[37]

The new method had much to commend it.[38] The Future Program Committee contended that the new approach was simple, permanent, responsible, unifying, ambitious, thoughtful, cooperative, visionary, biblical, and God honoring.[39] It brought greater efficiency to the SBC immediately, and, though more financial difficulties lay ahead,[40] the Cooperative Program did become the vehicle by which the SBC was able to accomplish great successes in missions and church growth over the next decades.[41] As one well-known Baptist historian put it, "The Cooperative Program is the greatest step forward in kingdom finance Southern Baptists have ever taken."[42]

In order for the new program to work as efficiently as possible, the SBC, over the next several years after the 1925 convention, made specific changes in the way the Executive Committee worked and to the way churches were represented and boards were rotated. Most of these changes were dictated by the incredible growth of the SBC.[43] This growth required greater efficiency. The Business Efficiency Committee was appointed in 1925 and completed its work in 1927.[44] Its recommendations were adopted by the Convention that year, establishing the SBC as a responsible business entity, helping to build confidence in the Convention's approach to doing business, making the Executive Committee responsible for administering the Cooperative Program, and systematizing Convention finances.[45]

Certainly there were many kinks to be worked out. McClellan noted eight major conflicts concerning the Cooperative Program in those early years.[46] First, states regularly altered distribution tables. In the early days some states altered the numbers regularly, sometimes annually. This caused the Executive Committee to challenge states not to alter the rates in the years 1928, 1929, 1930. Second, the SBC as a denomination now could appeal directly to churches. Third, state conventions still forwarded Cooperative Program gifts directly to the agencies. This changed when the New Financial Plan was approved in 1929, requiring states to send their funds directly to the Executive Committee.

Fourth, special solicitations continued to disrupt the Cooperative Program. The new rules prohibited agencies from making direct appeals for monies, but the problem of budget shortfalls made it tempting for them to return to pre-Cooperative Program methods. State conventions, of course, were not constrained by the New Financial Plan. Fifth, some SBC agencies did not promote the Cooperative Program. The Executive Committee in 1928 asked all agencies to be committed to the common cause of all for one and one for all. Sixth, there was a danger that the Cooperative Program would be terminated before it had the opportunity to prove itself. State conventions and their papers in particular were critical of the Cooperative Program. "In 1929, at a winter meeting of the state executive secretaries, it came to light that some agency executives were saying publicly that the Cooperative Program had failed."[47]

Seventh, there were different ideas about who was to pay for the Cooperative Program promotion—the states or the national SBC. In 1930 and again in 1934 state executives and the Executive Committee jointly agreed that there ought to be a fifty-fifty split in funds raised. Finally, there was also the need for an "effective promotional program for the Cooperative Program."[48] This problem was addressed directly by J. E. Dillard when he became chairman of the Executive Committee in 1936.

Major hurdles had been overcome. The SBC was coming of age, but the program was just getting settled in. Over the next several years, however, the Cooperative Program gained in acceptance by the churches and the entities, expanded with the addition of new SBC and state convention enterprises, and grew rapidly in income. The founders' dream of "one sacred effort" by Baptists for the kingdom of God now had a funding mechanism consistent with cooperative methodology and commensurate with the size of the missions challenge. The next two chapters will describe the current operation of the Southern Baptist Convention in general and the Cooperative Program in particular.

Chapter Six

Getting Down to Business:

The Southern Baptist Convention Annual Meeting

In 2004, Southern Baptists claimed a membership of 16,267,494 affiliated with 43,465 congregations. These congregations, by sending messengers and money, cause the Southern Baptist Convention to be a reality. The Southern Baptist Convention is a legal corporation but an unusual one. It has no assets. It has no employees. It owns no property. In fact, the Southern Baptist Convention only exists two days per year. It comes into existence when the presiding officer, elected in the previous year's session, calls the Southern Baptist Convention into session. It ceases to exist when the final session is adjourned.

This does not mean the work of the Southern Baptist Convention ceases to exist. It is carried out by trustees and employees of the various entities and committees of the Southern Baptist Convention. The work of these entities will be described specifically in subsequent chapters.

Because of the unique structure of the Southern Baptist Convention, the two-day annual meeting is pivotal to its work. During this meeting Southern Baptist Convention budgets are adopted, officers and trustees are elected, processes are set or amended, ministries are created or modified, and business necessary to the effective operation of the Southern Baptist Convention is conducted.

SCHEDULE

At its founding in 1845, the Southern Baptist Convention adopted the schedule of the Triennial Convention and met every three years. However, after only one cycle (1846–1849), the Convention changed its practice to a biennial meeting schedule. Following the Civil War, the Southern Baptist Convention began meeting annually, a practice that continues to the present. (The SBC did not meet in 1943 or 1945 due to World War II.)

The constitution of the Southern Baptist Convention states:

Article XI. Meetings:

1. The Convention shall hold its meetings annually at such time and place as it may choose.
2. The president may call special meetings with the concurrence of the other officers of the Convention and of the Executive Committee.
3. The Executive Committee may change the time and place of meeting if the entertaining city withdraws its invitation or is unable to fulfill its commitments.
4. The Convention officers, the Executive Committee, and the executive heads of the Convention's boards and institutions acting in a body may, in case of grave emergency, cancel a regular meeting or change the place of meeting.[1]

The length of the annual meeting was last modified in 1998 when the Convention voted to shorten the time frame from three days to two days beginning the next year. The trend across the years has been toward shorter annual meetings. In the 1800s the meetings convened for five to six days. From 1900 to 1949, the meetings lasted from four to five days, ordinarily conducting sessions throughout the weekend. From 1950 to 1970, the length was four days with all sessions held from Monday to Friday. In 1971, the SBC meeting began following a three-day Tuesday through Thursday schedule. This pattern continued until 1999 when the time frame was altered to a two-day Tuesday-Wednesday format.

The reasons for shorter meetings, especially by the mid 1900s, were due to improved communication and travel as well as the continued improvement in efficiency by the various boards of trustees, denominational workers, and the Executive Committee. During the foundational decades, the annual meeting was often a work session with *ad hoc* committees being appointed at the beginning of the Convention, deliberating for several days, and reporting by the end of the same Convention. For the last century the more common practice has been for committees to do their work in the months between annual sessions. With the growing organizational efficiencies and other improvements, shorter sessions were sufficient. Additionally, auxiliary meetings (SBC Pastors' Conference, WMU, etc.) added extra days to the Convention goers' itineraries. Shorter Convention schedules allowed time both for conducting the Convention's business and participating in other events without requiring the attendees to be away from their home fields for too long.

Additional factors affected the decision to adopt the two-day meeting schedule. In actuality, the schedule was reduced by only one session: the three-hour Thursday morning session. The Convention had been ending at noon on Thursday for several years prior to the change. This abbreviation was manageable because the adoption of the Program and Structure Study Committee Report in 1995 (called "Covenant for a New Century") had reduced the number of Convention entities from nineteen to twelve. With seven less entities, the time needed in the annual sessions for reports was significantly reduced, leaving as much time for all other ordinary Convention business in two days as had been available in the three-day format.

The Annual Meeting Study Committee, which recommended the shorter schedule, also "noted that, in recent years, many messengers have adopted the practice of leaving before the Thursday morning session, sometimes resulting in the lack of a quorum and usually a low attendance for the keynote speaker. By adjourning on Wednesday night rather than Thursday noon, the messengers' time expenditure would be lessened, and the committee believes a larger percentage of the participants would be present for the entire meeting."[2] The attendance of the SBC since 1998 has been 11,608 (1999), 11,959 (2000), 9,584 (2001), 9,645 (2002), 7,077 (2003), and 8,600 (2004).

MESSENGERS

The annual meeting of the SBC is comprised of messengers sent from qualified Southern Baptist churches. At the onset of the opening session, the Convention constitutes itself by seating all registered messengers and those who will report during the course of the meeting. Churches customarily receive messenger certification cards in advance of the meeting.

They send these cards with the messengers they have elected. In recent years churches have been able to register their messengers via the Internet. Only very rarely have challenges been raised concerning the qualification of certain messengers. Objections to sending any messengers are handled by the Credentials Committee, which is appointed by the president of the Southern Baptist Convention. This committee recommends to the Convention whether these "challenged" messengers should be granted or denied messengers status.

Until the 1930s, messengers were qualified by financial contributions to the work of the Convention. This included messengers from contributing churches as well as from other Baptist bodies (associations, societies, etc.) or even individual Baptists who had made a minimum contribution. This practice was challenged for a number of years by those who insisted messengers should only come from local churches. A minor schism occurred in the early 1900s when the Southern Baptist Convention would not modify its pattern of seating messengers who did not represent local churches. Finally, in 1931 the Southern Baptist Convention constitution was amended to state that messengers to the SBC must have been elected by a qualified local Baptist church.

The constitution currently provides:

8. Messenger Credentials and Registration:

    A. Each person elected by a church cooperating with the Southern Baptist Convention as a messenger to the Southern Baptist Convention shall be registered as a messenger to the Convention upon presentation of proper credentials. Credentials shall be presented by each messenger, in person, at the Convention registration desk and shall be in the following form:

        (1) A completed and signed Southern Baptist Convention registration card, certifying the messenger's election in accordance with Article III. Membership, of the Constitution of the Southern Baptist Convention; but if the messenger does not have the messenger registration card,

        (2) A letter from the messenger's church, signed by the clerk or moderator of the church, certifying the messenger's election in accordance with

Article III. Membership, of the Constitution of
the Southern Baptist Convention; or

(3) A telegram from the messenger's church certi-
fying the messenger's election in
accordance with Article III. Membership,
of the Constitution of the Southern Baptist
Convention.

Messengers registered in accordance with this section
shall constitute the Convention.

B. The president of the Convention, in consultation
with the vice presidents, shall appoint, at least thirty
(30) days before the annual session, a Credentials
Committee to serve at the forthcoming sessions of the
Convention. This committee shall review and rule upon
any questions which may arise in registration concerning the credentials of messengers. Any such ruling may
be appealed to the Convention during business session.
Any contention arising on the floor concerning seating
of messengers shall be referred to the committee for
consideration and the committee shall report back to
the Convention.

C. The registration secretary shall be at the place of the
annual meeting at least one (1) day prior to the con-
vening of the first session of the Southern Baptist
Convention for the purpose of opening the registration desk and registering messengers. The registration
secretary also shall convene the Credentials Committee
at least one day prior to the annual meeting and shall
assist the committee in reviewing questions concerning messenger credentials. The registration secretary
shall report to the Convention the number of registered
messengers.[3]

Also, in the early years of the Convention, messengers were called
"delegates." That designation was subsequently changed to "messengers."
Southern Baptists came to the understanding, after some years of debate,
that messengers were designated by the churches but "did not officially
represent their churches, nor possess any delegated authority from the
churches, nor corporately exercise any authority over the churches."[4] This

distinction is often lost to secular media reporting on the annual meeting who often substitute the word *delegate* when referring to the action of the messengers. It is important that Baptists do not miss the distinction. The messengers are *designated* by the churches but not *delegated*. Therefore, the annual meeting is a gathering of Baptists from the churches, not a gathering of the churches per se. The autonomy of the local church as well as the autonomy of the Southern Baptist Convention is preserved by this process.

The SBC annual meeting is a large parliamentary meeting. In its years of record attendance, it was the largest parliamentary meeting in the world. Every messenger gets one vote. Proxies are not permitted. Messengers must be in the designated meeting hall(s) at the time of a vote in order to cast a ballot. The vote of the messengers in annual session is the final authority.

DOCUMENTS

The SBC has adopted several documents that govern the conduct of the annual meeting as well as provide guidance for the various ministries of Southern Baptist entities. These documents are the SBC Constitution, the SBC Bylaws, the SBC Business and Financial Plan, and the SBC Organization Manual. Copies of the first three are provided to messengers each year in the *Book of Reports*, which is prepared by the Executive Committee.

All these documents can be and have been amended by the SBC in the annual meeting. The process for amending the documents is contained in the documents themselves. In addition, the messengers are provided with several issues of the *SBC Bulletin* which contains pertinent information on the annual meeting in progress.

OFFICERS

The Southern Baptist Convention Constitution provides for the election of officers.

Article V. Officers:
1. The officers of the Convention shall be a president, a first and a second vice president, a recording secretary, a registration secretary, and a treasurer.

2. The officers shall be elected annually and shall hold office until their successors are elected and qualified. The term of office for the president is limited to two (2) years, and a president shall not be eligible for re-election until as much as one (1) year has elapsed from the time a successor is named. The first vice president shall be voted upon and elected after the election of the president has taken place; and the second vice president shall be voted upon and elected after the election of the first vice president has taken place.

3. The president shall be a member of the several boards and of the Executive Committee.

4. The treasurer of the Executive Committee shall be the treasurer of the Convention.

5. In case of death or disability of the president, the vice presidents shall automatically succeed to the office of president in the order of their election.[5]

The president has a number of official duties prior to the annual meeting. He serves as an *ex officio* trustee of the Executive Committee and the boards of the Convention. He appoints the Committee on Committees, Resolutions Committee, Tellers Committee, and the Credentials Committee. He serves on the Committee on Order of Business. He chooses the Convention parliamentarian(s).

At the meeting itself the president is the presiding officer. He is assisted in the conducting of the annual meeting by the other officers, the parliamentarians, and the Committee on Order of Business. The president also acts as a goodwill ambassador and spokesman for the Southern Baptist Convention between annual meetings. His activities in this regard are not mandated by the Convention, but each president has functioned well in this "informal" duty.

The power of the Southern Baptist Convention president has been debated in recent years. James Sullivan, a former SBC president himself, lists as a "myth" the idea that the president occupies a position of tremendous power.[6] While it is true the president must abide by the rules of the Convention, and the messengers, by voting, have the final authority, the appointed duties of the president have had far-reaching impact in the past twenty-five years. This is particularly true in his role in selecting the Committee on Committees.

This committee, chosen at the prerogative of the president, nominates the Committee on Nominations. Once elected by the Convention, the Committee on Nominations nominates trustees for SBC entities and the Executive Committee and members of any standing committees for Convention consideration. This system has proven so effective in the eventual election of trustees nominated by this process that Southern Baptists who wanted the Convention entities to move in a more theologically conservative direction came to believe the election of the Convention president was the key to change.

In the last quarter of the twentieth century, a concentrated, announced effort to elect particular presidential candidates was undertaken. These conservative candidates were successfully elected. Even though the Convention was free to elect trustees other than those nominated, it ratified every nominee presented by the process. It is arguable that, while the presidency has limited authority, it does have tremendous power.

The duties of the first and second vice presidents are to preside over the annual meeting in the absence of the president. The recording secretary, assisted by the Executive Committee staff, keeps the minutes of the meeting, makes reports to the Convention, and subsequently causes the proceedings of the minutes to be published in the *SBC Annual*. The recording secretary is an *ex officio* member of the Executive Committee. The registration secretary prepares and conducts the registration process working with the Credentials Committee and also works with the Tellers Committee in tabulating and reporting ballot votes of the Convention. The treasurer of the Convention is always, by virtue of office, the president of the Executive Committee.

BUSINESS OF THE CONVENTION

While the Convention has always included singing, preaching, prayer, and other inspirational and devotional elements, its primary purpose is to conduct the business of the Convention. It must elect trustees to Convention entities. It must approve a Cooperative Program Allocation Budget and a Convention Operating Budget. It may adopt resolutions presented by the Resolutions Committee. Its entities are required to report to the Convention in writing and orally each year. It must act on any substantial changes in assignments to the respective entities. It must allow time for messengers to introduce business and make motions.

All of this business is scheduled according to an agenda recommended by the Committee on Order of Business. In the adoption of the agenda, the Convention makes time for the necessary business of the Southern Baptist Convention, including time for general business. All of the business of the Convention is conducted according to parliamentary procedure as dictated by the Convention documents and *Robert's Rules of Order.* Every messenger has the right and opportunity to make motions, ask questions, debate, vote, and otherwise engage the process of the meeting.

In 1986, after a record 45,000-plus messenger registration in 1985 in Dallas, Texas, the Executive Committee, at the president's request, began employing a certified parliamentarian to serve the annual meeting. This has helped to ensure a more orderly disposition of the business in the unusually large parliamentary gathering of the Southern Baptist Convention.

In addition, the same year brought the implementation of the microphone-ordering box (MOB). This technological tool allows the president to recognize messengers at the several floor microphones in chronological order. With the large number of messengers desiring to speak, especially in hotly debated topics, and the limited business time, the system has been a great asset. As one messenger noted, the MOB has kept the Southern Baptist Convention from becoming a mob.

When those wishing to debate have been heard, or when time expires for debate, the vote is taken. The action of the Convention is subsequently announced, recorded, and implemented. When the Convention has completed its agenda, the meeting is adjourned. The work of the SBC is carried on by those to whom it has been assigned until the following year when the Southern Baptist Convention is gaveled into existence once again at the annual meeting.

AUTHORITY

It is important to reiterate that the final authority over the SBC is the messengers sent by the churches. Once they seat themselves as the Convention, they speak with authority on all matters they address. In particular they elect trustees to each entity board. This is critical because virtually all the work of the Southern Baptist Convention between annual meetings is conducted by the various entities and the Convention's Executive Committee. These trustees are accountable to the Convention for the management of the entity they are elected to serve. They are responsible to set policies, adopt budgets, secure and maintain a president and supporting staff, and ensure the entity operates according to its SBC-approved charter and performs its SBC assigned ministries. Each SBC entity is directly accountable to its SBC-elected board. Each board is directly accountable to the SBC. This system of governance is consistent with Baptists' understanding of the autonomy of the local church and the appropriateness of intercongregational ministries.

Chapter Seven

The Distribution System:
Allocating the Cooperative Program

The Southern Baptist Convention and the state Baptist conventions have a prescribed plan for distributing Cooperative Program gifts. This is called the allocation process. Before a discussion of Convention allocation, it is important to understand how the Cooperative Program dollars get to the conventions.

INDIVIDUAL BAPTIST CHURCH MEMBERS

The Cooperative Program begins with individual stewardship. Stewardship encompasses all of life.[1] As Paul put it, "If we live, we live for the Lord, or if we die, we die for the Lord; therefore whether we live or die, we are the Lord's" (Rom. 14:8 NASB). Christians must learn to live all of life with a personal commitment to the lordship of Jesus Christ. They need to allow that kind of passion to permeate all they do, so that in every area of life they will be stewards of his gifts to them. Once they make such a general commitment, it is a logical matter to follow that through in stewardship of their personal finances. Those who have not committed their money to the Lord show thereby that they are not living lives of consistent discipleship. As Luther noted, it is those persons whose pocketbooks are converted who are truly saved.

Scripture also shows that the early disciples gave to and through their churches (1 Cor. 16:1–2; 2 Cor. 9). Believers have an obligation to share all good things with those who teach them the Word of God (Gal. 6:6) and to support the work of ministry both locally and in far-off places. Each Baptist decides the amount the Lord desires to be given from his financial resources to his local church. The Bible encourages a tithe (10 percent) of income as the model for giving. Many Christians give larger percentages. Church members generally have the opportunity to contribute their regular tithes to a unified budget adopted by the church. This "general" budget supports all the regular ministries of the church: personnel, debt retirement, operational costs, ministries, and missions including the Cooperative Program.

Church members can also contribute to special causes like the Lottie Moon Christmas Offering for International Missions, the Annie Armstrong Offering for North American Missions, the state missions offering, and so forth. Gifts to special causes are called "designated" giving because they are utilized only for the specific purpose the donor intended. Gifts to the general budget are called "undesignated" giving. They are utilized according to the decision of the church in its budget. Cooperative Program gifts come from the "undesignated" giving of the church members. It is important to note that individual members decide the amount given to special causes. The church decides the amount given through the Cooperative Program.

Each church sets the amount it will send through the Cooperative Program. Ordinarily, the amount is a set percentage of the church's total undesignated income. Although the Convention cannot and does not set a required percentage for congregations to give, the percentage of Southern Baptists churches' aggregate undesignated receipts given through the Cooperative Program from the 1930s to the 1980s was consistently in the 10.5 to 11 percent range. (Recent trends will be discussed in a later chapter.) Although some churches set a dollar amount for the Cooperative Program, most still utilize a percentage to determine the gifts for Cooperative Program ministries. Setting the Cooperative Program gift as a percentage of church receipts has been the preferred method across the years.

Although churches' gifts to the Cooperative Program are not subject to *tithing* regulations in the Scriptures, percentage giving produces some of the same positive effects that individual tithing does. It enforces the idea that a certain proportion should always be reserved for the Cooperative Program and is not available for other budget needs. Also, a gift based on percentage causes Cooperative Program gifts to grow automatically with the church's income growth. Furthermore, percentage giving sets a benchmark from which to increase to a higher percentage.

COOPERATIVE PROGRAM AND THE STATE CONVENTION

Once a month the treasurer of each Baptist congregation tabulates the amount of the previous month's general budget receipts. A check is made for the percentage of those receipts committed to the Cooperative Program. This check is sent with a remittance form to the Baptist state convention office. This one check is for Cooperative Program ministries at both the state and the Southern Baptist Convention level. The decision was made in the beginning of the Cooperative Program in 1925 that the state convention would be the "collecting agent" for both the Southern Baptist Convention and the state convention. Although some churches send gifts directly to the Executive Committee of the Southern Baptist Convention, the vast preponderance contribute through their state conventions. The state convention treasurers are responsible for keeping track of the local churches' giving. The state convention offices send the Southern Baptist Convention portion to the Executive Committee of the Southern Baptist Convention at least once a month.[2]

How does the state convention decide how much to forward to the Southern Baptist Convention? The messengers from the churches to the state convention annual meeting vote the percentage division each year. Again, this has been the agreement with the Southern Baptist Convention since 1925.[3] Each state convention sets the percentage for that state convention. The average percentage of all Cooperative Program funds forwarded to the Southern Baptist Convention the last twenty years has been about 36 percent with a low of 35 percent and a high of 39 percent.

The portion of the churches' Cooperative Program gifts retained for state convention ministries is allocated according to a budget adopted by the messengers from the churches to the annual state convention meeting. The budget preparation process varies from state convention to state convention but would be similar to the Southern Baptist Convention process described below. The receipt, disbursement, accounting, and auditing of Cooperative Program gifts is the responsibility of the state convention Executive Board and its employees.

One might ask, "Where in all of this mix is the local *association* of Baptist churches? Does the association receive Cooperative Program funds?" The answer is no, at least not directly, though some convention (state and SBC) programs are carried out partly through the associations. Churches give directly to their associations apart from their Cooperative Program gifts. Often this is in the form of another percentage formula, such as 1 to 3 percent of their revenue over and above that given to the conventions. Some churches make a flat dollar contribution to the association each year. But associational gifts are separate from the Cooperative Program.

THE COOPERATIVE PROGRAM AND THE SOUTHERN BAPTIST CONVENTION

How are the Cooperative Program receipts divided among the mission boards and other ministries of the Southern Baptist Convention? They are divided according to the Cooperative Program Allocation Budget. This budget is developed by the Executive Committee each year and recommended to the Southern Baptist Convention meeting in June for adoption. Upon approval of the Convention, this becomes the Allocation Budget for the following fiscal year. The fiscal year for the SBC is October 1–September 30.

As the state conventions forward the Cooperative Program gifts from the churches to the Southern Baptist Convention, those gifts are distributed to the entities of the Convention on a *pro rata* basis. It is important to note only those gifts identified as "Cooperative Program" by the state conventions are distributed according to the Cooperative Program Allocation Budget formula. Gifts that are "designated" by churches or individuals to be given to a particular SBC cause are forwarded in their entirety to that cause. The Southern Baptist Convention Bylaw 18.E. (3) reads, "To disperse all undesignated funds, according to the percentages fixed by the Convention and all the designated funds according to the stipulations of the donors." This is a policy that is scrupulously honored.

CP ALLOCATION BUDGET PROCESS

The development of the Cooperative Program Allocation Budget involves a number of steps beginning several months before the annual meeting.

In the September meeting of the Executive Committee, each entity leader gives an oral report to the plenary session regarding the status of that entity's work. These brief remarks allow the leaders the opportunity to summarize their work, share successes and challenges, and appeal for appropriate Cooperative Program support.

By October 1, Ministry Report Forms are mailed to entities by the Executive Committee for return to the Executive Committee offices by December 1. These forms are designed to obtain a written summary of the work of each entity, an evaluation of ministry goals achieved, a forecast of goals for the coming fiscal year, and financial data of the entity. These Ministry Report Forms are compiled by the Executive Committee staff and mailed to the SBC Executive Committee members in January for their study.

In the February meeting of the Cooperative Program Subcommittee, the entity executives discuss the ministry reports, financial data, and budget requests with the committee. It then becomes the responsibility of the Cooperative Program Subcommittee to develop a budget proposal for consideration by the full Executive Committee.

The Cooperative Program Subcommittee is guided by several Executive Committee policies as it prepares its recommendation. One policy, adopted in 1989, requires the Executive Committee to adopt a budget no larger than the total receipts of the last fiscal year of record. This means, in its February budget preparation meeting, the Cooperative Program Subcommittee refers to the total receipts tabulated through the previous September 30. That amount becomes the maximum budget that can be recommended to the Southern Baptist Convention the following June. Most consider this a wise, though very fiscally conservative, policy.

Prior to the adoption of this policy, the Executive Committee was free to set any amount for the budget total, even if it greatly exceeded what had been previously received in one year. It was easier to grant an unusual increase to one or more entities because the total budget goal could simply be expanded to accommodate the increase. Those who liked this practice saw it as a way to challenge the churches to give sacrificially to meet the increase. However, unlike challenging a local church to give "over and above" to underwrite a budget increase, the Southern Baptist Convention is too complex and far-flung to execute successfully that kind of appeal in a short time frame. When the projected increases were not met, the entities had to revise their expectations, and spending plans had to be reduced.

Also, because the receipts are distributed on a *pro rata* basis, entities that were not granted large increases could actually receive a lesser dollar allocation than the previous year. Under current policy, because all receipts over 100 percent of the budget are distributed to the entities just like the first 100 percent, every entity usually receives more from the Cooperative Program than it budgeted.

In 1998, the Executive Committee adopted other new policies that have changed the budget process. The first was the use of a two-year allocation cycle. The Executive Committee agreed that it would recommend a budget for one year, as is customary. However, in the following year each entity would receive the same percentage of the whole that it had in the previous year. If entity A was granted an allocation in the first year totaling 10 percent of the whole, it would know the following year it would receive 10 percent of the whole regardless of the total dollars received by the Southern Baptist Convention.

In the third year the cycle would begin again, and the Executive Committee could recommend a budget which caused entity A to receive 11 percent (or some different percentage) of the total. This "new" percentage would be fixed for the following (fourth) year. Entities would still file reports for evaluation by the Cooperative Program Subcommittee of the Executive Committee every year, although budget requests and budget allocations would be made every other year. The Executive Committee asserted this two-year cycle was beneficial because:

- The budget process for each SBC entity would become more personalized and purposeful.
- Southern Baptist Convention entities could do more long-range planning, by being assured of a fixed budget percentage for twenty-four months.
- Through the use of improved reporting procedures, the Cooperative Program Subcommittee could more adequately evaluate the expenditures of Cooperative Program funds, understand the results of ministries, assist in future mission projects and strategies, and encourage cooperative partnerships among the entities.
- The budget process would emphasize the evaluation of planning, accountability, and effectiveness of the entities as well as allocation of Cooperative Program receipts.[4]

Another change made in 1998 altered a longtime practice of the Cooperative Program. Capital needs allocations were eliminated from the Cooperative Program process. Capital needs are those expansions and improvements to the physical facilities of the entities (new buildings, equipment, renovations, etc.) which are too expensive to be paid out of a normal annual operating budget. When the Cooperative Program was adopted in 1925, capital needs were given a place in the allocations. Capital projects were ordinarily funded by retaining 50 percent of the Cooperative Program proceeds in excess of 100 percent of the adopted budget.

For example, the 1997–98 Cooperative Program Allocation Budget was $148,185,077. Actual receipts were $159,583,743. That year $5,699,333 was available for capital needs. The other half of the $11,398,666 was distributed according to the Cooperative Program Allocation Budget percentages. Each entity made application for available funds by having its project, including costs, approved by the SBC. A capital needs budget for a certain period was adopted, and the entities received the funds on a pro rata basis until the total was distributed.

The last capital needs budget was adopted in 1984 in the amount of $6,874,000. It was scheduled to be completed in 1988. Because of shortfalls in the Cooperative Program budget goals, there were not sufficient receipts to fund the scheduled needs until 1999, long after the projects had been completed through borrowing or other means. The Executive Committee decided it was not prudent for the entities to plan their capital projects on funds that may not materialize in a timely fashion. Capital needs would no longer be considered by the Southern Baptist Convention in the Cooperative Program allocation process. All of the receipts in excess of the budget goal would be distributed to every entity according to the budget percentages.

Once the Cooperative Program Subcommittee has decided on an allocation budget, it is presented to the full Executive Committee for approval. The recommended budget is printed in the *Book of Reports* for consideration by the Southern Baptist Convention. The annual convention has the final say. It may alter the budget from the "floor" by a simple majority of the messengers present and voting. It seldom does. Once the Convention has given its approval, even the Executive Committee may not change the budget. The Cooperative Program receipts for the following fiscal year will be distributed by the treasurer of the Convention according to the adopted budget.

SUMMARY

The Cooperative Program dollar originates with the undesignated gift of the individual Baptist to his church's general budget. The church votes annually for a set percentage to be contributed through the Cooperative Program. One check is sent each month to the state convention office. The total of all Cooperative Program gifts from all churches in 2002–03 was $501,199,697. The state convention treasurer retains the percentage voted by the state convention for state convention Cooperative Program ministries. (The aggregate amount retained by the state conventions in 2002–03 was 63.45 percent of the total.) The balance is sent to the Executive Committee of the Southern Baptist Convention for distribution to the SBC ministries according to the Cooperative Program Allocation Budget adopted by messengers in the Southern Baptist Convention annual meeting.

For the years since 1997, the SBC portion of the allocation has maintained a uniform percentage distribution among the entities. The International Mission Board allocation is 50 percent, the North American Mission Board allocation is 22.79 percent, the Theological Education allocation (for the six seminaries and the Historical Library and Archives) is 21.64 percent, the Ethics and Religious Liberty Commission allocation is 1.49 percent, the GuideStone Financial Resources (for ministerial relief) allocation is 0.76 percent, and the SBC Operating Budget allocation is 3.32 percent. LifeWay Christian Resources and the Woman's Missionary Union do not receive Cooperative Program funds.

The financial processes of the Cooperative Program are to be commended. Every step of the process (allocation, disbursement, reporting) is guided by the churches and their representatives. Annual professional audits are performed at every level and by every entity receiving Cooperative Program dollars. Full reports are made several times a year to the executive bodies and annually to each convention. And the whole process is extremely efficient. Administrative costs, including all accounting as well as promotion, are estimated at about 2 percent. This compares to as much as 20 percent costs of independent missions organizations and even more in many other charitable organizations.

Cecil Ray wrote, "The Cooperative Program is a bargain. It is the most effective and most efficient method Baptists have ever used for gathering and distributing money to mission causes. It costs less for promotion, postage, bookkeeping, and administration than any other known method."[5]

Chapter Eight

Network to the World:
Southern Baptist Organization

aptist churches in America have formed intercongregational organizations for ministry as far back as the Philadelphia Association, which
was organized in 1707. As Baptists spread across the United States, they
continued to create additional associations of churches in new geographical areas. Beginning with South Carolina in 1821, Baptists in the South
formed statewide associations or state conventions. When the Southern
Baptist Convention was founded in 1845, there were already nine state
conventions.

In contemporary Southern Baptist life, local congregations generally
belong to three distinct intercongregational organizations based on geography: (1) the local association which is usually comprised of churches in the
same county or local region; (2) the state convention comprised of churches
in the state; (3) the Southern Baptist Convention comprised of churches in
all the United States and its territories. Each of these organizations, while
working cooperatively with the same churches and with one another, maintains its own autonomy. Southern Baptist ecclesiology is not hierarchical.
The churches do not relate through the association to the state convention
to the Southern Baptist Convention. The churches relate directly to each
of these Baptist bodies. None of the bodies (churches, associations, state
conventions, national convention) rules over any other body.

The purpose of each of these organizations is to multiply the ministries of the individual churches. In 1971, a Cooperative Program Study

Committee recited the philosophy of Southern Baptist organization: "These presumptions generally have been followed in determining the areas of responsibility in the work of general bodies with the churches: (a) Any program which can be conducted effectively by the local church should be sponsored by the local church. (b) Associations and state conventions should sponsor only programs which cannot be carried out as effectively by the local churches. (c) The Southern Baptist Convention should sponsor only programs which cannot be conducted effectively by state conventions, associations, and local churches."[1]

THE BAPTIST ASSOCIATION

Baptist associations have historically provided a platform for fellowship, edification, and expansion of ministries among Baptist churches in a given area. In 2002–03, there were 1,194 associations of churches among Southern Baptists. Most of these associations are led by directors of missions (sometimes called associational missionaries). These men are responsible for coordinating the work of the local association, which involves any number of endeavors from operating food and clothing ministries, conducting training clinics, sponsoring abortion alternative ministries, working with Baptist collegiate ministries at local colleges, organizing area-wide evangelistic efforts, and so forth. The associations regularly partner with the state conventions and the North American Mission Board in planting new churches within the association. One association has recently changed its official name to the "Spartanburg County Baptist Network" in order to emphasize its function of being a catalyst for various joint ministries among the churches.[2]

Associations receive their financial support directly from their member churches and not through the Cooperative Program. In some associations, especially in the regions where Southern Baptist work is not as strong, the associations are assisted financially by the state conventions or the North American Mission Board.

THE STATE BAPTIST CONVENTION

The two partners who share Cooperative Program gifts from the churches are Baptist state conventions and the Southern Baptist Convention.

Southern Baptists currently have forty-two state conventions. The conventions are ordinarily referred to as state conventions even if their geographical territory extends beyond one state. Six of the state conventions are comprised of more than one state (e.g., the Baptist Convention of New England is made of churches in all six New England states). Thirty-four state conventions represent only one U.S. state. Two states (Virginia and Texas) have two state conventions, both of which serve churches in the whole geographical area of those states.

These state conventions are voluntary ecclesiastical organizations representing the Southern Baptist churches in that region. As with the Southern Baptist Convention, the Baptist state conventions have annual meetings (usually in the fall of the year) of two to three days in length, which are comprised of "messengers" sent by participating churches. Each state convention, while having cooperative ventures with the Southern Baptist Convention, is "autonomous in its own sphere." It adopts its own constitution, bylaws, and other governing documents, sets its own ministries, approves it own budgets, and secures and supervises its own employees.

Most Baptist state conventions have an elected executive board. Unlike the Executive Committee of the Southern Baptist Convention, these executive boards have broad authority to act for the Baptist state convention.[3] The state executive board generally employs an executive director who oversees the various ministries and employees of the executive board.

The state conventions vary in size from the Baptist General Convention of Texas, which reported in 2003 a membership of 4,322 churches and 2,385,936 members to the new Puerto Rico Southern Baptist Convention with 47 churches and 5,500 members. The ten largest state conventions, located in the Southeastern and Southern United States make up 63 percent of the Southern Baptist churches, 70 percent of the total Southern Baptist membership, and 71 percent of all the gifts to Southern Baptist causes.

The original states that were already organized into state Baptist conventions and sent messengers to the first Southern Baptist Convention were: Alabama Baptist State Convention (1823), Baptist Convention of the State of Georgia (1822), Kentucky Baptist Convention (1837), Baptist Convention of Maryland-Delaware (1836), Mississippi Baptist Convention (1836), Missouri Baptist Convention (1834), Baptist State Convention of North Carolina (1830), South Carolina Baptist Convention (1821), and the

Baptist General Association of Virginia (1823). By 1900, there were fifteen state conventions, and by 1950 there were twenty-four state conventions, reaching the current total of forty-two state conventions in 2004. The newest are: Puerto Rico Southern Baptist Convention—2004, Dakota Baptist Convention—2004, Montana Southern Baptist Convention—2002, Southern Baptists of Texas Convention—1998, and Southern Baptist Conservatives of Virginia—1996.

State Convention Ministries

The state conventions conduct a wide array of ministries and sponsor various institutions. Historically Baptist state conventions have concentrated on the following tasks:

- provide programmatic assistance such as Sunday school training, music promotion and planning, etc. to the churches;
- assist churches in planting new churches;
- own and operate institutions such as children's homes, senior adult homes, colleges and universities, and hospitals; and
- lead in stewardship and Cooperative Program development.[4]

Not every state convention has the same ministries. The older and larger conventions of the Southeast have many more institutions (primarily children's homes and colleges) than the other conventions. In 2004, there were forty-seven children's homes operated by the various state conventions and forty-nine colleges or universities as well as several academies and Bible schools. Thirty-three state conventions operate foundations whose purpose is to procure and manage investments for Baptist causes.

In addition to these institutions, state conventions have retirement homes, encampments, and counseling centers. Most state conventions that operated hospitals have severed those relationships, allowing the hospitals to direct their own work. Another important ministry performed by the state conventions is to college students. The state conventions, in 2004, employed 638 full-time and part-time campus ministers who minister on 880 campuses.

The state conventions also provide regular news and information through Baptist state papers. The papers are published weekly, biweekly, or monthly. There are forty-one Baptist state papers with a total readership of approximately 1.2 million. Two particularly effective ministries of recent years are partnership missions and disaster relief. The state conventions coordinate with the North American Mission Board and the International Mission Board in performing these ministries. Most state conventions have partnerships with other state conventions and with nations overseas. They involve local churches in ministering to these regions through short-term trips, prayer groups, and other projects. Forty-one states have disaster relief programs, which respond to regional and national emergencies such as hurricanes, tornadoes, fires, and crises like "9/11." In 2003, there were 497 disaster relief units with 12,871 volunteers. It has been estimated that Southern Baptist volunteers are responsible for providing and serving 90 percent of all hot meals served in the United States to victims of disasters.

A survey of state convention executive directors indicated about fifty different kinds of ministries carried out by the conventions. In addition to the ministries already mentioned, the states are involved in missions education, support of bivocational ministers, media/library training, ministry to families, and annuity supplements for pastors and other ministers. The ministries most commonly considered the highest priorities of the state conventions are evangelism, church planting, partnership missions, and language/ethnic ministries. According to state convention executive directors, the greatest value of the state convention is strengthening and challenging local Baptist churches for the work of evangelizing the many lost persons in their states and for the work of spreading the gospel around the globe.

COOPERATIVE AGREEMENTS BETWEEN STATE CONVENTIONS AND THE NORTH AMERICAN MISSION BOARD

For years Baptist state conventions and the North American Mission Board of the Southern Baptist Convention (formerly the Home Mission Board) have planned and coordinated their joint ministries through the use of cooperative agreements. The cooperative agreement is the instrument that facilitates the harmonious development of a uniform, national missions strategy. These agreements are especially vital to a nationwide strategy for missions and evangelism. They fulfill the Southern Baptist Convention directive to develop a single, unified missions plan of work.

Cooperative agreements (1) call for joint planning of NAMB work in the states, (2) authorize the joint selection and employment of missionaries and (3) include a unified budget with annual agreements on amounts of funding, ratio of participation, and other understandings. The vast majority of the approximately five thousand North American Mission Board missionaries are jointly sponsored and supervised by the state conventions. It was never intended that cooperative agreements be legal documents, but rather a basis of understanding and a plan for working together. In the planning process, ministry leaders of both the North American Mission Board and state conventions decide upon state strategies of missions and evangelism. At the same time North American Mission Board ministry leaders develop a continental strategy for missions and evangelism. These two strategies are compatible and not in conflict.[5]

COVENANT FOR A NEW CENTURY: THE RESTRUCTURING OF THE SBC

The other Cooperative Program partner is the Southern Baptist Convention. The Southern Baptist Convention was organized in 1845 with two ministries: the Foreign Mission Board and the Domestic Mission Board. The founders anticipated additional enterprises would be started as the Convention deemed them needed and possible. Over the next half century, theological education (The Southern Baptist Theological Seminary in 1859) and Christian publishing (the Sunday School Board in 1891) became a part of Southern Baptist Convention work. Other ministries were added throughout the first half of the twentieth century. These were the American Baptist Seminary Commission (1913), the Christian Life Commission (1913), the Education Commission (1915), the Executive Committee (1917), the Annuity Board (1918), the Radio and Television Commission (1946), the Southern Baptist Foundation (1947), the Historical Commission (1951), and the Stewardship Commission (1960).

Southern Baptists also expanded their efforts in theological education. Five theological seminaries joined Southern Seminary in the Southern Baptist constellation. They were Southwestern Baptist Theological Seminary (1908), New Orleans Baptist Theological Seminary (1917), Golden Gate Baptist Theological Seminary (1944), Southeastern Baptist Theological Seminary (1950), and Midwestern Baptist Theological Seminary (1957). Some ministries, such as the Baptist Hospital Commission, served for a period of time but were discontinued.

As the 150th anniversary of the Southern Baptist Convention approached, the Convention had a total of nineteen boards, commissions, and institutions as well as one auxiliary (Woman's Missionary Union). In 1993, a motion was made at the Southern Baptist Convention meeting in Houston, Texas, that a committee be appointed to study the structures and processes of the Convention. This motion resulted in the appointment of the Program and Structure Study Committee (informally called the Brister Committee after its chair, Louisiana pastor Mark Brister). The Brister Committee recommended to the Southern Baptist Convention in 1995 a report entitled the "Covenant for a New Century" which called for a wide-ranging restructuring of Southern Baptist Convention work. The report was adopted overwhelmingly by the Convention.

The Brister Committee wrote in the report: "Our concern is that the Convention keep its primary focus on its founding vision—and on our shared mission. Every question, no matter how difficult; every issue no matter how complex, must be measured by this standard: How can Southern Baptists accomplish our mission to the greatest level of faithfulness and the highest standard of stewardship?"[6] They suggested the mission of the Southern Baptist Convention be expressed as follows:

> The Southern Baptist Convention exists to facilitate, extend, and enlarge, the Great Commission ministries of Southern Baptist churches, to the glory of God the Father, under the Lordship of Jesus Christ, upon the authority of the Holy Scripture, and by the empowerment of the Holy Spirit.[7]

The committee was convinced the Convention needed a "streamlined structure"[8] in order to fulfill the principles of the mission statement. Their report recommended the dissolution or merger of eight of the Convention's nineteen ministries. Those entities that were dissolved were the American Baptist Seminary Commission, the Education Commission, the Historical Commission, and the Stewardship Commission.

The ministries of the Historical Commission (preserving Southern Baptist history and operating the Southern Baptist Library and Archives in Nashville, Tennessee) were assigned to the six seminaries. The ministries of the Stewardship Commission were assigned to the Sunday School Board (teaching stewardship and providing capital fund-raising assistance to churches) and to the Executive Committee (promoting the Cooperative Program). The work of the other commissions was not reassigned. The Southern Baptist Foundation was made a subsidiary of the Executive Committee and continues its duties under that administrative framework.

The most complex of the covenant's recommendations was the creation of the North American Mission Board. The Brotherhood Commission, the Radio and Television Commission, and the Home Mission Board were merged to form this new entity. NAMB was to combine the ministries of the former entities as it concentrated on assisting Southern Baptists in evangelism and church planting. Two other ministries received new names: The Foreign Mission Board became the International Mission Board, and the Christian Life Commission became the Ethics and Religious Liberty Commission (the Christian Life Commission had received the assignment for "religious liberty concerns" in 1991 when the Southern Baptist Convention withdrew its participation from the Baptist Joint Committee on Public Affairs).

When the "covenant" was implemented in 1997, the Convention had a total of twelve corporations plus one auxiliary to conduct its work. The Implementation Task Force (ITF), which had been elected by the Executive Committee to implement the recommendations of the Covenant for a New Century, reported to the Southern Baptist Convention in 1997 that as of June 19 of that year, the new ministries:

> have been transferred . . . and the respective boards of trustees,
> including the new NAMB, are authorized and positioned to
> carry out the ministries assigned to them. . . . The Executive
> Committee and the ITF affirm the goals of the Covenant for a
> New Century and are convinced that, by God's grace, they are
> attainable, workable, and full of promise.[9]

The largest reorganization in SBC history was completed. The streamlined ministries were underway. Two more changes came later. The Sunday School Board's name change to LifeWay Christian Resources was not a recommendation of the Brister Committee. It occurred later as a recommendation of the Sunday School Board in 1998. Also, the Annuity Board trustees asked the Southern Baptist Convention in 2004 for a charter amendment changing that entity's name to GuideStone Financial Resources. The following chapter contains a brief history and description of each of the ministries of the Southern Baptist Convention.

Chapter Nine

The Entities That Serve Southern Baptists

The nineteenth century was a remarkable time for Christians of all kinds, in America and around the world. New technologies made way for innovative approaches to ministry. The industrial revolution made missions expansion possible in a way previously unanticipated. Also, the nineteenth century witnessed urban sprawl, a situation that both created new problems and provided new opportunities for churches and their ministries. The increasing proliferation and rapidly expanding size of cities brought about the rise of many new colleges for the training of ministers; at the same time the flight of farmers to the cities created many new social and moral problems heretofore unanticipated. This led to the rise of societies for coping with moral and social ills.

Urbanization also led to an increasing concern for literacy since it became clear that in the city, much more so than on the farm, the key to financial security and career mobility lay in having a good education. All of this led to the rapid development of new approaches to evangelism, mission, the training of ministers, and even such matter as the architecture of church buildings. This chapter will explore these issues in their early general developments. It will then proceed to show how Southern Baptists adapted to these new situations. The chapter will conclude with a brief description of the current status of SBC entities.

THE NINETEENTH CENTURY AND AMERICAN CHRISTIANITY

Publishing societies abounded as the American Bible Society was formed in 1816 and the American Sunday School Union the following year. The American Tract Society was formed in 1825, one year after Baptists had established the Baptist General Tract Society. In addition societies dedicated to moral reform sprang up in the second quarter of the century. Some of these were by-products of the reforming passions associated with the Second Great Awakening, a movement which included college revivals, camp meetings, and early forms of crusade evangelism from about the 1790s through about the 1810s. In 1826 the American Society for the Promotion of Temperance was formed as a response to what appeared to be an increasing problem with drunkenness in America. Other similar organizations followed, with the state of Maine enacting prohibition in 1846.

Slavery also grabbed the attention of some reform-minded persons. Quaker John Woolman published *Some Considerations on Keeping of Negroes* in 1754, a book that led Philadelphia Quakers to abandon slavery and which would later influence northern and southern abolitionists. Prominent Virginians, including some Baptists, freed their slaves in 1782, when it became legal for them to do so. The General Committee of Baptists in Virginia passed a resolution against slavery in 1789. Later, in 1833, the same year that slavery was abolished in Great Britain and its colonial holdings in the West Indies, Northerner Theodore Dwight established the American Anti-Slavery Society.[1]

Church denominations and other Christian groups planted many new Christian colleges in the early to mid-nineteenth century. Colleges had been founded by Christian groups from the earliest days. Harvard College, named for benefactor John Harvard, who had been a teaching elder in the Congregational church at Charlestown, was founded by the General Court of Massachusetts in 1636.[2] James Blair arrived in Virginia from England in 1685 and discovered that Anglicanism was at a low ebb in the colonies. He labored to bring new life to the churches, but his most lasting contribution was the securing of a charter in 1693 for establishing the College of William and Mary, which he then served as first president.[3]

Committed to giving Connecticut its own institution for education, Puritans in New Haven, in consultation with Increase and Cotton Mather, founded Yale College in 1701.[4] William Tennent Sr. set up what he called the "log college" in 1726. Tennent, an Irish Presbyterian, established this school near Philadelphia to educate his sons and other Presbyterians in the Christian ministry. Eventually the school relocated to New Jersey, changing its name to The College of New Jersey, and later to Princeton College.[5] Baptists established Rhode Island College in 1764 "as an institution that would teach religion and the sciences without regard to sectarian differences,"[6] and yet at the same time with the goal that "religion and learning should unite their forces to elevate and save the race."[7] Morgan Edwards was its first president; later presidents included Francis Wayland and Ezekiel Gilman Robinson. This early Baptist college in America would later take the name of Brown University.

To these early colleges the nineteenth century would add many new names. Wheaton College was formed in 1860 under the leadership of evangelical pioneer John Blanchard. He believed the task of education to be a moral one and that "institutions of learning are the forts" at which our battles are being fought.[8] Blanchard was committed to anti-Masonry, he was opposed to secret societies, he lobbied the government for stronger Sabbath laws and laws against drink, he sought greater justice for American Indians, and he argued for the abolition of the Electoral College.[9] Oberlin College was founded in 1835 with Charles Finney as its first professor of theology and later, from 1851 to 1866, as president. Because of the influence of Finney, Oberlin became identified with revival theology, with the "new measures" that Finney had introduced to revivalism,[10] with the confidence in the possibility of Christian "perfectionism," and with political activism primarily in the realm of abolitionist sentiments. These two schools would be characteristic of different moods within evangelicalism developing from the middle of the nineteenth century.

Baptists in the South were starting up new colleges at breathtaking speed. Richmond College, later the University of Richmond, was formed in 1840 with sixty-eight students and three teachers. The school was closed during the Civil War, and its endowment was invested in Confederate bonds. It reopened in 1866. But with no endowment, with buildings ravaged by the fortunes of war, and with students scattered and lives ruined by the conflict, the outlook was bleak. A new president, Tiberius Gracchus Jones, was instrumental in rescuing the school.[11]

Richard Furman was passionately committed to theological education. In 1786 he called for the churches of the Charleston Association to take an annual offering for ministerial education. He formed what came to be known as the General Committee, a committee whose purpose was to raise funds for theological education. "By this simple act, the seed of Baptist education was planted."[12] In 1826 Baptists in South Carolina would establish a university that bore his name.[13]

Jesse Mercer was the most influential Baptist leader in Georgia in the nineteenth century. Mercer was a tireless proponent of missions, both foreign and domestic. He formed the Powelton Baptist Society for Foreign Missions in 1815 and was corresponding secretary for a mission to the Creek Indians for a number of years. Mercer University was established in 1833 as a testament to both Jesse Mercer and his father, Silas.[14]

Many other such colleges could be listed. Carson College was founded in 1850, Union University in 1844 (it previously had been Jackson Male Academy since 1825), Mississippi College in 1850 (when Baptists took it, it had begun in 1826 and was the first college to graduate a woman in 1831), Baylor in 1846, and William Jewell in 1849. Baptists in the South demonstrated by example and certainly by hard work that they were committed to the ideal of an educated ministry.

Sunday schools grew in prominence during this period. Robert Raikes was the early enthusiastic supporter and innovator in the development of Sunday schools in Great Britain beginning in 1780. His idea was to educate the children of the poor by teaching them to read on Sundays. He chose Sunday because many English children, whether on the farm or in the cities, worked up to twelve hours a day, six days a week. Sundays were free days. His desire and goal was to teach them to read the Bible, but before he could do that he had to teach them the general skill of reading.[15] By 1786 patrons of the movement enrolled some 200,000 children in English Sunday schools, and the movement had gained the support of John Wesley, Christian poet William Cowper, philosopher Adam Smith, and Queen Charlotte.[16] Within a few years it spread to America.

Until about 1815 most American children who attended Sunday schools were from the very poorest children in the country, children who had no other prospect of learning to read. Increasingly, with the aid of the American Sunday School Union, this new institution was taken over by churches and became part of their educational program, though it would still be a long time before the Sunday schools would look anything like what we have known in the twentieth century and beyond.

By the 1880s Sunday schools focused great attention on conversion, and they became the primary avenues for entry into church membership.[17] Uniform Sunday school lessons were published beginning in the early 1900s. Tensions between denominations divided over the modernism/fundamentalism debate resulted in the founding in 1945 of the evangelical National Sunday School Association. Since the 1960s mainline denominations have experienced a serious decline in their Sunday school enrollments while most of the more conservative churches held their own through the century.[18] Sunday schools in other nations have experienced declines as well, with attendance in the Church of Scotland, for instance, dropping off in 1971 to half of what it had been in 1900.[19]

In chapter 4 we dealt in detail with the rise of foreign missions through the centuries and into the nineteenth century. Domestic missions had also long been a major concern for American Christians. Right through the late nineteenth century domestic, or home, missions was mainly ministry to American Indians, black slaves, and frontier work. In 1636 Congregationalist minister John Eliot began his work among the Northeastern Indian tribes, followed not long after by the mission work of Roger Williams.

American Baptists established the American Baptist Home Missionary Society in 1832. The driving force behind this society was John Mason Peck. Peck observed that 40 percent of the Baptist churches in America had no pastor, but when he made a tour of the West, he discovered the situation there to be far worse. He then led Baptists to form the new society to help meet the pressing need of churches on the frontier for leadership. By 1844 this society had ninety-seven missionaries and had started 551 churches.[20] For a variety of reasons, Baptists in the South were never heavily involved in the work of this society but when they formed the new work in 1845, southern commitment to domestic missions would leap forward monumentally.

SOUTHERN BAPTISTS ORGANIZE TO MAKE THE GREATEST IMPACT

The first meeting of Southern Baptists occurred in 1845, and their first official convention came a year later. Between these two meetings Baptist leaders worked very hard to set the mission work of the new denomination in place.

International Mission Board

Since we discussed foreign missions in some detail in chapters 4 and 5, we will only sketch a few important details here. Jeremiah B. Jeter was appointed to be president of the Foreign Mission Board at the Consultative Convention in 1845. Eight days later he called the newly appointed members of the board together for their first meeting in Richmond, Virginia. The board selected James B. Taylor to be the corresponding secretary, that is, the hands-on leader of the mission board. Adoniram Judson, the famous missionary who had served so long in Burma under the Triennial Convention, visited Taylor and encouraged him in the work.[21] Taylor was deeply moved and greatly helped by this kind visit from American Baptists' greatest missionary. From the earliest days of the SBC, it was clear to many that the Convention was almost completely identified with its commitment to foreign missions.

Where would the new mission board find its first missionaries? That was actually not a problem at all since the first three missionaries were already on the field. They were southerners under appointment to the existing mission board of the Triennial Convention, and they quickly agreed to transfer their support to the new Southern Baptist board. By December 1845, six missionaries were under appointment and the new work was moving forward as quickly as anyone could have hoped. In 1847 the Southern American Negro missionary, John Day, also joined the SBC. The Board needed of course to raise funds to carry out its work, and Southern Baptists demonstrated an eagerness to support the missionaries. In 1846 Southern Baptists gave just under $12,000 to foreign missions; in 1859 those gifts had risen to nearly $80,000.[22]

One of the most remarkable early missionaries was R. H. Graves, missionary to Canton (China). Graves served as missionary from 1856 to 1912 and was instrumental in leading thousands of Chinese people to Christ.[23] The Foreign Mission Board saw its resources grow dramatically in the twentieth century. In 1900 it employed ninety-four full-time missionaries on the field. By 1910 that number had swelled to 246, and by 1960, there were 1,381 missionaries under appointment in forty-five nations.[24]

North American Mission Board

The Consultative Convention that appointed members for a board of foreign missions also appointed a board of domestic missions. (This

Domestic Mission Board later became the Home Mission Board; then, more recently, the North American Mission Board.) Basil Manly Sr. was appointed first president and J. L. Reynolds the first corresponding secretary, but neither of these men stayed through the first year. Russell Holman then took the leadership, but the early years of the Domestic Mission Board were filled with problems, problems largely related to the fact that Baptists in the North were still very much involved in work in Southern states. The presence of Baptists from the North in these states made many Baptists reluctant to contribute to the work of Southern Baptists there.

During the first fifteen years of the SBC, leadership of the Domestic Mission Board changed four times; during the same period the Foreign Mission Board had been led by the same man, J. B. Taylor. The early work of the board was primarily with Blacks, Indians, Chinese in California, and Germans in Maryland and Missouri, along with the white Catholic population of southern Louisiana.[25] But it did more than that. It gave itself to "provide gospel preaching where none existed; to plant churches in destitute areas; to strengthen weak churches by helping support their pastors and providing funds for buildings; to provide schools, especially in mountain areas, before the coming of public high schools; . . . [and] to develop an urban mission to share the gospel in the mushrooming cities."[26]

Then came the War Between the States. The war threatened to bring Southern Baptist domestic missions to a standstill since funds were even harder to come by than in the previous lean years. But the new secretary, Martin T. Sumner, was undaunted. The total income for the board in the year 1862 was only $15,000. But the board directed its major energies to ministry among the Confederate soldiers. Many of those who served as full-time missionaries during these war years served for no salary at all.[27] Great work was accomplished as tens of thousands of the South's military men were converted through the ministry of the Domestic Mission Board—renamed the Home Mission Board in 1874—and other Christian agencies. At the end of the war, though, the board was completely out of funds. Kentucky Baptist churches extended a call to all SBC agencies to come to the state for financial help. In six weeks Kentucky Baptists collected $10,000 toward convention causes; other border states and some southern states followed suit.[28]

The years of reconstruction still weighed heavily on the SBC, but in 1882 the board moved to Atlanta from its previous home in Marion,

Alabama, and it appointed Isaac Taylor Tichenor to be its secretary. He traveled extensively and worked feverishly with the state conventions in the South to such a degree that within five years all of the home missionaries in the South were working with the HMB and the southern state conventions. This one development, the reclaiming of the southern field, "probably preserved the existence of the SBC itself," even though it did not "secure the existence of the Home Mission Board."[29] "Seldom has a leadership change achieved such a dramatic turnaround as did that which brought" Tichenor to the HMB.[30]

Even through the first half of the twentieth century, the HMB had to fight off several challenges to its existence. Critics arose at key junctures and called on the SBC to eliminate the Home Mission Board. The board faced several financial crises in the past century, the worst of which coincided with the Great Depression and an embezzlement scandal that happened at the same time. Opponents at such times argued that the HMB was unnecessary. Some of them alleged that the entity did nothing more than duplicate the efforts of state conventions. There certainly is an overlap between the HMB and some state convention activities, but wiser heads have prevailed and Southern Baptists are still deeply committed to the mission work at home as well as abroad. The purpose of it all can be summed up in one word—*evangelism.*[31]

LifeWay Christian Resources

In 1885 I. T. Tichenor called upon Southern Baptists to appoint a committee to study the best way to provide literature for the churches of the Convention. This was not a new idea; Southern Baptists had been debating this notion for years. John Waller, editor of Kentucky's *Western Recorder*, and J. S. Baker, editor of *The Christian Index* of Georgia, had lobbed editorials at each other on several occasions about this issue, Waller being opposed to a Southern publication house and Baker being for it. Four previous attempts to establish such a venture had been attempted, the first in 1847. All had failed for one reason or another. But Tichenor was adamant, and his lofty oratory carried the day at the Convention in Richmond in 1888, though it took three years before the dream became a reality.[32]

The creation of the Sunday School Board in 1891 "completed the schism with its northern counterparts."[33] The new board, located in Nashville, Tennessee, prevailed upon James Marion Frost, a pastor in Baltimore, to become its first secretary. Because the Sunday School Board received no financial support from the Convention, Frost took out a loan to begin operation until revenues from sale of literature could provide financial stability. Within a year the board was in good financial shape.[34] Frost was convinced that the Sunday School Board was crucial to the existence and strength of Southern Baptists, that it "carries within itself . . . the very life of the Convention." He went on to say, "We are working at the very base of things" related to the progress of kingdom work.[35]

It is difficult to overestimate the impact of Sunday schools on the churches of America. Churches had to adapt their architecture and building plans now to make room for large educational facilities. Prior to the rise of Sunday schools, this was generally not necessary. The Sunday school also called for multiple staffing of churches, even of smaller or mid-size churches. Educational ministries, children and youth ministries called for more specialization, both in training at the seminaries and execution at the local church.[36]

Shurden has pointed out four ways in which the Sunday School Board itself has impacted the SBC. First, it has provided education for laypersons within Baptist churches. Second, it has made an impact on missions and evangelism, since it has published literature related to missions and since many people converted in SBC churches have been converted through Sunday schools. Third, the board has had a financial impact since the Sunday school became the primary agent for collecting offerings in most Baptist churches. Fourth, it brought some amount of unity to the churches since most of them used the Sunday school literature published by the board.[37]

GuideStone Financial Resources

Baptist ministers in the early days in England and in America were often poorly paid. This was largely due to the fact that Baptist people often came from the poorer parts of society and so were unable to provide for their pastors in the manner that some other denominations were. That situation was compounded when pastors became too ill or too feeble to continue their work since they then had no salary at all. Baptist individuals and associations made various attempts to remedy this situation. In 1717 Baptists in England formed the Particular Baptist Fund to provide some relief for ill or retired pastors or their widows. In Kentucky the Baptist Ministers Aid Society was established in 1884 with an endowment of

$65,000, while in Maryland William Crane and J. H. Deems organized the Widows and Superannuated Ministers Fund in 1893.[38]

Nashville pastor William Lunsford became convinced that more could be done and that the SBC should step up to the plate and do so on a Convention-wide basis. He and a group of other Nashville pastors convinced the Sunday School Board to set aside $100,000 for ministerial relief, and the same year the SBC organized a committee to study the situation.[39] The next year the Convention voted to establish the Relief and Annuity Board, located in Dallas, and the board then chose Lunsford to be its first Secretary. Northern Baptist oil magnate John D. Rockefeller assisted the fledgling organization with a one million-dollar gift from his foundation, and by 1923 the board had a million and a half dollars in assets.[40]

The Annuity Board (now GuideStone) has made a very large impact on Southern Baptists. McBeth cites three major contributions. First, it has enabled a "financial safety net for the pastor and his family."[41] Those who follow the Lord's call into full-time ministry do not generally do so out of any ambition to become wealthy. Many, in fact, consciously abandon other professions that would probably provide a better living. But it is helpful to know that one does not necessarily have to live out the final years of one's life in virtual poverty. Second, the retirement program has likely caused ministers to think in a more businesslike manner about the financial aspects of church ministry. The fact that a pastor thinks about his own life in responsible financial terms spills over into how he thinks about the church and its financial stewardship. Third, the Annuity Board has had a unifying effect on the SBC. Even those who have become dissatisfied with some aspect or other of SBC life find it hard to break away entirely since that break, for good or ill, might impact their financial future.[42]

The Ethics and Religious Liberty Commission

Baptist people have long been passionate about ethical and social issues, and they have also been deeply committed to involvement in political life, while at the same time holding their own views on the relationship between church and government. It ought to come as no surprise then that at some point they would appoint a commission to study these issues and to keep Baptists apprised of what is happening in our culture on these matters. In 1907 the Convention appointed two new organizations—the Committee on Civic Righteousness and the Temperance Committee. Six years later Southern Baptists organized the Social Service Commission. It combined the work of the previous committees into one entity, but in practice tended only to address issues of alcohol abuse, lynching, Sabbath neglect, and the sale of obscene literature.[43]

In 1946 the chairman of this commission, J. B. Weatherspoon, urged Southern Baptists to adopt a wider focus on social issues, to appoint a full-time secretary, and to expand the work of the commission. This plan was enacted in 1947, and the name of the commission was later changed to the Christian Life Commission and, later still, to its present designation. The SBC assigned two functions to the CLC in 1961—to assist churches in understanding the moral demands of the gospel and to help them to apply those principles to moral and social problems.[44] In the early 1990s, the Southern Baptist Convention severed its relations with the organization The Baptist Joint Committee on Public Affairs, and the assignment for teaching and promoting religious liberty was assigned to the Christian Life Commission, now the ERLC.

Seminaries

Earlier in this chapter we discussed the rise of Baptist colleges across the South in the early nineteenth century. By 1850 more than a score of these institutions had been formed, but Baptists in the South still had no seminary. Seminaries began to crop up in America in the early 1800s largely because of the rise of liberalism and unitarianism in American institutions. When Harvard College hired Henry Ware to teach theology in 1805, it sent shock waves through many churches in the Congregationalist denomination since Ware was a professed Unitarian. Conservatives in that denomination established Andover Theological Seminary in 1808 to counter Harvard's move to the left.[45] Presbyterians formed Princeton Seminary four years later, and a spate of similar schools sprang up in the decade or so that followed.

Baptists had opened a seminary in Covington, Kentucky, as a joint effort between Northern and Southern Baptists, but it lasted only three years. During its first decade of existence, the SBC meeting frequently witnessed debate over forming a southwide seminary, but not until 1856 were any definitive plans set in motion. Furman University offered its facilities predicated on fulfillment of certain stipulations, which were met, and the seminary opened in 1859 with four faculty and twenty-six students.[46] James Petigru Boyce had been appointed professor of theology at Furman University in 1856, and in his now-famous inaugural address to that position, he proposed three significant changes in Baptist theological schools: (1) not only college graduates but men with less general education, even a common English education, should be offered such opportunities of theological study as they were prepared for and desired; (2) special courses should be provided so that the ablest and most aspiring of students might be prepared for service as instructors and original authors; (3) there should be prepared an abstract of principles, or careful statement of theological belief, which every professor in such an institution must sign when inducted into office so as to guard against erroneous and injurious instruction.[47]

Boyce implemented all of these proposals into the new seminary three years later. The seminary, then, offered instruction to all persons who had a sufficient education to that point to be able to enroll in class and do the work even if their prior education was limited. It also provided advanced study, by century's end right up to doctoral degrees, for the more qualified. And all teaching was to be "in accordance with and not contrary to" the Abstract of Principles which was drawn up by Basil Manly Jr. and affirmed by faculty and trustees.[48]

Due to the Civil War, the Southern Baptist Theological Seminary fell on hard times almost right away. It closed for a period but then reopened in the fall of 1865, due mainly to the faculty. They had stated that the school might die, but they would die first.[49] James P. Boyce almost singlehandedly kept the school open for a time in the antebellum years, even paying the faculty's salary out of his own pocket.[50] By the mid-1870s Boyce and others sensed that the school needed to be relocated. The expansion of Southern Baptists into the Southwest made it difficult for many potential pastors to receive an education, so in 1877 the school relocated to Louisville, Kentucky.

As the seminary moved through the late nineteenth and then twentieth centuries, it entered several major crossroads. There were several periods in which struggles with liberalism on the faculty resulted in professors' terminations, either by firing or resignation, especially in 1879, 1958, and in the late twentieth century. Southern Seminary has also been blessed with some of the best scholars in Baptist history serving on its faculty. John Albert Broadus, Archibald Thomas Robertson, and Edgar Young Mullins are legends in Baptist life and scholarship, and the list of other names is too long to include here.

By the turn of the twentieth century, many Southern Baptists in the West and Southwest saw the need for a seminary closer to them. In 1907 the Baptist General Convention of Texas approved the founding of a new seminary in Waco, Texas, and handed the task to the man who had already laid the plans in place—Benajah Harvey Carroll, pastor of First Baptist Church, Waco. Carroll had already been operating a seminary there since 1905, but in 1908 it received official sanction, and then, two years later, moved to its present location in Fort Worth, Texas.[51] Carroll gathered a high-quality faculty to the school, and after his death his hand-picked successor, Lee Rutland Scarborough, continued the tradition.

Southwestern pioneered in several areas, including religious education, church music, and evangelism. In the latter area Scarborough's intense work as an evangelist gave to the chair of evangelism its distinctive name, "The Chair of Fire." This focus on practical ministry often caused Baptists to see Southwestern as the "preachers' seminary," while they viewed Southern as the "scholars' seminary." But that characterization was far too broad and general, because Southern produced great preachers (i.e., Criswell and Hobbs), and Southwestern also produced great scholars (i.e., Walter Thomas Conner, who graduated in the first commencement, Robert Andrew Baker, and James Leo Garrett Jr.).

The Baptist Bible Institute was chartered in New Orleans in 1917 to train pastors to minister in Louisiana and the Mississippi Valley and also to train ministers for the Latin countries and for reaching Roman Catholics at home with the gospel.[52] At the time the institute was chartered there were only six Baptist churches in New Orleans, and only one of them was self-supporting.[53] In contrast, then, to the first two Baptist seminaries, this institute was founded here not because of Baptist strength but because of Baptist weakness. Bryan Hoover DeMent, its first president, previously pastor of First Baptist Church, Greenwood, South Carolina, stated, "Our motto is, 'The enthronement of the Bible as the Word of God.'"[54]

The faculty was presented to the SBC in its annual meeting in Hot Springs, June 1918, before the opening class session in the fall of that year. It was opened by the authority of the SBC in 1917 and then came fully under SBC direction in 1925.[55] The school became New Orleans Baptist Theological Seminary in 1946. It eventually opened a satellite campus in Atlanta and energetically serves many parts of the Gulf Coast and Florida with extension campuses.

Southern Baptists had begun moving to California in the 1849 gold rush. The War between the States, though, brought Southern Baptist work in California to an end; it would take another migration prompted by the Great Depression to bring Southern Baptists back to the West Coast.[56] In 1941 Baptist churches in California petitioned to join the SBC, a petition that was granted the following year. Isam B. Hodges, a pastor in Oakland with degrees from Ouachita Baptist College and Southwestern Seminary, established the Golden Gate Baptist Theological Seminary in 1944, and it was adopted by the SBC in 1950.[57] In 1959 the seminary moved to its present campus on Strawberry Point, Marin County. The seminary also has satellite campuses in Phoenix, Portland, Los Angeles, and Denver. Golden Gate has focused special attention on ministry in the Pacific Rim and in the western United States.

No sooner had Golden Gate Seminary been adopted by the SBC than others began asking the question, "Are four seminaries enough?"[58] The Convention that met in Chicago in June 1950 decided to purchase the campus of Wake Forest University in North Carolina and to open a new seminary there the following year.[59] This school was modeled after Southern Seminary in many ways, even adopting its Abstract of Principles as the doctrinal statement. It filled the need that had been left open when Southern Seminary moved to Kentucky in 1877—the need for a Baptist seminary to serve the Southeast.

The one part of the country left without a seminary was the Midwest. In advance of the Chicago Convention in 1957, advocates of several possible sites debated the location of the sixth seminary, including Denver, Cleveland, Memphis, Chicago, and Kansas City. Kansas City was finally selected, though not without considerable controversy.[60] Midwestern Seminary opened in 1958 and the next year moved to its beautiful campus. The seminary early on faced a conflict over the publication of the book *The Message of Genesis* by Midwestern Old Testament professor Ralph Elliott, an event we discussed earlier in this volume. The criticism addressed to the seminary over this event hurt the school in its infancy. But Midwestern has done well since that time and has been an important component of Southern Baptist presence in the heart of America. It offers extension studies in Kansas, South Dakota, and Wisconsin, with others in development.

Woman's Missionary Union

Another organization that deserves mention is one that is not an entity of the SBC but very integral to it. This is the Woman's Missionary Union (WMU). Founded in 1888, Woman's Missionary Union is an auxiliary of the Southern Baptist Convention. Its board is not elected by the Southern Baptist Convention, nor does it receive Cooperative Program funds. However, the president of WMU is an *ex officio* member of the Executive Committee of the SBC. "The task of WMU is to equip adults, youth, children and preschoolers with missions education to become radically involved in the mission of God. Headquartered in Birmingham, Alabama, WMU is a nonprofit organization that offers an array of missions resources including conferences, ministry ideas and models, volunteer opportunities, curriculum for age-level organizations, leadership training, books and more."[61] The WMU is also a valuable partner to the mission boards in promoting missions in general and the mission offerings in particular.

During the meeting of the Southern Baptist Convention in Richmond, Virginia, in May of 1888, a group of women delegates from twelve states gathered at the Broad Street United Methodist Church and organized the Executive Committee of the Woman's Mission Societies, Auxiliary to Southern Baptist Convention. In previous years women had been meeting during the convention to discuss the possibilities of creating a missions organization. During the 1888 meeting, a constitution was adopted, and the first officers were elected. Baltimore, Maryland, was chosen as headquarters. In 1890 the women adopted the name Woman's Missionary Union, Auxiliary to Southern Baptist Convention. The headquarters of WMU was originally stationed in the Maryland Baptist Missions Reading Room where Annie Armstrong had an already established office. In 1921, under the guidance of Kathleen Mallory, the national headquarters was moved to 1111 Comer Building, Birmingham, Alabama.

The 1970s brought changes to the organizations of WMU. In October of that year, WMS, YWA, Girls' Auxiliary, and Sunbeams were changed to Baptist Women (BW), Baptist Young Women (BYW), Acteens, Girls in Action (GA), and Mission Friends. Change in publications followed as *Contempo, Accent, Discovery, Aware,* and *Dimension* were introduced into the WMU publications family. In 1984, the national headquarters moved once again to New Hope Mountain on U.S. Highway 280, just outside the Birmingham city limits.[62]

THE SBC ENTITIES AT WORK TODAY

International Mission Board

Jerry Rankin, president of the IMB, recently wrote: "The vision of the IMB is to lead Southern Baptists to be on mission with God to bring all the peoples of the world to saving faith in Jesus Christ."[63] He reported that, at the beginning of 2004, a total of 1,194 people groups were being engaged by the personnel and strategies of the International Mission Board. The number of missionaries was approaching 5,300. These missionaries and the overseas groups they work with started 21,000 new churches and baptized more than 600,000 in 2004. The total 2004 budget of the IMB was $242,526,532. Cooperative Program support provides about 35 percent of this budget while the Lottie Moon Christmas Offering for International Missions provides about 55 percent.

North American Mission Board

Evangelism and church planting in the U.S. and Canada continue to be the twin objectives of the NAMB of the Southern Baptist Convention. In conjunction with the Baptist state conventions, NAMB supports approximately five thousand missionaries in North America. These missionaries are involved in numerous assignments such as church planting, chaplaincy, resort missions, social ministries, and so forth. Southern Baptists, under the NAMB's strategy, have been starting approximately seventeen hundred new churches a year for the last several years. The 2004 budget was $118,285,000. The Cooperative Program provided 36 percent of that total while the Annie Armstrong Easter Offering for North American Missions provided 43 percent.

In 2004, Southern Baptists continued to operate six seminaries. The seminaries offer a full range of quality theological studies and ministry preparation for the thousands of students God has called to mission and ministry vocations. Courses of study are available at baccalaureate and graduate levels. A few statistics about the seminaries will provide some perspective.

Seminaries

Golden Gate Baptist Theological Seminary, Mill Valley, California, reported 715 Full Time Equivalent (FTE) students in 2003–04.[64] Its total operating budget was $8,690,000 with 37 percent provided by the Cooperative Program. Midwestern Baptist Theological Seminary in Kansas City reported 302 FTEs in 2003–04 with a budget of $5,015,101. The Cooperative Program provided 57 percent. New Orleans Baptist Theological Seminary had 2,230 FTEs in 2003–04 and a budget of $16,707,968. The Cooperative Program provided 46 percent of the budget.

Southeastern Baptist Theological Seminary in Wake Forest, North Carolina, reported 1,631 FTEs in 2003–04. Its budget was $20,818,718 with 46 percent provided by the Cooperative Program. The Southern Baptist Theological Seminary in Louisville, Kentucky, had 1,973 FTEs in 2003–04 and a budget of $28,322,189. Cooperative Program funds provided 31 percent of the budget. Southwestern Baptist Theological Seminary in Ft. Worth, Texas, had 2,202 FTEs in 2003–04. Its budget was $30,173,093 with 31 percent provided by the Cooperative Program.

The six seminaries educated over fifteen thousand different students (9,000 Full Time Equivalent) in 2003–04 at a cost of about $110,000,000. The Southern Baptist Cooperative Program provided over $40,000,000 to this cause.

Ethics and Religious Liberty Commission

With twenty-four staff members and a 2003–04 CP allocation of $2,825,268, the Ethics and Religious Liberty Commission is Southern Baptists' smallest entity. However, with offices in Nashville, Tennessee, and Washington, D.C., it provides a service far beyond its size. With regular print and electronic media and a daily radio broadcast, the ERLC endeavors to keep Baptists and others informed and motivated about moral, cultural, and civic concerns. The total budget in 2003–04 was $3,385,177.

GuideStone Financial Resources

With the second consecutive affirmative vote of the Southern Baptist Convention, 2005, the Annuity Board officially became GuideStone Financial Resources of the SBC. One of the latest changes made in GuideStone's ministry assignment from the SBC was the granting of permission to market their products to persons not affiliated with the SBC.

The corporation reported a record amount of assets under management of $8.3 billion at the close of 2004. GuideStone provides retirement plans known as the Church Annuity Plan and Convention Annuity Plan, where church staff and denominational workers and their employers can set aside funds for employee retirement. At year end 2004 there were 23,226 active churches for a total of 54,942 active member participants in the Church Annuity Plan, and a total of 260 agencies and institutions with 33,813 employees in the Convention Annuity Plan.

GuideStone also provides various types of insurance coverage (medical, dental, life, disability, etc.) for those individuals, churches, or entities that wish to purchase them. In addition, a relief program for qualifying retired Baptist ministers and their widows is operated by GuideStone. Nearly fifteen hundred persons received financial support in 2004. GuideStone spent $5,271,148 for relief in 2004. Cooperative Program contributed $1,456,328 of this amount. No other programs of GuideStone receive any Cooperative Program money. The entity's $47 million operating budget is funded by fees from the participants.[65]

LifeWay Christian Resources

The Sunday School Board became LifeWay Christian Resources of the Southern Baptist Convention in 1998 in order more accurately to describe its array of products and services. It is one of the largest producers of Christian materials in the world. LifeWay, located in Nashville, Tennessee, operates three major divisions: Church Resources, Broadman & Holman Publishers, and LifeWay Christian Stores. The activities of this organization are too numerous even to list here. It produces literature, Bible studies, training materials, conferences, music, and much more for all age groups and sizes of churches and organizations. LifeWay is a very large corporation with a budget over $450,000,000 (2004) and around fifteen hundred employees. LifeWay Christian Resources has never received Cooperative Program funds from the Southern Baptist Convention but is self-supporting. It invests a significant amount in Southern Baptist missions and ministries worldwide.[66]

Woman's Missionary Union

Since its beginning in 1888, WMU has become the largest Protestant missions organization for women in the world, with a membership of approximately one million. WMU's main purpose is to educate and involve adults, youth, children, and preschoolers in the cause of Christian missions. Although originally geared toward women, girls, and preschoolers, both genders are active participants in WMU organizations and ministries today. These ministries are: Baptist Nursing Fellowship[SM], Christian Women's Job Corps[®], International Initiatives[SM], Missionary Housing, Project HELP[SM], Pure Water, Pure Love[SM], Volunteer Connection[SM], and WorldCrafts[SM].

Woman's Missionary Union, SBC, as the WMU vision statement states, "continues to look towards the future, to challenge Christian believers to understand and be radically involved in the mission of God. National WMU provides mission resources that rekindle a passion for God's mission among God's people."[67]

The organizations described above have been created and supported by Southern Baptists to conduct their national and international ministries. They continue to render valuable ministry effectively and efficiently under the directions of their Baptist-elected boards. The next chapter will address a unique organization in the SBC, the Executive Committee.

Chapter Ten

Inspiring Confidence in Cooperation:

The Executive Committee of the Southern Baptist Convention

As discussed earlier, the Southern Baptist Convention can be found only two days per year. It is brought into existence when its presiding officer calls to order the duly elected messengers from the churches. Two days later, when the final gavel is brought down, the messengers disperse to their homes and churches across the country, and the convention is over. If one searched for the Southern Baptist Convention, it would not be found.

But the Convention's ministries, perpetuated by the messengers, continued unabated. The trustees the messengers had elected assumed their roles on the governing boards of the Convention's entities. The officers and employees of those entities, including thousands of missionaries and hundreds of professors, performed their ministries of evangelizing, teaching, administering, and serving with a singular purpose: to seek first the King and his kingdom.

Between one annual meeting and the next, the Executive Committee of the Southern Baptist Convention is an important link for the work of the Southern Baptist Convention. The Executive Committee performs its ministries and conducts and administers the work of the Convention that is, in the language of SBC documents, *"not otherwise assigned."* The Executive Committee has been doing this since the Southern Baptist Convention, upon the recommendation of the Business Efficiency Committee in 1927, reorganized it, made it a legal corporation, and commissioned it:

- to create orderly financial management procedures for all Southern Baptist work,
- to provide a systematic approach to problem solving,
- and to advise and recommend on all matters involving cooperation among and between the several Baptist entities and state conventions.

HISTORY

The Executive Committee of the Southern Baptist Convention was created because of a concern among Baptists for organizational efficiency and accountability. With the growing ministries of the boards and the growing number of agencies in the early years of the twentieth century, a more coordinated system was seen as a necessity. At its founding in 1845, the Southern Baptist Convention determined that it would carry out whatever work it deemed important through "separate and distinct boards" under the direction of managers elected by the Convention's messengers for that purpose. In the nineteenth century the size of the annual Convention meetings and the limited number of boards made it possible for extensive interaction between the messengers and the leadership of the boards so that the Convention in some ways acted as a committee of the whole.[1]

However, for fifty years, in the hallways of the convention meeting, there was a running debate as to whether the separate boards ought to be consolidated (especially the two mission boards) into one central board. The reasons given most often by those favoring consolidation were efficiency and economy. At the 1880 Southern Baptist Convention, a motion was made to consolidate the boards. Although it was defeated, the issue did not go away.

The issue of consolidation came to a head in 1913. Some Baptists believed the growing complexity of the convention meeting and the expanding work of Southern Baptists needed more coordination and business efficiency. They called for a new organizational approach. A motion was made to appoint seven men to study whether the existing organization of Southern Baptist work was sufficient. When the committee was appointed, a further motion added the four agency heads (Foreign Missions, Home Missions, Sunday School Board, and Southern Seminary) to the committee, which became known as the Efficiency Commission. Their recommendations, which were adopted by the Convention over the next two years, struck a compromise and set in place the practice that continues in the Southern Baptist Convention until today. Processes were implemented which would ensure the entities would maintain a high level of coordination and accountability to the churches through the Convention. The report of the Efficiency Commission set in motion changes in the Southern Baptist Convention that brought increased organization, coordination, efficiency, and accountability.

These changes, as important as they were in the development of the relationship between the Southern Baptist Convention and its entities, did not resolve the issue. Those who desired more coordination and efficiency in Convention work spoke again. In 1916, one year after the Efficiency Commission's recommendations, a constitutional amendment was proposed that would create "one strong Executive Board which shall direct all the work and enterprises fostered by this Convention." A "Consolidation Committee" was named which reported to the 1917 Southern Baptist Convention. The report did not recommend the original idea to consolidate all the boards (although a substitute motion to that effect was offered, hotly debated, and, then, defeated). What it did recommend was a compromise between those who believed "consolidation" was best for the Convention and those who wanted to maintain "separate and distinct boards."

The result of several years of wrangling, debating, and proposing at the annual meetings was the creation of the *Executive Committee.* Southern Baptists had struck a balance between centralized authority and board prerogatives. The Executive Committee was proposed in order to bring *more* coordination and accountability to the ministries of the various boards of the Southern Baptist Convention. The Executive Committee became a unique feature of Southern Baptist life, first as a committee of pastoral and lay leaders in 1917 and then as a legal corporation with paid staff beginning in 1927. It alleviated fears of a single board while providing for a neutral body, without authority over the entities, to act for the Convention in matters of efficiency and coordination. As Albert McClellan concluded:

In the strengthening of the Executive Committee, another step
was taken in Southern Baptist organizational growth. Not needed
or possible in 1845, the Executive Committee's time finally
arrived in 1917 and 1927, when the complexity and maturity of
the Southern Baptist Convention made it necessary. The founders
in 1845 had made room for it with the phrase, "and other important objects connected with the Redeemer's kingdom." It was
the final and essential step in the Convention reforming process
begun by the Business Efficiency Commission (1913–1915).[2]

The Executive Committee's name has some significance. When it was
organized, the concerns about centralized power caused the Convention
to call it a *committee* and not a *board*. Many Baptist state conventions have
an executive *board* that has broad centralized authority. The Executive
Committee of the Southern Baptist Convention is much more limited in its
authority. Therefore, though they are legally the "trustees" of the Executive
Committee, a Tennessee not-for-profit corporation, Executive Committee
trustees are called "members" because the Executive Committee is a committee and not a board. The Executive Committee is always careful to
recognize the limitations of its authority in the SBC structure. Although
the Executive Committee functions as the Southern Baptist Convention
ad interim, it can only exercise authority in matters not otherwise assigned.
Most of the actions of the Southern Baptist Convention have already been
otherwise assigned to itself in annual meeting or to one of the several entities of the Convention.

For example, the Executive Committee is not the Convention *ad
interim* for approving the Cooperative Program Allocation Budget because
the SBC has reserved that assignment for itself in its annual meeting. Also,
the Executive Committee does not appoint missionaries for overseas duty
because the SBC has assigned that function to the International Mission
Board. The documents of the Southern Baptist Convention address the
relationship of the Executive Committee to the other entities as follows:

> To maintain open channels of communication between the
> Executive Committee and the trustees of the entities of the
> Convention, to study and make recommendations to entities
> concerning adjustments required by ministry statements or by
> established Convention policies and practices, and, whenever
> deemed advisable, to make recommendations to the Convention.
> The Executive Committee shall not have authority to control

or direct the several boards, entities, and institutions of the Convention. This is the responsibility of trustees elected by the Convention and accountable directly to the Convention.[3]

The trustees of the Executive Committee have a unique responsibility among all the trustees elected by the Southern Baptist Convention. In certain ways they function like all other trustees. For example, they set policy and employ a management team to carry out policies and assignments and function in ways unique to other boards of trustees. However, unlike trustees of the entities, the members of the Executive Committee regularly interact with the leadership of all the entities and the elected leadership of the Southern Baptist Convention.

While the Executive Committee is instructed by the Southern Baptist Convention to oversee the Convention's ministries, it does not supervise the work of the entities. Each entity is governed by the board of trustees elected by the Convention. The Executive Committee takes special care to respect this separation of power built into SBC polity.

The Executive Committee *is* specifically assigned the following duties in relation to the entities:

- The Executive Committee is told by the Convention to notify the entities of the actions of the Convention and to advise with the entities as to the best way of promoting all the Convention's interests.
- The Executive Committee is responsible for acting in an advisory capacity on issues regarding cooperation among the entities of the Convention and among the Convention's entities and those of the state conventions.
- The Executive Committee is directed to secure from the entities information about ministry plans, accomplishments, and financial data. It presents to the Convention each year a comprehensive financial statement and audit of the Convention and all its entities. It monitors compliance with the Convention's bylaws, ministry statements, and Business and Financial Plan.
- The Executive Committee receives, studies, and reports to the Convention the budgets of the entities and recommends to the Convention the amount of Convention funds to be allocated to each cause.

The Convention has chosen a rather deliberate approach in dealing with matters that come before it. The Executive Committee performs a valuable function in this regard. This allows the Convention to make a careful, informed decision in matters of significance assisted by the study of the Executive Committee on behalf of the Convention. The Executive Committee is able to give the time and attention to weighty matters that would not be possible in the two-day annual meeting format.

In the months between annual meetings, the Executive Committee, in partnership with the several entities, carries out its duty of deliberation so that recommendations may be brought for the Convention's consideration. The Executive Committee endeavors to ask the questions messengers might ask. The Executive Committee seeks the answers the Convention wants to have. The more important the issue, the more intense the study. In 1958, The Total Program Study Committee (the Branch Committee), the first major study of Convention structure in SBC history, reaffirmed the very necessary role of the Executive Committee. It wrote:

> The Convention must have extensive, detailed knowledge of the
> entities' ministries. The Convention cannot do its work prop-
> erly without the Executive Committee. The Convention meet-
> ing once a year does not have ample time or information neces-
> sary to carry out detailed operation of its many ministries. The
> Executive Committee is established to assist the Convention
> in carrying out its programs without assuming either the
> Convention's responsibilities or those of the agencies.[4]

The Executive Committee of the Southern Baptist Convention continues to perform that valuable role today.

The work of the Executive Committee can be divided into two broad categories: (1) the work conducted by the members of the Executive Committee, assisted by the staff, and (2) the work assigned by the Convention and carried out by the staff. The second category is similar to the function of all the entities. The first category is unique to the work of the Executive Committee.

WORK CONDUCTED BY MEMBERS OF THE EXECUTIVE COMMITTEE, ASSISTED BY THE STAFF

The Executive Committee of the Southern Baptist Convention has adopted its own bylaws in keeping with the instructions of the Southern Baptist Convention, elects its own officers, and organizes itself to carry out its assignment from the Southern Baptist Convention. Through the years the Executive Committee has organized itself into subcommittees and workgroups in order to accomplish the assignments given to it by the Southern Baptist Convention. These subcommittees, which relate to the various tasks of the Executive Committee, have been modified from time to time in order to achieve more efficiency and accommodate changing needs in the Convention.

Currently, the Executive Committee has three subcommittees: Administrative, Business and Finance, and Cooperative Program. Each member of the Executive Committee serves on one subcommittee.

The Administrative Subcommittee is divided into three workgroups: Bylaws Workgroup, Communications Workgroup, and Personnel Workgroup. Each member of the Administrative Subcommittee serves on one workgroup. The Bylaws Workgroup handles all matters concerning Southern Baptist Convention documents such as the Charter, Bylaws, and the Business and Financial Plan as well as Southern Baptist entity charters. It also addresses legal and policy matters affecting the Southern Baptist Convention and other matters. The Communications Workgroup relates to the Convention Relations and Baptist Press assignments. It considers various matters when the Executive Committee needs to make official pronouncements such as resolutions regarding persons or events important to Southern Baptists. The Personnel Workgroup, as the name suggests, deals with matters related to administering the employees of the Executive Committee.

The Business and Finance Subcommittee is organized into three workgroups: Business and Financial Plan Workgroup, Audit Workgroup, and Convention Arrangements Workgroup. The Business and Financial Plan Workgroup makes recommendations concerning compliance with the provisions of the Business and Financial Plan of the Southern Baptist Convention. The Audit Workgroup reviews the audits of the Executive Committee as well as of the entities of the Southern Baptist Convention as required by the Business and Financial Plan of the Southern Baptist Convention. The Convention Arrangements Workgroup deals with issues related to the planning and execution of the annual meeting of the Southern Baptist Convention. The Business and Financial Subcommittee as a whole recommends each year the SBC Operating Budget to the plenary session of the Executive Committee. The SBC Operating Budget, which must be approved by the Southern Baptist Convention, provides funds for the work of the Executive Committee and the work of the Southern Baptist Convention (expenses of committees, the annual meeting, etc.).

The Cooperative Program Subcommittee has three workgroups: Convention Ministries Workgroup, Cooperative Program Development Workgroup, and Foundation Workgroup. The Convention Ministries Workgroup interacts with the leadership of the Southern Baptist seminaries and makes any recommendations relating to the work of theological education. The Convention Ministries Workgroup also interacts with the four boards (International Mission Board, North American Mission Board, Annuity Board, and LifeWay) and one commission (The Ethics and Religious Liberty Commission) of the Southern Baptist Convention. It makes recommendations concerning their ministry assignments and other aspects of this work when Executive Committee or Southern Baptist Convention action is needed. The Cooperative Program Development Workgroup relates to the Executive Committee's assignment of Cooperative Program promotion and to questions regarding the status of the Cooperative Program. The Foundation Workgroup interacts with the work of the Southern Baptist Foundation and is the first body to approve trustees of the Southern Baptist Foundation, which is a subsidiary corporation of the Executive Committee. The Cooperative Program Subcommittee as a whole prepares for the Executive Committee the annual Cooperative Program Allocation Budget.

From time to time the Executive Committee authorizes special *ad hoc* committees to study particular needs and make recommendations. From 1993 to 2003 the Executive Committee authorized eight special committees. The Theological Education Study Committee investigated various ways to improve the delivery of theological education in Southern Baptist life. The Program and Structure Study Committee was appointed in response to a motion from the Southern Baptist Convention. It met from 1993 to 1995 and ultimately recommended the wide-ranging restructuring of the Southern Baptist Convention called the "Covenant for a New Century." The Implementation Task Force met from 1995 to 1997 and made such recommendations necessary to enact the provisions of the Covenant for a New Century.

Another special committee was the SBC Annual Meeting Study Committee (1997), which recommended the elimination of the Thursday session of the annual meeting, making the Southern Baptist Convention a two-day meeting. The Baptist World Alliance Study Committee was appointed in 1997 with the assignment to monitor and evaluate the relationship between the BWA and the Southern Baptist Convention. This committee ultimately recommended to the Executive Committee in 2004 that the Southern Baptist Convention sever its relationship with the Baptist World Alliance.

The Budget Process Study Committee was asked to recommend improvements to the Cooperative Program Allocation Budget process. The Southern Baptist Council on Family Life was authorized by the Executive Committee to develop a denominationwide emphasis on strengthening marriages and families. Their work resulted in the Empowering Kingdom Families initiative. The SBC Funding Study Committee was commissioned to investigate the funding needs of Southern Baptist entities.

Schedule and Meetings

The Executive Committee has three regular meetings per year—in February, in June (at the Southern Baptist Convention annual meeting), and in September. The work groups meet first and forward any recommendations to their subcommittees. The subcommittees, in turn, present recommendations to the plenary session of the Executive Committee. Each June the Executive Committee presents all motions requiring Southern Baptist Convention action to the annual meeting comprised of the messengers from the churches.

Actions of the Executive Committee

The Executive Committee considers three major kinds of motions: (1) those referred to it in a given year by the SBC in session; (2) those regularly assigned to it by the SBC; and (3) those requested by an entity of the Convention. The Executive Committee may also generate actions on its own initiative.

Some regular actions of the Executive Committee by assignment are: (1) recommendation of the Cooperative Program Allocation Budget; (2) recommendation of the SBC Operating Budget; (3) recommendation of the *SBC Calendar of Activities*; and (4) preparation of the *SBC Book of Reports*.

In the ten-year period from 1993 to 2003, the Executive Committee recommended 120 motions on behalf of the entities of the Southern Baptist Convention, such as ministry assignment changes, name changes, and charter changes. In the same period the Executive Committee responded to 124 referred motions from the Southern Baptist Convention on a variety of subjects.

TASKS OF THE EXECUTIVE COMMITTEE STAFF ON BEHALF OF THE SBC

The Executive Committee staff is headed by the president and chief executive officer, who is responsible to the members (board of trustees) of the Executive Committee. Morris H. Chapman has served in this capacity since 1992. The past presidents of the Executive Committee were: Harold C. Bennett 1979–92, Porter Routh 1951–79, Duke K. McCall 1946–51, and Austin Crouch 1927–46. In addition to his duties of reporting to the Executive Committee and the Southern Baptist Convention and representing Southern Baptists in various Baptist, religious, civic, and government groups, the president leads a team of vice presidents and other staff in performing a number of tasks for Southern Baptists. In 2003, the Executive Committee employed thirty-two persons to carry out these assignments.

1. Finance

The Executive Committee staff is responsible for receiving, disbursing, and accounting for all the gifts the churches and individuals forward to the Executive Committee for the ministries of the Southern Baptist Convention. The preponderance of these gifts is sent by the several state or regional Baptist conventions that have collected the gifts from the churches in their respective areas. The main categories of receipts are: (1) the Cooperative Program, (2) special offerings for international and North American missions, and (3) other designated gifts. The Executive Committee receives and disburses only gifts for approved Southern Baptist causes. All gifts are disbursed electronically to the entities of the Convention according to the Cooperative Program Allocation Budget or donor designation every five business days. Financial reports are prepared monthly and distributed to Baptist leaders and reported through Baptist Press.

2. Arrangement and Management of the Annual Meeting

The vice president of business and finance also acts as the Convention manager for the annual meeting of the Southern Baptist Convention.

An assistant Convention manager, housing director, and other staff aid him. This team negotiates contracts with the host city's facilities managers, hotels, transportation providers, and other vendors in arranging for the Southern Baptist Convention meeting. Host cities are selected four to six years in advance of the meetings and approved by the Southern Baptist Convention. The arrangement team travels to the host city numerous times both in selecting the city and in preparing for the meeting. Relationships are developed with local officials as a part of creating secure, hospitable, and efficient meeting conditions. Southern Baptist volunteers from the host city are selected to be the Local Arrangements Committee and work closely with the Executive Committee staff. In recent years the average cost to the SBC Operating Budget of arranging and conducting the annual meeting has been from $850,000 to $890,000.

3. Legal

An aspect of Executive Committee action on behalf of the Convention that is often overlooked has to do with legal matters. On the rare occasion when the Convention is sued, or when property needs to be received or conveyed, and on other occasions, the Executive Committee, in its "ad interim" capacity, acts in a fiduciary role in the legal realm to protect the interests of the Convention. Examples of specific "legal" actions taken would include:

- Requesting legal specialists to render opinions in legal matters brought to the Executive Committee for deliberation and determination, such as in the case of corporate reorganization, charter amendment at any of the SBC subsidiaries, or assessment of regulatory compliance or corporate practice by the SBC or any of its entities
- Hiring and overseeing defense counsel representing the Convention when it is sued for damages (usually as one of several defendants, the principal one of which is normally the entity or church where the damage or injury is alleged to have occurred)
- Negotiating and documenting contractual agreements
- Representing the SBC in connection with property matters and in regard to estates
- Relating to the Internal Revenue Service
- Complying with governmental regulation, both state and federal, and defending against its illegal or excessive intrusion into

matters of faith protected by the free exercise clause of the U.S. Constitution

- Joining in *Amicus Curiae* briefs before various courts in matters of concern to Christendom in general and the Southern Baptist Convention in particular (when a "Convention presence" is deemed necessary in addition to the Ethics and Religious Liberty Commission)
- Protecting the intellectual property rights of the Southern Baptist Convention
- Reviewing and assuring parliamentary propriety

4. Convention News

Baptist Press (BP) was formed in 1946 at the suggestion of Baptist state paper editors and is supported with Cooperative Program funds. It has been the daily national news service of Southern Baptists since that time. Partnering with Southern Baptist entities, state Baptist papers, and a network of freelance professionals, Baptist Press deploys writers and photographers around the globe in order to get the news and to report it with a Christian perspective that is largely absent in other media reports.

BP operates as a wire service and reaches about 1.2 million Southern Baptists in print through forty-one state Baptist newspapers and journals. Agreements with other Christian print publications add hundreds of thousands more readers in the broader evangelical market. BP receives a number of "spot" reprint requests from Christian and secular media outlets as well.

In 1996, Baptist Press began publishing via the Internet. Now also known as *BP News*, Baptist Press reaches a rapidly expanding Internet constituency via www.BPNews.net, various "electronic reprint" agreements with Christian Web sites, a daily e-mail dispatch, and *BP News* headline links that are hosted on church Internet sites. In 2000, Baptist Press launched a Christian sports service, *BP Sports* (www.BPSports.net), to provide daily scores and sports features from the more than fifty colleges and universities traditionally affiliated with Southern Baptists. *BP Sports* also presents special features about the witness of Christ through believers of various Christian traditions involved in all sports at all levels of competition.

Baptist Press maintains a central office in Nashville, Tennessee (Southern Baptist Convention Executive Committee) and has four partner bureaus in Richmond, Virginia (International Mission Board), Atlanta,

Georgia (North American Mission Board), Washington, D.C. (The Ethics and Religious Liberty Commission), and Nashville, Tennessee (LifeWay Christian Resources).

5. Convention Relations

The task of the Convention Relations Office is to describe and interpret Southern Baptist Convention decisions, actions, statements, beliefs, and policies to Southern Baptists and to the public at large. Within the Southern Baptist family this office describes and reports motions and resolutions from annual meetings, explaining SBC beliefs and positions taken on key issues. The Convention Relations Office also provides information and encouragement for churches and their members. To aid in these responsibilities, the office publishes three brochures that summarize SBC beliefs, mission endeavors, polity, and heritage.

The office also publishes *SBC Life*, the official journal of the Executive Committee. *SBC Life* is published ten times per year and is provided free of charge to Southern Baptist pastors, church staff members, denominational leaders, missionaries, and vocational evangelists. Paid subscriptions are also available to the public.

As a liaison with the general public, the Convention Relations Office describes and interprets SBC decisions, actions, statements, beliefs, and policies, responding to inquiries from network television programs, television stations, network radio programs, radio stations, newspapers, and magazines. In addition, the office responds to inquiries from non-Southern Baptist churches, as well as from private individuals, who wish to better understand the SBC.

6. Cooperative Program Development

With the creation of the Stewardship Commission of the Southern Baptist Convention in 1960, promotion of the Cooperative Program at the Southern Baptist Convention level shifted from the Executive Committee, where it had been assigned since the late 1920s, to this new entity. The assignment reverted to the Executive Committee in 1997 when, as part of the restructuring of the Convention, the Stewardship Commission was dissolved. The Cooperative Program Development Division was formed in 1997. It focuses not only on the procurement of funds but also on developing vision and relationships which, in turn, lead to increased participation from the churches. The primary mission is to champion the benefits and potential of cooperation among SBC entities, state conventions, and churches. Enhanced cooperation between all these parties maximizes Southern Baptists' efforts to fulfill Christ's Great Commission.

Developing this vision includes repositioning the Cooperative Program from being perceived as basically bureaucratic and administrative, a common opinion of Baptists according to recent surveys. To aid in this repositioning, the slogan "Caring people, partnering together, to touch the world" has been utilized to define the missions opportunity through the Cooperative Program. The Cooperative Program Development staff creates resources that focus on people and missions—preparing people, sending people, and reaching people. Multimedia resources (pamphlets, brochures, videos, CDs, DVDs, etc.) are produced and made available to state conventions and the churches.

7. Southern Baptist Foundation

The Southern Baptist Foundation was established in 1947 to provide a wide range of investment and estate planning services for Southern Baptist Convention agencies, institutions, and individuals. In 1997, the Southern Baptist Foundation became a subsidiary of the Executive Committee of the Southern Baptist Convention although its method of operation was not altered. The object of the Southern Baptist Foundation is to support the Convention in spreading the gospel by securing and managing financial gifts and investments whose earnings benefit Southern Baptist Convention work.

The foundation offers a program of investment management to the *various entities and institutions of the Southern Baptist Convention.* This service may include investing temporary funds, reserve funds, and endowment assets. The investment objective may vary widely depending on the type of funds or the particular agency or institution responsible for them, and the foundation develops a program to meet those specific objectives. As needs or objectives change, the foundation works with the particular entity or institution to ensure that the programs are adapted.

The *various state foundations* may, from time to time, require supportive information regarding taxes, investments, or estate planning. The SBC Foundation assists the state foundations as they might request. The Southern Baptist Foundation also serves *individuals who express a desire to provide perpetual support for denominational causes* through an outright gift, trust, will, deed, or gift annuity. Assistance in estate planning services is offered to aid Baptists in making gifts either during one's lifetime or by will. Current tax information is provided and appropriate legal advice is available through counsel to donors who wish to provide a permanent source of income to Baptist institutions and causes.

SUMMARY

The Executive Committee was identified by the Program and Structure Study Committee as a "facilitating" ministry. This means its primary role is to be a resource for the work of all the other entities of the Southern Baptist Convention as well as other Baptist bodies and the churches. The Executive Committee is not headquarters for Baptists. But it is a hub for coordination, communication, accountability, and evaluation. The ministry statement for the Executive Committee reads: "The Executive Committee exists to minister to the churches of the Southern Baptist Convention by acting for the Convention ad interim in all matters not otherwise provided for in a manner that encourages the cooperation and confidence of the churches, associations, and state conventions and facilitates maximum support for world-wide missions and ministries." In carrying out this assignment, the Executive Committee aims to "inspire confidence in cooperation" so the churches and entities of the Southern Baptist Convention which it serves may find unlimited success in advancing the kingdom of God.

Chapter Eleven

Tensions, Trends, and Troubles

What is the current status of the Cooperative Program? How has it fared in recent years? What problems, if any, have appeared in its operation and performance? Are there emphases or trends that are becoming apparent? What are the implications of these issues for the future of the Cooperative Program? These questions frame the content of this chapter.

DECLINE IN PERCENT GIVEN

After a bumpy start (due to its newness and the onset of the Great Depression four years after its inception), the Cooperative Program settled in for fifty years of steady growth, not only in dollars but in the confidence of the churches. From the early 1930s until the mid-1980s, gifts to the Cooperative Program grew from $2,421,118 to $325,436,882. The percentage of the churches' aggregate undesignated receipts given through the Cooperative Program was consistently in the 10.5 to 11 percent range. Faithful support of the Cooperative Program was a nearly universal practice. Such widespread, aggressive support of the Cooperative Program made it the premier missions funding methodology among denominations.

For decades the regular increase in a church's Cooperative Program percentage was promoted as a virtue and was a sign of a healthy Southern Baptist congregation. Since 1984, however, there has been a marked change in support for the Cooperative Program from the churches. The total dollars continued to grow, reaching $501,000,000 in 2003. In addition, the percentage of churches giving through the Cooperative Program remained at a remarkably high 95 percent, according to recent surveys.[1] However, the percentage of the churches' undesignated receipts contributed through the Cooperative Program began a serious decline in 1985. The most significant factor about the Cooperative Program's performance over the last twenty years concerns this decline. The average percentage of undesignated receipts sent by the churches through the Cooperative Program from 1984 to 2004 declined from 10.6 percent to 6.99 percent.

This nearly twenty-year trend represents a startling 33 percent reduction in the average Cooperative Program percentage of the churches. A random review seems to indicate the decline in percentage giving is occurring in all varieties of churches—large and small, city and rural. Many who gave double-digit percentages have reduced to single digits, and many who gave modest percentages have reduced them further. What is the explanation for this downward trend in the percentage given through the Cooperative Program?

TENSIONS IN THE DENOMINATION

The Conservative Resurgence

Some would attribute the decline to controversy in the Southern Baptist Convention. Cecil Ray noted in *Cooperation: The Baptist Way to a Lost World*, "The success level of Baptists' cooperative mission endeavors parallels their trust level." Maintaining a cooperative spirit in Convention life "has tended to swing from trust and unity to renewed independence and separateness." Are Southern Baptists on a "separateness" trend, and, if so, will a return to unity follow?

Most any observer of religious life in the United States in the last quarter of the twentieth century would know that a major upheaval was occurring in the Southern Baptist Convention. This upheaval has been variously described by its opponents as a "fundamentalist takeover" and by its proponents as a "Conservative Resurgence."[2] The aim of the conservatives was a return of the Southern Baptist Convention and its entities to traditional biblical standards in doctrine and practice. Over a twenty-five-year period, the proponents of this movement prevailed, and succeeding meetings of the Southern Baptist Convention saw trustees and other leaders elected who reflected the views of the conservative resurgence. These leaders caused these same conservative standards to be applied to the personnel and policies of Southern Baptist Convention entities. By the mid-1990s, the conservative resurgence was a *fait accompli* in Southern Baptist Convention life.

In the midst of this controversy, some pre-conservative resurgence denominational leaders tended to downplay the necessity of doctrinal consensus for Southern Baptists, insisting that the basis for cooperation has always been missions, not doctrine. James L. Sullivan expressed a common view held by "moderate" Southern Baptists: "It is most important to observe that the basis on which the Convention was brought into being was not Christian doctrine but Christian action. As necessary as doctrine is, it was not the original basis for our cooperation as a denomination. Not only was missions and ministry action that original motivation, it still remains the major emphasis."[3] The implication of this line of thinking is that Southern Baptists viewed doctrinal concerns as secondary matters and were always willing to compromise or accommodate in order to organize for missions.

Conservative Southern Baptists, however, argued that a consensus of primary theological convictions always existed among Southern Baptists and was a prerequisite to forming common organizational structures for missions.[4] They asserted Southern Baptists did not band together in spite of doctrinal differences but because of doctrinal consensus. That consensus is evident in the confessions of faith adopted by Baptists (such as the New Hampshire Confession, 1833) and affirmed from time to time when the doctrinal integrity of the common work was threatened. The Baptist Faith and Message, through its various editions (1925, 1963, 1998, 2000), codifies the effort of Southern Baptists to define those commonly held beliefs.

The insistence on the primacy of Baptist principles has also been evident in Baptists' constant aversion to ecumenical organizations. "There are times when the sin lies at the door of those who refuse to separate. In short, Baptists do not subscribe to an uncritical ecumenical philosophy of union at any cost."[5] Baptists generally choose to work toward their mission with those who hold the same convictions about that mission.

Thus, the conservative resurgence rejected the premise that mission action, not doctrine, is the basis for Southern Baptist work. Southern Baptists have frequently debated where to "set the boundaries" of Baptist cooperation *vis a vis* Baptist doctrine. They have not, however, been unconcerned about sound doctrine. On the contrary, they understood that cooperative missions flows from common convictions. Southern Baptists have insisted unity of action is dependent on common belief and cannot be sustained apart from it.

What was the impact of the conservative resurgence on the Cooperative Program? Some critics attribute the decline in percentage giving to the denominational conflict. Nancy Ammerman, a sociology and theology professor at Boston University and author of the book *Baptist Battles*, said that "after 20 years of telling their congregations that (the Cooperative Program is) a bad system and doing bad things, in some sense they've reaped that harvest."[6] While some may have had complaints about the way the Cooperative Program works, most conservative resurgence supporters were not concerned with the methodology of the Cooperative Program (i.e., that it was a "bad system"). They were concerned the entities receiving the funds were not being faithful to historic Baptist theology and principles.

A number of Baptist congregations and individuals began about 1992 diverting their mission giving to the theologically moderate Cooperative Baptist Fellowship, which had been organized as an alternative to the now conservative-led SBC. In its first year of operation in 1991, the CBF received donations of about $10 million. In 2003, it reported income of about $17 million. It is likely most of these dollars would have been contributed through the Cooperative Program if not for the controversy. In the years 1991–1993, Cooperative Program receipts of the Southern Baptist Convention actually declined.

Although many state conventions will not receive funds for the Cooperative Baptist Fellowship, some such as the Baptist General Convention of Texas, the Baptist State Convention of North Carolina, and the Baptist General Association of Virginia receive contributions for the CBF and count them as ordinary Cooperative Program receipts before being forwarded. Since much of the money diverted to the Cooperative Baptist Fellowship continues to be counted as Cooperative Program, it is not as significant a factor in the percentage decline as might initially be assumed.

Baptist Colleges

Another symptom of tension in the denomination is the relation between Baptist colleges and state conventions. In the years of the conservative resurgence, a number of Baptist colleges altered their relationship with their state Baptist conventions. (It is to be remembered that colleges and universities in Baptist life ordinarily are affiliated with state conventions and not the Southern Baptist Convention.) Some of these decisions were made unilaterally, over the objections of the Baptist state convention, while others reached a compromise with the state convention in order to avoid legal or convention battles. In every incidence the degree of authority or legal control of the institution by the state convention was lessened. This was usually accomplished by defeating the state convention's absolute right to elect trustees. In every case theological/convention controversy played a role. The institutions did not want the state conventions to be able to direct their theological stances.

These institutional defections were both the result of controversy (institutions preempting potential actions by the state conventions) and the cause of controversy (churches and conventions seeking to change institutions they believed to be unsuitable). In many cases the schools that severed the control of the state convention continue to receive support from the Cooperative Program through the state convention budget. This has produced tension in many state conventions.

Negative Designations

The standard practice across the years for contributions through the Cooperative Program was for churches' contributions to be "undesignated." This meant a church's monthly gift would be a single amount sent to its state convention office. Of the amount sent a set percentage (approved by the annual meeting of the state convention) would be forwarded to the Southern Baptist Convention Executive Committee. Both the amount forwarded to the Executive Committee and the amount retained by the state convention would be distributed according to the respective approved budgets at each level. Churches were encouraged to give to the "whole program," that is, without designations. Of course, a congregation could give designated money if it so decided, but generally those "designated" portions were not considered "Cooperative Program."

With rising tensions in the conventions, many more congregations clamored for the freedom to withhold funds from certain entities of which they disapproved. Others wanted a disproportionate share of their gift to go to entities with which they were more pleased. There were movements in some state conventions to severely restrict the amounts to be forwarded to the Southern Baptist Convention. Other congregations began giving directly through the Executive Committee of the Southern Baptist Convention, skipping the state convention entirely. Several "new" Cooperative Program practices generally described as "negative designations" began to appear because of these pressures.

One "new practice" was designated giving provisions *within* state convention Cooperative Program accounting. In 1995, the Baptist General Convention of Texas (BGCT) began allowing churches to negatively designate up to five recipients in the state convention budget and still count the gift as "Cooperative Program." For example, a church that did not wish any of its gifts to go to Baylor University or to the Texas Christian Life Commission could so indicate and adjustments would be made. The gift, even with the designations, was still counted as Cooperative Program.

A corollary to this practice was the creation of multiple Cooperative Program plans within certain state conventions. A church could direct its gift to any of the approved plans, and it would be counted as "Cooperative Program." The BGCT, Baptist Convention of North Carolina, and Baptist General Association of Virginia developed multiple giving options in the mid-1990s. A common feature of all these state conventions' multiple plans was the option for churches to select a "Cooperative Program" option which sent little or no money to the Southern Baptist Convention and which allowed worldwide gifts to be distributed to the Cooperative Baptist Fellowship.

Other plans allowed churches to give more to the SBC and less to the state convention. In addition, the Executive Committee of the Southern Baptist Convention changed its policy on designated giving in 1993. All gifts that were sent directly to the Executive Committee by churches for the SBC Cooperative Program Allocation Budget in its entirety (no designations)—even though the gift was not shared with the respective state convention—began to be counted as "Cooperative Program." Negative designations continue to create tension for Cooperative Program allocation and promotion.

Second State Conventions

Another anomaly resulting from the controversy was the creation of new state Baptist conventions in states where a Baptist convention already existed. In 1996, churches in Virginia formed the Southern Baptist Conservatives of Virginia Convention. The *causus belli* was the perception that the older state convention, The Baptist General Association of Virginia, was becomingly increasingly adversarial toward the Southern Baptist Convention. Baptists who wished to be more supportive of the Southern Baptist Convention formed the new convention. Some churches hold affiliation with both state conventions. The Southern Baptist Convention and its entities currently relate to both conventions.

A similar situation occurred in Texas with the creation of the Southern Baptists of Texas Convention in 1998. Again, this was in reaction to the decidedly anti-SBC direction of the older Baptist General Convention of Texas. The BGCT, in particular, adopted a variety of peculiar budgets (over the protests of the Executive Committee of the Southern Baptist Convention), which attempted to direct funds away from certain SBC agencies. By the 2004 fiscal year, the BGCT budget removed the peculiarities and returned to a straightforward division between the state convention and the Southern Baptist Convention. However, the percentage forwarded to the SBC was sharply reduced to 21 percent. For the years prior to 1999, the adopted percentage in the BGCT budget to the SBC had been in the 33–36 percent range.

Other actions were taken by the BGCT which were seen by many as anti-SBC. In recent years the leadership of the older Texas convention produced reports highly critical of Southern Baptist Convention mission boards and seminaries, refused to allow SBC seminaries to be present in the exhibit area of their annual meeting, authorized the production of literature in competition with LifeWay Christian Resources (the SBC's publisher), and generally attempted to persuade Southern Baptist churches in Texas to reduce or eliminate their financial support of the Southern Baptist Convention.

Whether or not cooperative relations, including the unified collection of Cooperative Program funds, can be maintained between the Baptist General Convention of Texas and the Southern Baptist Convention is an uncertainty.

Even relations between the Baptist General Association of Virginia and the Southern Baptist Convention could deteriorate if churches are forced to choose between support for the Southern Baptist Convention or the BGAV. The working relationships are definitely stressed. The two *new* conventions in those states practice a standard division of the Cooperative Program receipts with the Southern Baptist Convention, both forwarding at least 50 percent to the SBC. The older conventions, as noted above, have approved plans discouraging congregations from historic support of the SBC. Because so many participating churches in Texas chose against the Baptist General Convention of Texas's proposed giving plan or moved to the new Southern Baptists of Texas Convention, the SBC has continued to receive as much or more financial support from churches in Texas as in the past. The results in Virginia have been similar.

A third incident of a second Baptist convention in one state occurred in Missouri. The political situation was the reverse of the Virginia and Texas situations. In Missouri, the older convention, The Missouri Baptist Convention, was turned in a more conservative and decidedly pro-SBC direction. A new convention, the Baptist General Convention of Missouri, was formed in 2002 in opposition to the older convention. It proposed to be a state organization for churches dissatisfied with the direction of the older convention. When the new Missouri convention began to collect Cooperative Program funds for forwarding to the Southern Baptist Convention, the Executive Committee of the Southern Baptist Convention refused to recognize the Baptist General Convention of Missouri as an approved collecting agent for the Southern Baptist Convention. Money forwarded through that organization was returned.

What was the rationale for this decision, especially when the Executive Committee was already receiving funds collected by newer state conventions in Virginia and Texas? Executive Committee leadership outlined its rationale as follows:

1. It is the prerogative of the SBC to decide who will represent its interests to the churches and collect its contributions.

2. A single state Baptist convention per area is the ideal and best serves the interests of the Southern Baptist Convention for the collection of funds and other cooperative functions.

3. The expectation is any state convention acting as collection agent for the Southern Baptist Convention will vigorously promote the ministries of the Southern Baptist Convention and encourage churches to give undesignated gifts through the

Cooperative Program exclusively for the state convention and
the SBC.

4. There should be a compelling reason to vary from the *status
quo*.

These principles are based in part on a 1928 document entitled "Relation
of Southern Baptist Convention to Other Baptist Bodies." This document
concluded:

1. The cooperative relations between this Convention and state
bodies as now established are limited to the one matter of collecting funds for Southwide and state objects in conjunction
with a unified appeal for the objects. The state convention
boards are at present recognized by this Convention as collecting agencies for Southwide as well as for state funds. This
arrangement, however, is not an essential in Baptist organization, but is made simply as a matter of convenience and
economy, and may be changed at any time.

2. The fact that the state bodies first handle the funds and are
more directly related to the churches in the matter of collections does not alter the basic relations involved. For the practical
ends in view this Convention cooperates in the unified appeal
for funds through state agencies. But in principle it retains as
inalienable and inherent the right to direct appeal to the
churches. Furthermore, in all matters other than money raising
it retains complete control of its own affairs, with the right to
fix its own objectives and to determine the amounts of money
allocated to its various objects.[7]

It was determined the new Missouri convention was unnecessary
because, unlike Virginia and Texas, the older Missouri convention was
faithfully supportive of the interests of the Southern Baptist Convention.
There was no compelling reason to vary from the *status quo* and to have
more than one group in Missouri collecting funds on behalf of the
Southern Baptist Convention. It was further determined the principal
proponents of the new Missouri convention were not in sympathy with
the direction of the Southern Baptist Convention, and, therefore, it was
not in the best interests of the Southern Baptist Convention to enter into
a cooperative relationship with this new group.

Even though these practices affect only a handful of state conventions and a minority of the churches in Southern Baptist life, they have

the potential for changing the meaning of *Cooperative Program*. They, on one hand, are the *result* of strained relationships. On the other hand, they *contribute* to the deterioration of relationships. The standard definition of *Cooperative Program* is "a financial channel of cooperation between the state conventions and the Southern Baptist Convention which makes it possible for all persons making undesignated gifts through their church to support the missionary, education, and benevolent work in their state convention, and also the work of the Southern Baptist Convention."[8]

Each of these new variations violates at least one basic premise of the Cooperative Program: (1) penalizes one of the two partners of Cooperative Program, the SBC or the state convention; (2) one partner allocating the gifts intended for the other partner; (3) adding other unauthorized "partners" into Cooperative Program; (4) fails to equitably share receipts among the partners; (5) ignores the unified budgeting process that is at the heart of the Cooperative Program method.

It is not a matter of local congregations or autonomous conventions having the right to alter their giving plans and budgets. They most certainly have that right. It is whether these changes are truly a cooperative methodology justifiably called the Cooperative Program. For most of the history of the Cooperative Program, these kinds of variations were discouraged by church and convention leaders in favor of standard Cooperative Program practices.

State/SBC Division of Cooperative Program Funds

Another source of tension is the division of Cooperative Program funds between the state convention and the Southern Baptist Convention. From the inception of the Cooperative Program, it was agreed the state conventions would set the percentage of division. The Southern Baptist Convention was satisfied with this arrangement with the understanding the state convention would always set an equitable percentage. Through the years, the goal of a fifty-fifty split was offered as the ideal. Although a few state conventions from time to time have set this percentage division, currently only two state conventions forward at least fifty percent of all Cooperative Program receipts to the Southern Baptist Convention. The average percentage of all Cooperative Program receipts forwarded to the Southern Baptist Convention the last twenty years has been about 36 percent with a low of 35 percent and a high of 39 percent.

Some argue the fifty-fifty ideal should include Lottie Moon
International Missions Offerings and Annie Armstrong North American
Mission Offerings forwarded by the state conventions. Under this inter-
pretation, many more state conventions forward at least 50 percent to the
Southern Baptist Convention. Cecil Ray noted the following:

> The Woman's Missionary Union report for 1927 referred to
> the foreign missions offering as "Cooperative Program funds."
> Austin Crouch, the first executive secretary of the Southern
> Baptist Executive Committee, wrote: "The Cooperative
> Program includes all distributable funds, all designated funds,
> and all special offerings, such as the Woman's Missionary
> Union's Lottie Moon Offering for Foreign Missions, the
> Annie Armstrong Offering for Home Missions, etc. In reality,
> all funds received for any cause included in the Cooperative
> Program, whether they be distributable, designated, or spe-
> cial funds, belong to the Cooperative Program." Was the
> Cooperative Program meant to be one among Baptists' several
> systems of support or an umbrella covering all systems?[9]

The 1925 report to the Southern Baptist Convention, however, seems
to make clear that the mission offerings were not to be considered when
determining a percentage division:

> The special thank-offerings for state and home missions and
> the Christmas offering for foreign missions ingathered during
> the Week of Prayer of the Woman's Missionary Union for these
> respective causes shall be recognized as gifts in addition to the
> regular contributions to the Co-Operative Program and shall
> not be subject to expense deduction or *percentage basis* (emphasis
> added).[10]

The report also stated:

> That we fix as our financial goal for Southwide purposes in
> 1926 a minimum of $5,000,000 and we recommend to our con-
> stituents that they divide their offerings for denominational
> purposes upon a basis of 50% for Southwide purposes and 50%
> for State purposes. In the event that any find it impracticable
> at present to make this division, such brethren are urged to
> provide as much as possible of the $5,000,000 for Southwide
> purposes.[11]

Regardless of which opinion is correct for the early decades, Lottie Moon and Annie Armstrong receipts certainly have not been understood as Cooperative Program for at least the last forty years. And the fifty-fifty ideal has historically been promoted. For example, the 1983 Cooperative Program Study Committee called on each state convention to work toward a fifty-fifty division (with the understanding the mission offerings were not a part of the equation).[12]

This issue is getting more attention in recent years. The creation by a few state conventions of alternative giving plans (mentioned above) and the larger convention controversy has caused some Southern Baptists to call for shifts in the percentages going to the state conventions. A recent survey indicated 60 percent of pastors believe the division of Cooperative Program funds between the state and the SBC is "just about right." About 24 percent believed the SBC should receive a larger portion. About 11 percent believe the state convention should receive a larger percent.

With the exception of churches in Texas, there does not appear to be a widespread trend of churches opting out of normal Cooperative Program processes by sending their gifts directly to the Executive Committee for the Southern Baptist Convention. From 2000 to 2003, Cooperative Program gifts coming directly to the Executive Committee from churches in Texas grew from approximately $1,928,124 to $4,858,684. The Texas situation can be attributed to the conflict over budgeting decisions by the Baptist General Convention of Texas that penalized Southern Baptist Convention recipients. Through the years, for the most part, the leaders of the Southern Baptist Convention have been sympathetic with the financial needs of the state conventions and have not criticized the level of receipts forwarded by the state conventions. As noted above, they have requested the states consider increasing the percentage for the Southern Baptist Convention on a regular basis, moving toward the fifty-fifty ideal.[13]

It is difficult to determine exactly the level of impact the denominational controversy has had on Cooperative Program giving. Neither contributions diverted elsewhere from the Cooperative Program because of the controversy nor contributions added to the Cooperative Program because of the controversy have been measured. Furthermore, in a survey of Baptists conducted for the Cooperative Program Development Division of the Executive Committee of the Southern Baptist Convention, only a small minority of the respondents indicated the controversy had affected the level of their Cooperative Program support. It is probably fair to conclude there has been an erosion of Cooperative Program giving due to the controversy by those who are no longer satisfied with the direction of the Southern Baptist Convention. The degree to which those who are pleased with the conservative resurgence have made up the loss is yet to be measured.

TRENDS IN THE CHURCHES

Some of the decline in percentage giving to the Cooperative Program can be attributed to some changing attitudes about contributing to a common fund such as the Cooperative Program. These attitudes could shape the trends in giving. The existence of these trends is indicated by surveys, financial results, observations, conversations, and interpretations.

Direct Versus Indirect Giving

The first of these trends could be called "direct versus indirect giving." Many churches and individuals desire to have immediate connection to the ministry or mission they are funding. Because the ministries supported by the Cooperative Program have grown large and are far-flung geographically, the criticism has come that the churches have lost touch with the people who carry out the mission. They feel they are giving to an endeavor without a name or face. They have a sense of detachment. Some leaders complain their people no longer are willing to give if they don't have a close connection.

This is not a new complaint. Cecil Ray noted this objection to the Cooperative Program in 1984 when he wrote, "Human nature, when mixed with Baptists' particular values, creates a strong tendency to prefer individualistic giving over team giving. Baptists, of course, know from experience that cooperation is more effective in producing a greater outreach in Christian ministries. But in spite of the past record of disappointments, the love of freedom and fear of centralization make individual, one-cause giving appealing to many."[14]

These churches want a direct tie to a ministry. They want to know specifically who is benefiting from their gifts. This may involve communicating directly with a missionary, traveling to the location of the mission endeavor for mission projects, having mission/ministry personnel in the local church setting, or engaging in designing the strategies, budgets, and outcomes of the ministry. The great popularity of mission volunteers and mission trips is an indicator of this desire for hands-on, direct involvement. Being personally connected with the mission has some positive values. Strong personal relationships can result, which bring a sense of satisfaction and accomplishment and spiritual growth. The participant may become more highly motivated to pray, to give, and, even, to commit to a life in mission service. A high degree of confidence in the worth of the ministry is fostered.

However, this desire for personal involvement can have other consequences. For example, some churches have begun to direct financial support to the cause they are personally connected with and away from the Cooperative Program. If this trend of directed giving becomes more prominent, it could have a negative impact on the mission and ministry enterprises of Southern Baptists. Churches, while concentrating on a few ministries that attract them, may neglect a wide array of ministries supported by the Cooperative Program. The personalized ministries may actually be less efficient and less accountable than those directed and supervised by the Convention.

Less prominent, but still important, ministries may suffer from lack of attention. Mission boards, schools, and other ministries may begin to engage in more intentional fund-raising work to compensate for declining Cooperative Program support. This could instigate a return to the "societal" method of funding from decades ago where each ministry independently campaigned in the churches for support. The challenge is to provide the positive values of personal involvement without causing harm to the larger cooperative work.

Donor Versus Owner

Another developing trend concerns the churches' attitude about denominational ministries compared to extradenominational or parachurch ministries. No longer is it automatically the default practice of a Southern Baptist church to choose to engage in denominational mission or ministry projects. Many opt instead for those managed or promoted by independent or parachurch leadership. It should be noted that individual Baptist churches have always been free to work with anyone they chose and, to some degree, have always done this. However, there seems to be more of a willingness now to ignore denominational identification in choosing ministry avenues. Some would describe this as the loss of "brand loyalty." Other critics worry that Cooperative Program ministries cannot react quickly to immediate opportunities. They are not designed to be able to adapt to changing needs and, therefore, are out of step. They take too long to gear up and to respond and to make decisions.

Other observers believe this trend is a natural consequence of the burgeoning market of evangelical ministry outlets and opportunities such as those created by the megachurch phenomenon in the last quarter of the twentieth century. Many large churches (Baptists and others) have their own seminars, publications, and mission organizations. A wide array of opportunities beyond the usual denominational process is available to Baptist churches.

Some churches have begun to view the denomination mission opportunities as just "another option" for their support. No distinction is made between parachurch groups to which they may contribute and the denominational enterprise. Their relationship to either is as a "donor." No longer do they sense an obligation as the "owner" of the Convention and thus responsible for its health and success. The relationship is more akin to that of a vendor whose services they contract rather than that of a company of which they are stockholders. A church that adopts the "donor" mentality toward the Convention continues the relationship as long as it seems beneficial but probably senses no duty to ensure the overall success and vitality of the Convention work. The Convention must make a "pitch" each year for support rather than being able to count on an automatic continuation of support. A church that sees itself as "owner" of the Convention is more likely to do whatever it takes to make the Convention strong. It is not likely to withdraw support from the Cooperative Program in favor of some other mission organization. Said another way, a declining sense of ownership will ultimately result in a declining level of support. The implications of this trend for the Cooperative Program are obvious.

People Versus Institutions

Another trend in attitudes among churches and their members is a disinclination to give their support to institutions rather than to people. Some have assumed, because the Cooperative Program ministries are large and varied, they must be cumbersome, inefficient bureaucracies. These critics see the personnel and offices of Cooperative Program ministries as majoring on *rear echelon* work having to do with policies, budgets, and red tape rather than frontline, cutting-edge missions. They worry about wasted time and resources and lack of accountability. This trend may be more affected by perception than any of the others.

For example, a church is highly responsive to supporting a missionary but not a mission board. Or it is responsive to supporting a seminarian but not seminaries. It is motivated to respond financially to people in crises (war, poverty, etc.) but not to budgets (even if those budgets are dedicated to supporting people in crises). If the Cooperative Program is perceived as primarily institutions, agencies, bureaucracy, and budgets, churches energized by "people needs" are less likely to be highly motivated in their support.

Recent surveys have revealed that the Cooperative Program indeed is perceived by many Southern Baptists as a necessary but stodgy bureaucratic system of budgeting. This does not bode well for Cooperative Program support from people who want to help people, not institutions.

TROUBLE IN THE PEW

The tensions in the denomination and the trends in the churches just noted are serious. They must be addressed. However, by far the most serious problem threatening the Cooperative Program is the minimal church giving of many Southern Baptist church members. Even if the challenges above are successfully met, the stewardship problem alone is enough to cripple the Cooperative Program.

The report on the state of giving by American churches produced by *empty tomb, inc.* in 2000 indicates that per-member giving as a percentage of income decreased between 1968 and 1998. The 1968–98 church giving data contained in this report indicates that giving as a percentage of income for congregational finances declined from 2.45 percent in 1968 to 2.12 percent in 1998, a decline of 13 percent. Southern Baptists, according to this report, gave 2.03 percent of their earnings to their churches in 1998. This figure is derived by multiplying the total membership (data from the Annual Church Profile) by the median per capita income in the USA. That total is divided into the gross receipts reported by the churches.

The alarming fact is not just that the 2.03 percent giving average falls miserably short of the tithe (10 percent) but that the percentage has dropped dramatically in the last thirty years. In a time when Southern Baptist members arguably were experiencing financial prosperity, they have been giving a shrinking percentage of their available income to the local church.

Churches have reacted by shrinking the percentage the church gives to missions. The report by *empty tomb, inc.* states that contributions to the category of benevolences (their term for any kind of missions outside the local congregation) between 1968 and 1998 have been declining proportionately faster than those to congregational finances.[15] Not only are American church members giving smaller percentages to their churches; their churches are giving smaller percentages to anything outside the congregation's needs. Southern Baptist churches are no exception to this trend. In 1985, Southern Baptist churches gave on average 17 percent of their total gifts to "missions" (the "missions" category on the Annual Church Profile is anything the church calls missions including Cooperative Program, denominational mission offerings, parachurch efforts, local church mission trips and projects). In 2003, that percentage had dropped to 11 percent. The following facts are startling:

From 1987 to 2001, undesignated receipts in SBC churches
grew from $3.2 billion to $6.5 billion (101 percent) and total
receipts in SBC churches grew 108 percent over that same
period, from $4.3 billion to $8.9 billion.

In the same period, total missions expenditures reported by
churches, including Cooperative Program, special offerings
and local missions, grew only 47.9 percent from $662 million to
$980 million.

Furthermore, gifts to the Cooperative Program nationwide,
including both the portion retained by state conventions and
the portion forwarded to the SBC, grew at a lower rate (47.8
percent), from $337 million to $487 million. In the same period,
Lottie Moon receipts went from $68 million to $104 million
(51.9 percent) and Annie Armstrong receipts grew from $30
million to $48 million (60 percent).

Three trends are clear, all of which indicate serious challenges for Southern Baptists' financial support through the Cooperative Program: (1) Church members are giving smaller percentages of their income to their local churches; (2) From this smaller percentage, local churches are spending an even smaller percentage of their income outside the congregation on any form of missions; (3) From this even smaller percentage, the

Cooperative Program is receiving a slightly smaller percentage of the local churches' mission expenditure.

Tensions in the denomination have eroded trust. Trends in the churches have eroded commitment. Trouble in the pews has eroded resources. All of these have eroded support for the Cooperative Program. The following chapter will address potential measures for reversing this erosion in the future.

Chapter Twelve

Future Challenges:
The Cooperative Program in the Twenty-first Century

What will be the future of the Cooperative Program? Can it survive the tensions, trends, and troubles discussed in the previous chapter? Will it remain the foundational support mechanism for missions and ministries for both the Baptist state conventions and the Southern Baptist Convention? Will new generations of Southern Baptists embrace the Cooperative Program as the most efficient method for accomplishing the corporate work of the churches? Can the declining percentage giving to the Cooperative Program be reversed? These are serious challenges, but they can be met.

Before looking at the various challenges that must be met, it must be asserted that the fundamental key to the success of the Cooperative Program and all Convention ministries is *the local church*. The oft-repeated phrase "Southern Baptist headquarters is the local church" is not merely posturing. It is the truth—both theologically (as we have noted earlier) and practically. Unless local Baptist churches find value and sense ownership in the Cooperative Program and the endeavors it supports, the vitality of the effort cannot be sustained. The following evaluations and suggestions will attempt to help local churches address pertinent issues about the value of the Cooperative Program to their mission. Six areas of challenge for the future are identified.

THE THEOLOGICAL CHALLENGE: ESTABLISHING COMMON GROUND

Southern Baptist churches once again must become confident in the primary theological affirmations that not only allow but also mandate their common work. This is the theological challenge for the Cooperative Program. The denomination must renew the consensus founded on the truthfulness and authority of the Bible that also values liberty of interpretation on non-essential or "disputable matters" (Rom. 14:1 NIV) in church life. Southern Baptists must articulate for themselves and the world what ought to be believed and practiced and what is optional to be believed and practiced. If, as Cecil Ray noted twenty years ago, trust is the linchpin of the success of the Cooperative Program, a clear delineation of those principles and doctrines which define and guide Southern Baptists can provide a platform for the trust necessary to motivate Southern Baptists' far-reaching, united endeavors in Christian ministry.

The mistrust in Southern Baptist life that reached its zenith from about 1960 to 1980 (and threatened the desire to cooperate) stemmed in large measure from an inability or an unwillingness to identify and affirm a common set of basic beliefs. The 1963 revision of the Baptist Faith and Message statement, the Southern Baptist Convention's statement of faith, was an effort to alleviate the problem. While attempting to build consensus theologically, the rewrite tended more to accommodate rather than correct the leftward drift among certain sectors of influential Southern Baptists. The attempt to maintain a consensus for ministry without a consensus on theology was doomed to fail eventually. *Without* that consensus, cooperative missions by Southern Baptists will not be vigorously attempted, much less succeed. *With* that consensus, Southern Baptists can be rallied to go together to the ends of the earth.

This "truism" needs to be understood clearly by those who desire a strong Cooperative Program. Appeals for Cooperative Program support do not *ignore* common beliefs but *assume* common beliefs. Southern Baptists are not expecting those who do not share the basic convictions of the SBC to participate. More importantly, Southern Baptists are not willing to compromise basic convictions in order to garner financial support. Such an idea is antithetical to Southern Baptist theology.

In the most recent theological controversy, conservatives denied that uniformity in every theological detail has been or should be the position of Southern Baptists. A common phrase describing the role of doctrine in Baptist cooperation is, "Unity in essentials; diversity in nonessentials." Many issues about which various Southern Baptists disagree heatedly (e.g., eschatology, alien baptism, Calvinism) have not become matters of fellowship and cooperation for the Southern Baptist Convention. In the early years of the conservative resurgence, Jimmy Draper, then president of the Southern Baptist Convention, set out what he termed "irreducible minimums" of Southern Baptist doctrine. He stated:

I would suggest that the first basic parameter be the undiminished Deity and the genuine humanity of Jesus Christ in one person—the hypostatic union.

Secondly, I would suggest the doctrine of the substitutionary atonement of Christ, that He actually died in our place, in our stead, and that He suffered a penal judgment from the Father on behalf of us, for our sins. Man is eternally lost apart from Christ, thus such atonement is absolutely necessary.

Thirdly, I would suggest that we require a belief in the literal, bodily resurrection of Jesus Christ from the grave, a literal, bodily ascension into heaven and a literal, bodily return of Jesus Christ to earth. Eschatological views would not be required. Whether or not one held to a view of premillennialism or amillennialism, for instance, should not be a test in any way. That is a matter of interpretation that has always been widely diverse among Southern Baptists.

Fourthly, I would suggest that we require a person to believe in the doctrine of justification by God's grace through faith.[1]

Draper concluded that, without these common beliefs, Southern Baptists could not remain vital, nor should they remain unified.

Southern Baptists should be encouraged by the recent reemphasis on biblical conservatism on three fronts. First, it guards against those (most commonly called theological liberals) who, due to their low view of Scripture, would diminish or discard orthodox Christian doctrines. Second, it guards against heterodoxy, i.e., those who advocate erroneous doctrines or practices based on misinterpretation of Scripture. Third, with a clear definition (such as The Baptist Faith and Message) of what is believed and promoted through Convention enterprises, an environment of trust can be reestablished.

It is significant that the *churches* have set the parameters of what is generally believed and practiced by Southern Baptists. The *churches* have declared what is important and unvarying in Baptist doctrine as well as those things where wide latitude of interpretation is allowed. Now, people who share those convictions are motivated to cooperate because they are confident in the theological commitments underlying the mission and ministry ventures. The cloud of suspicion that, at times, has hovered over the Convention's enterprises has been lifted, and the way is clear for unreserved enthusiastic support.

THE ECCLESIOLOGICAL CHALLENGE: COOPERATING CONGREGATIONS

The ecclesiological challenge is for churches to recognize their duty of cooperation with other congregations of like faith and order. Southern Baptist theology affirms the importance of Bible-believing congregations working together for the kingdom's sake. Cooperative methodology is more than a matter of pragmatism. It is a New Testament principle. A consensus about the cooperative ministries of the churches is, also, a necessary component to the effectiveness of the Cooperative Program.

This is the subject matter of ecclesiology. Southern Baptist ecclesiology is centered in the autonomy of the local church. Each congregation is free under Christ to conduct its own ministry with no ecclesial authority over it. For Baptists, no practice or organization or endeavor is permissible if it impinges on local church autonomy. Some Baptist groups have understood the doctrine of local church autonomy to prohibit congregations from sponsoring Convention enterprises. In the first half of the nineteenth century, many Baptists in America opposed a model of cooperation like the one the Southern Baptist Convention and Baptist state conventions adopted. They had concluded the local church was the only legitimate organization to carry out missionary and benevolent endeavors and, therefore, could not turn over these functions to some other ecclesiastical body.

At its founding, however, the Southern Baptist Convention rejected this hyper "high church" view of some people that says *only* a local church may accomplish the kingdom's work. The Southern Baptist Convention adopted an organizational model whereby the churches, through the messengers they send annually to the Convention meeting, jointly operate any number of missionary, educational, and benevolent ministries. Several state conventions had already organized along these lines. Early Southern Baptists did not believe the "Convention" model violated in any way the autonomy of the local church. This is a different practice from independents and separatists on the issue of denominational cooperation.

Southern Baptist theology of the church affirms both the freedom of the local church and the necessity of cooperation. In fact, Southern Baptists insist that a "separatist" view is not only counterproductive to the work of the gospel, but, more importantly, is a misunderstanding of New Testament ecclesiology. It is clear from the New Testament that the congregations in various regions understood they had an obligation to the ministry outside their own locale. The council at Jerusalem (Acts 15) in AD 50 indicates "doctrinal concerns" were to be considered by the larger Christian family.

Another example of multicongregational cooperation was the commissioning of missionaries. The famine in Jerusalem evoked the collection of a freewill offering from among the Gentile churches. Both John's epistles and the book of Hebrews insisted that hospitality for other Christians was a congregational duty. Furthermore, a proper understanding of Jesus' admonition in Matthew 28:19–20 and Acts 1:8 requires local churches to work in concert with other congregations. Christian congregations have a New Testament duty to engage, by their own autonomous action, in cooperative mission and ministry with the larger body of Christ.

In a 1980 speech to the Southern Baptist Convention, Morris Chapman, the current president and chief executive officer of the Executive Committee of the Southern Baptist Convention, remarked on the necessity of maintaining not only *conservative theology* but also *cooperative methodology*:

> Our conservative heritage is based upon the belief that the Bible
> is the authoritative, inspired, infallible Word of God, inerrant
> in the original autographs. . . . We also know deep in our hearts
> that our enthusiasm for evangelism and missions will not exceed
> our convictions about biblical authority. . . . Just as we are a
> people of the Book, we are also a people who are one in the bond
> of love. This tie that binds our hearts in Christian love has given
> birth to the cooperative program, cooperative missions, cooperative education, cooperative literature, and above all, a cooperative spirit. . . . In our Convention there are some who tend to be
> conservative, but not cooperative, and there are others who tend

to be cooperative, but not conservative. However, the rank and file of Southern Baptists is both conservative and cooperative.[2] Southern Baptists are not only conservatives; they are cooperating conservatives. The concern for correct "faith and practice" does not negate the obligation to cooperate in worldwide ministries. The duty of Christian congregations to pursue joint ministry is a core value that does not in any way compromise the autonomy of the local church.

The future success of the Cooperative Program depends on a proper understanding of the correctness and utility of intercongregational cooperation. Whether motivated by theological concerns, pragmatism, or inattention, if the churches adopt an independent-separatist mind-set, the cooperative ministries of Southern Baptists will naturally diminish. Southern Baptist churches must continue to be taught that, while they are free to choose their own ministries, they are under the mandate of Christ to find ways to work with other like-minded congregations for the sake of the kingdom. Finding and funding ways for Southern Baptist congregations to work together to fulfill the Great Commission is the function of the Cooperative Program. The Cooperative Program is a natural consequence of cooperative methodology and is consistent with Southern Baptist ecclesiology.

THE MISSIOLOGICAL CHALLENGE: A VISION FOR THE WHOLE WORLD

Another key challenge for Southern Baptist congregations is to develop and maintain the proper balance between local church ministries and missions enterprises. This demands a biblical missiology. Missiology is a corollary to ecclesiology. Ecclesiology addresses *how* the church works, i.e., its methods and structures. Missiology addresses *why* the church works, i.e., its purpose. New Testament ecclesiology addresses the churches' need for cooperation. New Testament missiology addresses the churches' need for a worldwide perspective.

The Cooperative Program was designed to aid churches in implementing a New Testament missiology in congregational life. In 1925, the Future Program Commission noted that some of the churches, after five years of intensive denominational giving during the "Seventy-five Million Campaign," were holding back denominational support in order to take care of local needs. The commission opined: "We should view with alarm the possibility that along with the loss of idealism which has come to the nation, our churches, too, have lost something of the world outlook and the world consciousness." (The committee also reminded the Convention that local church receipts had grown by about 300 percent during the five-year period and churches were still "contributing more than twice as much to local expenses as to denominational objects.")[3] The tension between local needs and mission needs continues to be an issue for Southern Baptists. Adopting a New Testament "missiology" is the beginning place for resolving the tension.

The pivotal missiological affirmation of Southern Baptists is that local congregations ought to cooperate for worldwide evangelism. Southern Baptist leaders do not suggest that the churches neglect the ministry in the locale where they are planted. But they do insist that a proper understanding of Southern Baptist missiology requires that the churches give attention to the commission to be witnesses "in Jerusalem, in all Judea, in Samaria, and to the ends of the earth" (Acts 1:8). Missions is not only a matter of *content* but *extent*. Congregations, in obedience to Matthew 28:19–20 and Acts 1:8, are to pursue relationships with other congregations for the purpose of an intentional mission strategy of *global* proportion.

Nor do Southern Baptist leaders insist that the endeavors of the Southern Baptist Convention, state conventions, and associations are the only acceptable intercongregational efforts for Baptist congregations. They do, however, commend the missions and ministries of these bodies as some of the most effective, efficient, kingdom-focused, God-honoring opportunities available to the churches for extending their reach to the ends of the earth.

THE ACTS 1:8 CHALLENGE

Through the years Southern Baptists have developed strategies, promoted themes, and issued challenges intended to motivate the churches to maintain a worldwide focus. These emphases have served Baptists well, and the churches have responded enthusiastically and sacrificially. Southern Baptist leaders have recently designed a new process to assist churches in developing a comprehensive missions strategy. Its aim is to call Baptists once again to a global missions perspective and to sacrificial service. In May 2004, *The Acts 1:8 Challenge* was launched at a joint meeting of the

International Mission Board and the North American Mission Board. In cooperation with Baptist state conventions and associations, this initiative aims to challenge local SBC churches to embrace a comprehensive missions strategy in their community (Jerusalem), state (Judea), continent (Samaria), and world (ends of the earth). This strategy was piloted in 2002–2003 with IMB, NAMB, and four Baptist state conventions.

The Acts 1:8 Challenge is primarily a joint communication and enlistment process that is inspirational rather than programmatic. SBC churches are challenged to the following kingdom-growing responses:

- *Prepare*—empowering a designated leader of missions and developing mission teams, strategies, and plans to take the gospel to our community, state, continent, and world.
- *Learn*—bringing mission awareness and interaction to the entire church body, training members for service, and connecting them to missionaries and mission needs.
- *Pray*—asking God for kingdom perspective and worldwide vision, interceding for Christian workers and unevangelized peoples.
- *Give*—increasing the financial support of the Cooperative Program and other SBC cooperative missions.
- *Go*—enabling a growing number of members to participate directly in short-term, long-term, and marketplace opportunities to minister and spread the gospel beyond our church's walls.
- *Tell*—involving an increasing number of members in intentional, culturally relevant evangelism.
- *Send*—providing members with opportunities to hear God's call to vocational mission service.
- *Multiply*—participating in church planting, and facilitating church-planting movements, to reach people that existing churches do not.

The Acts 1:8 Challenge can help Southern Baptists emphasize cooperation and avoid competition. With local associations, state conventions, and national agencies all seeking to serve and assist local churches, and to mobilize people and resources to the mission fields for which they are passionate, it is possible for mixed or even conflicting communication and service opportunities to occur. The challenge for the local church is to maintain a comprehensive, balanced missions strategy and for denominational entities to communicate complementary, coordinated messages and services designed to assist the local church as a worldwide mission center.

Current Southern Baptist leaders believe embracing this "Acts 1:8 paradigm" can have significant practical advantages for local churches and for denominational entities. For denominational entities it calls for coordinated communication and services that continually reflect an understanding and respect for a comprehensive, balanced mission strategy for each local church. Each entity points enthusiastically to its sister entities, helping local churches discover their complete Acts 1:8 responsibility and urging balanced awareness, prayer, giving, and mobilization to each arena of mission involvement. As churches move people and resources from one mission field to another, cooperation and coordination characterize the relationships of all their Southern Baptist partners.

In essence, each denominational partner says to each local church: *"You, the local church, are the primary channel through which God's redemptive purposes flow. We are here to serve you as you fulfill the Great Commission. What are your strategies for doing so, and how may we assist you? May we help you reach the mission field in which we specialize, and point you to other mission partners who specialize in other fields?"*

And in essence, the Acts 1:8 paradigm would call for each local church to say: *"Our church has a Great Commission responsibility to reach our Jerusalem, our Judea, our Samaria, and our ends of the earth. Embracing this responsibility and 'giving ourselves away' in God's worldwide mission will both strengthen our church and help fulfill its true purpose. So we will embrace a comprehensive, integrated missions strategy that sends people and resources to each of these mission fields. And we will work cooperatively with and through our local association, state convention, and national agencies to maximize our impact because of the infrastructure, missionary force, expertise and resources these entities bring."*[4]

As churches adopt *The Acts 1:8 Challenge* or some strategy very similar to it, it will be apparent the Cooperative Program is a proven, effective method for undergirding, implementing, and energizing those strategies. The Cooperative Program is not the only means available to Southern Baptist churches for obeying the Great Commission, but something like it must be employed if they are to be true to their foundational principles. All who value biblical theology, all who understand the imperative of missions, and all who affirm the necessity of collaboration will find an indispensable ally in the Cooperative Program. It aids Bible-preaching, people-reaching, world-conscious Southern Baptist churches in accomplishing effectively what God has placed in their hearts to do. When Southern Baptist congregations think strategically about their mission goals and how to attain them, they will realize once again the value of the Cooperative Program.

THE OPERATIONAL CHALLENGE: DEVELOPING EFFECTIVE PARTNERSHIPS

The operational challenge is to demonstrate the effectiveness and efficiency of the Cooperative Program as a missions-funding process. Southern Baptist leaders through the years have asserted the value of Cooperative Program ministries with phrases like "the most effective, efficient, far-reaching, consistent, missionary funding enterprise in the history of Christian denominations."[5] Is this public relations hyperbole? Does an objective evaluation of the Cooperative Program show this to be true? Even if the Cooperative Program is theologically, ecclesiologically, and missiologically fit, churches must be convinced of its practical value and real-world contribution. This is the operational challenge.

Improving State Convention/SBC Relations

The Cooperative Program is primarily a partnership between the Southern Baptist Convention and the various state conventions for serving Southern Baptist churches in their mission enterprises. These working relationships between the several conventions must continue to be evaluated both for their consistency with Baptist polity and their usefulness to Baptist ministry. Baptist churches have the right and responsibility to know that the Cooperative Program enterprises they support are effective, efficient, and sound.

The principles that guide relationships between Baptist bodies is addressed by Southern Baptist ecclesiology. Southern Baptists affirm that each state Baptist convention as well as the Southern Baptist Convention is "autonomous in its own sphere." This means that each body is independent from the control of any other body. The state conventions are not accountable to the Southern Baptist Convention or to another state convention. The Southern Baptist Convention is not accountable to any state convention. Each convention has its own governing documents, elects its own officers, manages its own enterprises, and sets its own priorities and budgets. This has been termed by James Sullivan as our "governing" ecclesiology.[6]

All Baptist general bodies are voluntary organizations, established by individuals who wish to cooperate for some common

end or ends in the kingdom of God. This Convention is not an
ecclesiastical body composed of churches, nor a federal body
composed of state conventions. Churches may seek to fulfill
their obligation to extend Christ's kingdom by cooperating with
these general organizations, but always on a purely voluntary
basis, and without surrendering in any way or degree their right
of self-determination. These associations, unions, or conventions vary greatly in form, in size, in purpose, in territorial
extent and in conditions of membership. But they are all similar
to churches in the fundamental principle of their organization
and life in that each is independent of all others in its own work,
free, fraternal, autonomous, or self-determining in its own
sphere and activities.[7]

Southern Baptists, however, also have a "functional" ecclesiology.[8]
While not ignoring the autonomy of the various Baptist bodies (associations, state conventions, the Southern Baptist Convention), Southern
Baptists have constructed a way of working together among those organizations. It includes sharing resources and personnel, creating joint
planning processes, entering into cooperative agreements, and other
mechanisms whereby associations and state conventions, as well as state
conventions and the Southern Baptist Convention, regularly work in concert. Cooperation among these levels of Southern Baptist life is efficient,
wise, and necessary. After all, each body is derived from a common constituency: the churches.

The Cooperative Program is the most intensive and important feature
of Southern Baptist "functional" ecclesiology. Since 1925, it has been a
voluntary agreement between the Southern Baptist Convention and state
conventions. The Cooperative Program is primarily a way for state conventions of Southern Baptists and the national Southern Baptist Convention
to have a unified approach with the churches for funding ministries.

Some voices, especially in light of some of the recent controversies,
have called for the state conventions and the Southern Baptist Convention
each to collect their own gifts from the churches. This would create, in
effect, two Cooperative Programs: one for the state convention and one
for the SBC. Those calling for this division have suggested it is more
consistent with our polity since each convention is autonomous. They
also suggest it allows each local church to make its own determination on
how much each convention receives. In addition, the argument goes, it

eliminates the source of conflict between state conventions and the SBC because the funding is separate.

There are a number of reasons why this "dual Cooperative Program" concept is a bad idea:

1. It would weaken the desire for cooperation on shared ministries among the conventions and the churches.
2. It would immediately make the state conventions and the SBC competitors for the support from the churches.
3. Each convention would have to create separate "promotional" emphases for the churches as well as separate accounting systems.
4. It would weaken the unity of identity among Southern Baptists.
5. It would destabilize the Cooperative Program and the denomination in a time when they already need to be revitalized.
6. It would encourage a return to the societal method of funding with each enterprise seeking its own support.

In truth the matter rests on the desire of Southern Baptists to be one unified people with a comprehensive plan for extending the ministry of the churches everywhere. Of course, if common ground and common purpose cannot be maintained, the Cooperative Program is not going to last. However, if Southern Baptists affirm common doctrines, common goals, common heritage, and common methodology, the Cooperative Program is a self-evident blessing for the work. It certainly should not be discarded over turf battles, administrative wrangling, or power grabbing.

Convention leaders have a heavy responsibility in this regard. Since they share a common constituency, it has always been important for a high degree of cooperation and fraternity to exist among the denominational entities and organizations. Those responsible for encouraging this spirit are denominational employees, elected Convention officers, and entity board members. When the partners in the Cooperative Program process who receive and employ the resources provided by the churches are known for their spirit of working together across all levels of Baptist enterprise, it builds confidence among the churches. On the other hand, if the churches observe a spirit of competition or criticism between or within the state conventions and the Southern Baptist Convention, it lowers their enthusiasm for the Cooperative Program process.

Therefore, there are certain understandings that must be followed if the partnership is to function smoothly and effectively into the future. What protocol should be observed to maintain and improve the historic Cooperative Program partnership between the Southern Baptist Convention and the various state Baptist conventions?

Mutual Affirmation

State convention leaders and Southern Baptist Convention leaders (both those elected and employed) must affirm the basic premises of the Cooperative Program partnership. They must remember that each convention, respectively, has entered into the relationship voluntarily. The goal has always been to work together because of the advantages cooperation affords to the churches' mission. It is very important that each convention value the purpose and work of the other. Each party should desire to commend the other to the churches and to be as positive about the other's sphere of work as their own. The practice of one convention publicly criticizing the other or demeaning its ministries harms all efforts of challenging the churches to be enthusiastic about Cooperative Program methodology and support. This does not mean there can be no disagreements or that constructive criticism cannot be offered or that one convention has to please the other in every decision that is made. It does mean that adversarial, competitive, "us versus them" attitudes and actions ought to be avoided.

There should be an affirmation of the common identity of "Southern Baptist." Attempts to identify Baptists by region or state in order to diminish "Southern Baptist" identity ought to be avoided. A Southern Baptist in Texas is both a Texas Baptist and a Southern Baptist. However, it is divisive to suggest he is a Texas Baptist in contradistinction to being a Southern Baptist.

Careful Communication

In order for this to be more than lip service to Cooperative Program ideals, efforts should be made to work more closely together and to address concerns one party may have with the other. There should be a new enthusiasm for communication and coordination of ministries. Each convention ought regularly to involve representatives of the other conventions in annual meetings and other events. The protocol of staff interaction and planning that has existed across the years between the Southern Baptist Convention entities and the state convention entities should be strengthened and applauded. Opportunities for joint ministries and missions should be maximized while minimizing areas where duplication of ministries or services exist.

The Cooperative Program, by definition and nature, depends on the willingness of autonomous Baptist conventions to work together for the purpose of multiplying the effectiveness of the churches they represent. Most of the relationships between the Southern Baptist Convention and the state Baptist conventions are working very well. In those instances or on those points where there is a conflict, thoughtful, prayerful, respectful dialogue should allow the parties to reaffirm their mutual partnership. There should be a willingness to discuss any matters of concern. To act as if there is no obligation to talk about matters of concern could be *prima facie* evidence that the partnership really doesn't exist.

Although a breach could occur, it would be a serious step indeed for any Baptist state convention and the Southern Baptist Convention to abandon the Cooperative Program partnership. Churches and church leaders should encourage the denominational leaders at all levels to pursue the highest degree of cooperation possible.

Renewing the Cooperative Program Partnership

Rebuilding is necessary in this area. During the years of the conservative resurgence, in many regions the Baptists elected to lead the Southern Baptists at the national level were not the same folks elected to lead the respective state Baptist conventions. Where this occurred, it most often reflected a difference of opinion between the goals of the Southern Baptist Convention and the goals of the state convention. In 1983, representatives of the various state conventions and the Southern Baptist Convention renewed their commitment to the Cooperative Program. Because of the tensions in the denomination and the declining support for the Cooperative Program, it may be time for Baptist leaders who serve Cooperative Program-funded ministries to demonstrate a new show of unity. If, in fact, a consensus on theology has been reached and the churches still desire a coordinated multilevel denominational effort, it is incumbent on current leaders to sound the call for cooperation.

In July 2000, a historic meeting took place in the Southern Baptist Convention building in Nashville, Tennessee. It was attended by the executive leaders of all Baptist state conventions and all Southern Baptist Convention entities. Its purpose was to discuss the state convention-SBC partnership. One result of this meeting was the creation of the Task Force on Cooperation comprised of four state executive directors and four SBC entity presidents. Morris Chapman is the chairman of the task force. This group currently is working to reaffirm Baptist partnerships in general and the Cooperative Program in particular.

Pursuing Effectiveness and Efficiency

In addition to the need for Cooperative Program partners to affirm one another and the principles of the Cooperative Program, the churches expect that each Cooperative Program ministry be conducted in the most effective and efficient manner possible. This is a matter of good steward-ship of resources and opportunities. Through the years various criticisms in this regard have been leveled at Cooperative Program enterprises.

Cecil Ray pointed out seven criticisms of the Cooperative Program, such as that the Cooperative Program is inefficient, impersonal, too big, and unresponsive.[9] All of these criticisms have some substance. The size of the Cooperative Program enterprises and the large network of churches that underwrite it do demand careful processes and policies. Changes and decisions do have to go through channels, and sometimes that involves decision making at the Convention level, which can take months. There are levels of administration involving numerous people and offices. And the average Southern Baptist may not have very many opportunities for face-to-face encounters with those who are responsible for spending the money and conducting the ministry.

However, Ray concluded these criticisms should be considered "myths." He pointed out that the administrative costs of the Cooperative Program are much smaller by far than independent ministries. Furthermore, both the ministries of the Southern Baptist Convention and the state conven-tions have processes in place and functioning that ensure accountability for funds given by the churches as well as evaluating the effective use of those funds. Any perceptions that Cooperative Program-supported min-istries are not effective can be easily tested by giving attention to these evaluative processes. It is the contention of this evaluation that current Cooperative Program-funded ministries are in large measure very effec-tive and efficient.

This is not to say adjustments are not in order. State conventions and the Southern Baptist Convention need to look continually for areas where there is duplication of services, such as competitive educational opportuni-ties. Both Baptist colleges and Southern Baptist seminaries are currently engaged in offering undergraduate and graduate theological education for ministry. This needs further evaluation as to its impact on cooperative funding and mutual ministries. Other areas that may encourage competition rather than cooperation involve publishing, direct mission projects, promotion/communications, etc. It is probably not achievable or even desirable to eliminate every duplication. However, careful communication and cooperation between the several entities and conventions can aid in effective use of resources and accomplishment of common goals.

In 1995, the Southern Baptist Convention voted to restructure its ministries. One of the purposes of restructuring was to maximize effectiveness. The Southern Baptist Convention concentrated its efforts on its mission boards and its theological schools. These enterprises receive nearly 95 percent of the Cooperative Program gifts at the SBC level, and, of course, the two mission boards receive the entirety of the two primary special offerings. LifeWay Christian Resources' wide-ranging publications and other ministries are self-supporting and actually create revenue that is put back into Cooperative Program endeavors. The Southern Baptist Convention is committed to accountability, evaluation, and reporting that will ensure the continued effectiveness of its ministries. A number of Baptist state conventions have also restructured in order to maximize their ministry opportunities.

Cooperative Program-supported ministries should always be prepared to respond to questions and criticisms about their accomplishments. Churches should expect the following:

1. Conventions ought to affirm that each enterprise is faithful and accountable to the churches through the conventions.
2. There should be complete openness and accountability through the convention processes (committees, reports, audits, annual meetings, etc.) with unfettered involvement and access by the churches.
3. Ministries ought to set measurable goals and review and report regularly the progress toward achieving those goals.
4. Priority in funding ought to be given to those ministries deemed most valuable by the churches in accomplishing their mission.
5. Endeavors that are no longer faithful or effective in multiplying the ministries of the churches ought to be altered or discontinued.

As this kind of process is followed diligently, it accomplishes several purposes: It aids each enterprise in being highly successful. It answers unfounded criticisms. It inspires confidence in the churches for the Cooperative Program ministries.

Sharing Cooperative Program Gifts

The subject of the division of Cooperative Program receipts between the state conventions and the Southern Baptist Convention was discussed in the previous chapter. Are there issues to be resolved here? Other than the two or three state conventions where there is serious division between Southern Baptist Convention supporters and state convention supporters, is there any serious tension over the amount of Cooperative Program funds retained by the state conventions? What should be expected in the future on this subject? It should be noted that the challenge to improve the stewardship of individual Southern Baptists and the missions commitment of individual Southern Baptist churches is much more crucial for the success of the Cooperative Program than adjusting the percentage division between the Southern Baptist Convention and the state conventions. In fact, if progress is made in these other areas, it will be easier to modify any inequities that may exist in the SBC-state sharing of Cooperative Program.

Although there exists a difference of opinion as to "how" or "if" it should be reached, it is true the fifty-fifty split between the SBC and the state convention Cooperative Program receipts continues to be recognized as an ideal. Although a few state conventions have set this percentage, at least temporarily, it has never been reached for the total amount of Cooperative Program given in any year. Is it a realistic goal? Is it necessary? Will it help motivate Southern Baptists to be more generous in their support for the Cooperative Program? Since the state conventions historically have had the privilege and responsibility of setting the percentage division between the SBC and the state, what principles or guidelines should they follow? The following are suggestions from SBC Cooperative Program leaders:

1. Since each state convention is different (size, age, responsibilities, financial strength), a uniform percentage division may not be possible for each convention at a given time.
2. Each state convention should recognize the Cooperative Program gifts from the churches belong as much to the SBC as to the state. The gifts are not to be viewed as property of the state convention from which they grant an allocation to the SBC. The SBC should be treated as a full partner in the process.
3. Each state convention should view the ministries of the SBC to be as valuable as their own and should divide the Cooperative

Program equitably. Preferred items should be limited to those agreed upon with the SBC. (Preferred items are those that are funded "off the top" from Cooperative Program receipts by the state convention before calculating the percentage division with the SBC. Examples of preferred items are costs of promoting the Cooperative Program, state WMU and Baptist paper expenses, and annuity benefit supplements.)

4. No Cooperative Program plan should be approved that either defunds the Southern Baptist Convention and any of its entities or that allocates moneys to groups other than the Southern Baptist Convention and the state convention.

5. Each state convention should seek to communicate with SBC leadership before reducing the percentage allocated to the SBC. The SBC allocation should not be viewed as a resource from which state conventions may make up shortfalls in their budgetary needs.

6. Each state convention should develop a plan and a timetable for moving toward the fifty-fifty split with the SBC. This may eventually require the state convention to give the vast worldwide ministries of the Southern Baptist Convention priority over some of the enterprises of the state convention.

7. Each state convention should encourage churches to support the "whole program" rather than deselecting certain ministries they don't like. Churches certainly have the right to designate or otherwise alter their contributions. However, state conventions should acknowledge they prefer churches give one undesignated gift for the Cooperative Program. Designated giving should not be counted as Cooperative Program.

These guidelines, if followed, will strengthen the SBC-state partnership, will reaffirm historic Cooperative Program practices, and will build confidence and support from the churches.

THE STEWARDSHIP CHALLENGE: EVERY BAPTIST A TITHER

Although the challenges noted above are important, it is evident the key for reversing the trend in Cooperative Program gifts lies in the radical improvement of the financial stewardship of individual Southern Baptists. If Southern Baptists practiced biblical stewardship, it is not guaranteed that the Cooperative Program would receive greater support. However, if Southern Baptists do not practice biblical stewardship, it is almost guaranteed the Cooperative Program will not thrive.

The reason is obvious. With the expenses of local congregations growing at a faster rate than income, there is extreme pressure to squeeze the proportion of the church budget that had been allocated to missions in general and the Cooperative Program in particular. Appeals to churches to increase the percentage going to the Cooperative Program are, in effect, an attempt to get a larger piece of a smaller pie. The solution is for the "pie" to get larger. The churches' income must grow faster than their expenses. The only way for this to happen is for the individual members of the church to begin to practice biblical stewardship.

The Future Program Commission, which recommended the creation of the Cooperative Program in 1925, understood the relationship between successful missions support and individual stewardship, as the following excerpts from their report to the Southern Baptist Convention indicate:

> That every Baptist Church in the South be requested to put
> on a simultaneous thorough Every-Member Canvass from
> December 6 to 13, 1925, or as near thereto as possible for sub-
> scriptions to cover the needs for the calendar year 1926. It is
> advised that both individuals and churches maintain the pres-
> ent standards and regularity of giving until the program of the
> following year is full installed, that there be no break in the
> contributions and no lapse in the financial support of institu-
> tions and activities. . . . That renewed emphasis be placed upon
> permanency in financial plans through the Bible principles of
> stewardship and tithing. Every church is urged, after a care-
> ful study of local and denominational needs, to adopt a budget
> and install the weekly plan of giving, with the use of the duplex
> envelopes. . . . That there be a well co-ordinated program of
> teaching stewardship and promoting better financial methods
> in the churches, especially in assisting the churches to adopt the
> budget plan. We recommend that a committee . . . make a study
> of the whole work of teaching stewardship and promoting better
> financial methods, and recommend to all of the states a pro-
> gram of effort along these lines which cover a period of years,
> this program of effort to be recommended as the generally
> accepted plan of work for the entire South.[10]

The Seventy-five Million Campaign (1919–1924) had demonstrated to the churches the positive results of enlisting every member in stewardship and missions giving.[11] The early and the sustained success of the Cooperative Program was directly attributable to emphases on individual member commitments to the church and improved financial education and promotion by the churches.

What will be required to cause future generations of Southern Baptists to be more faithful in their financial commitments to their churches? Some have suggested it will demand an intensive reeducation regarding personal finances. They argue the spending habits of contemporary Americans, including Southern Baptists, has left them mired in debt. They are spending more than they make. The dollars available for charitable giving are not there, even when there is the desire to give.

Others argue the church will need to convince members of the great need and the potential for their church meeting that need. George Barna, of the Barna Research Group, offered opinions on motivations for church giving:

[To] significantly increase people's willingness to give generously, a church must speak to the issues that get people excited. The leader, first and foremost, must present a compelling vision for the ministry—not simply keeping the doors open and the programs running, but a clear and energizing goal that describes how lives will be transformed by the church if people will contribute their time, money, and skills. Related to that vision the church must then impress potential donors with its ability to minister in ways that are efficient, effective, satisfying urgent needs, providing personal benefits, and incorporating donors into the heart of the effort to bring about serious life-change.[12]

There is value in teaching money management and getting people excited about ministries. These actions may indeed make a positive impact in motivating Christians to become better givers. However, the proper starting point for developing biblical stewards is challenging Christians to deeper spiritual obedience. This is especially true for a denomination that insists it is committed to the authority of the Word of God. Southern Baptists must be taught the implications of the lordship of Christ for the use of their possessions. They must also be led to practice Jesus' admonition to "seek first the kingdom of God and His righteousness." Kingdom-focused Christians will be motivated to give their tithes and offerings in obedience to God's commands.

The biblical principle of tithing should become the starting place for Christian stewardship. All the downward trends in finances noted in the previous chapter are attributable to a failure of Christians to tithe. The difference between the calculated total of all American church members' tithes (10 percent) and the amounts actually given by church members is in the billions of dollars annually. For the Southern Baptist Convention membership, a conservative estimate of the difference between what was actually given in 2003 and the potential gifts if only the resident members had tithed was $10 billion. It is the duty of church leaders to address the failure forthrightly, in the same way they address other serious sins in the lives of Christians.

Certainly, debt-ridden Christians must be taught how to escape from and avoid crippling debt and other poor financial decisions. But it is the wrong starting place. The challenge to tithe is not only for the debt-free. In fact, Christians who have been struggling financially may find tithing to be the one practice that sets them free. Not only will they benefit from the spiritual promises (Mal. 3:10); they will also benefit from the practical financial lessons that come to those who are disciplined enough to tithe.

Likewise, getting people excited about ministry accomplishments is the wrong starting place. *Where* to give their gifts may be influenced by exciting ministries and effective management, but *whether* to give is a question of obedience. Christian stewardship is not merely fund-raising. It is a spiritual obligation. Southern Baptists ought to tithe through their churches because of their love for Jesus and in obedience to him. Church ministries ought to be challenging and exciting. Church members should be motivated by aggressive, Christ-honoring, far-reaching enterprises for which they are being asked to give. But appealing to the emotions of immature Christians in order to obtain a fraction of the Lord's required tithe is an ineffective strategy. It is also a flawed strategy. Nothing short of a spiritual commitment to live and give as God desires will create biblical stewards.

Southern Baptists must commit themselves to an unapologetic, intentional, intensive, continuous emphasis on biblical stewardship. It is the right thing to do, and it will benefit the kingdom of God. When Christians are healthy stewards, the churches will be healthy financially, and they can be challenged to accomplish all God intends in missions around the world.

In the Southern Baptist Convention structure, since the 1997 implementation of the Covenant for a New Century, stewardship education has been the responsibility of LifeWay Christian Resources. Additionally, each of the Baptist state conventions has a ministry of stewardship education, most with personnel assigned to the task. Their responsibility is heavy and crucial. In these early years of the twenty-first century, it may be time to heed the admonition of 1925 "to make a study of the whole work of teaching stewardship and promoting better financial methods, and recommend to all of the states a program of effort along these lines which cover a period of years."

Southern Baptists who live in this present affluent age surrounded by the benefits of a free and prosperous nation must be taught that everyone will answer to God. With all the blessings God has given, does he not wonder why his people quibble so much about the tithe? Pastors and other church leaders who read this book must hear the challenge to call Southern Baptists to obedience in stewardship.

THE EDUCATIONAL CHALLENGE: REVIVING THE DREAM

Second only to the challenge of developing biblical stewards is the challenge of reeducating contemporary Southern Baptists concerning the value of the Cooperative Program. This book is one such attempt. The Executive Committee's SBC Funding Study Committee noted in 2003:

> While more research is indicated, the factor that appears to
> be emerging as the most plausible explanation for the declining support for the Cooperative Program is a serious neglect
> of Cooperative Program education and promotion in the
> churches. Rather than widespread negative feelings about the
> Cooperative Program, there appears to be widespread ignorance about the Cooperative Program. . . . Southern Baptists,
> especially the younger generations, must be taught the value of
> the Cooperative Program. CP's image must be re-envisioned
> from a "necessary but stodgy bureaucratic finance system" to
> a "dynamic, comprehensive, effective, missions strategy for
> Southern Baptists." Unless Southern Baptist churches are led to
> see Cooperative Program as a tool they need and want in order
> to fulfill the Great Commission, CP will lose support to other
> initiatives that appear attractive but are likely to be less effective
> than Southern Baptist Convention ministries.[13]

The Committee recommended:

> That the SBC Funding Study Committee, in conjunction with
> the Task Force on Cooperation, enlist and engage pastors across
> the Convention in creating a pastor-led strategy for
> re-invigorating stewardship and the Cooperative Program in
> the churches.[14]

The rationale behind the preceding motion is that Southern Baptists have woefully neglected this subject, resulting in widespread ignorance about and emphasis on the wonderful opportunity Southern Baptists have to reach the world for Christ. A massive undertaking is needed now. If nothing is done, the temptation to go back to a societal method of missions support will only increase. Entities, both state and national, will tire of waiting around and hoping that cooperative funding efforts will be fruitful and will go directly to churches and individuals to fund their endeavors. People will choose more immediate but less effective methods for carrying out missions, and the Lord's work among Southern Baptists could be poorer for it.

How can the challenge of reeducating Southern Baptists about the Cooperative Program best be met?

CALLING ALL PASTORS

The SBC Funding Study Committee was not arbitrary when it recommended a "pastor-led" movement to reeducate Southern Baptists. They rightly concluded:

> Southern Baptist pastors are God's called leaders for the
> local churches and, by extension, for the work of the conven-
> tions. As such, their leadership in stewardship education and
> their confidence in the Cooperative Program methodology are
> critical. This Committee commends the leadership of our pas-
> tors to the churches and to the denomination, and beseeches the
> pastors to accept this crucial assignment.

If Southern Baptist churches give greater support for the Cooperative Program in the future, it will be because pastors lead them to do so. One of the main purposes of this present book is to challenge Southern Baptist pastors preparing for the ministry to be aware of the opportunities for world ministry through the Cooperative Program and to be committed to responsible Cooperative Program training in their future congregations. Convention leaders are envisioning a massive undertaking for Cooperative

Program enhancement. Its exact shape is not yet known. But its promise of success rests with the pastors.

REPOSITION THE COOPERATIVE PROGRAM AS MISSIONS

Southern Baptists are mission minded. The appeal to reach the world for Christ attracts their attention. If they can be led to understand that Cooperative Program is funding for missions, they will be much more easily led to give generously and sacrificially. On the other hand, if they think the Cooperative Program is a tax on the church or some obligation to pay for the denomination, they are more likely to be tepid in their support. Therefore, leading Southern Baptists to think of the Cooperative Program as missions has both a theological and a public relations objective.

Is the Cooperative Program missions? This is the theological question. The answer depends on your definition of missions. Some want to limit the term *missions* to those activities involving missionary personnel or travel to a distant place. A more comprehensive definition of missions includes all ministries conducted outside the local church.[15] Under this definition, church work is divided into two categories: (1) local: that done by the local church for the local church, and (2) missions: that done by the local church for the larger kingdom of God. The Cooperative Program funds joint enterprises on behalf of the churches that are beyond the domain of single local churches. Therefore, it is proper to say that the Cooperative Program is missions.

As to public relations, some observers say the word *program* in the name contributes to the perception that the Cooperative Program is bureaucracy rather than missions. There is no consensus on the need to find another name for the "Cooperative Program." It will probably be around for the foreseeable future. But there is a need to project the proper perception. The Executive Committee's Cooperative Program staff has used the shorthand phrase "CPMissions" in promotional material to attempt to connect the Cooperative Program and missions. Some state conventions use the term "Cooperative Missions Program" or simply "Cooperative Missions."

The main public relations point of talking about the Cooperative Program as missions is to remind the churches they are not paying for a "stodgy bureaucracy" but participating in New Testament missions. Even those who distinguish between missions and other endeavors funded by the Cooperative Program (such as educational institutions, benevolences, and so forth) must be careful to convey the "kingdom" value of each enterprise in the Cooperative Program. Every endeavor undergirded by the Cooperative Program multiplies the ministries of the churches in reaching their world.

It is technically correct to describe the Cooperative Program, as did the report of the 1973 Cooperative Program Study Committee, as "a plan for the orderly transfer of resources from the churches to the states and the Southern Baptist Convention for work which cannot effectively be done in the churches." But that sounds horribly bureaucratic. It is more dynamic to describe it as "caring people partnering together to touch the world." The Cooperative Program is missions.

Inspire as Well as Inform

The story of the Cooperative Program, both past and present, is exciting. The problem is that too many Baptists have not heard it or have not heard it in a way that captures their imaginations. One of the tasks of reeducating Southern Baptists is to tell the Cooperative Program story in such an informative and inspiring way that it becomes the vehicle of choice for local church missions support.

Cooperative Program leaders from the national and state conventions have suggested the following characteristics for teaching the Cooperative Program:

1. Humanization. Put a face on it. When speaking of the Cooperative Program, emphasize the human element. Budgets, buildings, and bureaucracies are not the important elements of CP. People are—both the thousands of people (missionaries, church planters, student workers, teachers) who give leadership to the ministries and the thousands more who are recipients of spiritual, emotional, and physical help. Connecting churches via print, multimedia, or personal presentations with real people with real names and faces is an important communication task.

2. Personalization. Make it hands-on. Let the Baptist in the pew see how he is personally involved in the Cooperative Program task whether by praying, giving, or going. The genius of cooperative missions is that even a person of limited means or opportunities can become a partner in monumental mission accomplishments.

3. Compassion. Show the needs. Because of technology, the world has become a smaller place. The troubles of people half a world away

are made immediate. Cooperative Program teaching opportunities must help Baptists sense the dramatic spiritual needs in the world.

4. Productivity. Show the results. Southern Baptists are not merely wringing their hands over the great troubles in the world. Millions of people are being helped. Approximately 600,000 people a year are now being baptized overseas through Southern Baptist missionary efforts. Thousands more are being fed and clothed. Students by the thousands in the USA and abroad are being equipped for ministry through Southern Baptist schools. And the list goes on. These results are even more exciting because they are being accomplished efficiently, maximizing the resources invested by the churches. Those who worry about the "waste" that might accompany a denominational bureaucracy will be very pleased. Southern Baptist missions succeed in their goals for a mere fraction of the cost of other ministries. It is one of the best mission "buys" available.

5. Creativity. Tell the story in an attractive, compelling way. Those responsible for Cooperative Program promotion in Southern Baptist life have begun to take advantage of first-rate communication resources (technical and human). There has been an explosion in recent years of electronic media available to local churches for telling the CP mission story in the churches through video, CD, DVD, Web sites, as well as educational materials in print. Each product is developed with a view to not only inform the mind but also to move the heart.

6. Contextualization. Reach multiple targets. Products and emphases are being developed to teach various demographic groups within the Southern Baptist family (ethnic, age, region) about the Cooperative Program.

Priority Planning

The Future Program Commission of 1925 began its report to the Southern Baptist Convention with this statement: "That ours is a critical situation as a denomination all must admit."[16] They understood very well the gravity of their assignment. The plan they recommended has many facets that should be incorporated by Southern Baptists in the beginning of the twenty-first century as they face similar funding challenges. The

1925 plan projected a multiyear emphasis. It involved every level of the denominational structure. It was given a place of priority, and it utilized the services of the denomination's best leaders. It was designed to be employed at the local church level and concentrated on individual and congregational as well as denominational finances.

As Southern Baptists enter the twenty-first century, it is time to enlist all Southern Baptist congregations in an intentional, intensive, and inspirational study of Baptist heritage, doctrine, missiology, and organization. The objectives of such an effort should be to bring:

- a renewed understanding of and appreciation for the convictions of Southern Baptists and the value of being a part of this denomination;
- a knowledge of the accomplishments, organizations, and opportunities for the kingdom of God through Southern Baptist ministries;
- a commitment by church members to personal stewardship expressed through congregational life;
- the development of the local church's world mission strategy for fulfilling Acts 1:8; and
- a renewed commitment for Cooperative Program participation and support.

Leaders from all levels of Southern Baptist life are beginning to work together to make Cooperative Program education a priority in denominational life. In the summer of 2004, state convention and Southern Baptist Convention executives launched a strategy *"to design and implement a Cooperative Program initiative for local Southern Baptist churches which will result in education about and commitment to Southern Baptist cooperative missions and ministries."* The vision of the strategy is to *"ignite celebration and support among Southern Baptists by telling the stories of how God has changed lives through the Cooperative Program."*[17]

If pastors and congregations across the Southern Baptist Convention will engage and implement this strategy as it develops, it promises to bring new vitality to the Cooperative Program. The prayer of SBC leaders is that the Cooperative Program methodology that has been so useful in the "one sacred effort" of Southern Baptists since 1925 will sustain the work for decades to come.

Conclusion

From Good to Great:

The Cooperative Program and the Kingdom of God

If you are a Southern Baptist pastor or other church leader, what do you tell your congregation about the Cooperative Program? We have endeavored in this book to set the Cooperative Program in its biblical, theological, and historical contexts. We have attempted to demonstrate its compatibility with Baptist principles and practices and to give a cogent explanation of how it operates as an integral part of Baptist missions and ministries. We have tried to examine areas of challenge and change for the continued usefulness of the Cooperative Program. Hopefully, all the information in this book could eventually be taught to every member of our churches. But how can you summarize the great opportunity for advancing the kingdom of God through the Cooperative Program?

The book *Good to Great* by Jim Collins[1] has captured the imagination of many leaders in both business and ministry. Its major thesis is that companies, even ordinary companies, can break out of the pack and move from being merely good to being great. It has spawned others works on "good to great leadership," "good to great churches," "good to great families," etc. It is our contention that the Cooperative Program has the potential, when rightly employed, for moving Southern Baptist ministries from the ordinary, the average, the good—to superlative, outstanding, *great* fruitfulness for the kingdom of God. Tell your people the Cooperative Program can help them move from good to great.

TELL THEM OF THE GREAT NEED

In Matthew 9:35–38, Jesus emphasizes to his disciples the great need of humanity. He was in the midst of ministry and began to be overwhelmed by the vast "lostness" of humanity. He was moved with compassion because they were "harassed and helpless." The word *harassed* means they were like sheep being devoured by the wolves. Jesus was moved with compassion. He said, "The harvest truly is plentiful" (NKJV). In a companion passage in John 4, the same idea is used when Jesus says to his disciples, "The harvest is ripe." It is ready. Don't say in four months. Don't say next year. Don't say in another decade. Don't say when things get better. Right now the harvest is ready.

Lost people are everywhere. They are hurting. They are ready. In the twenty-first century, the words that Jesus spoke two thousand years ago have never been truer than they are today. When the new millennium began, the earth had reached a population of six billion people. Statisticians say half of the people who have ever lived in human history are alive today. The continuous news stories from CNN or FOX News take the viewer to people and events around the globe in real time. The lives and struggles of the earth's inhabitants are not abstract ideas but concrete, visible realities.

Modern Christians in the West have no delusions about the fact of the world's pain. It is as Jesus saw it. People are everywhere, and they are hurting. And they are ready for the gospel. The harvest truly is plentiful. Charles Spurgeon has a wonderful sermon on Matthew 9:38 entitled "Harvest Men Wanted." He says in the sermon that he believes there has never been a time when the world has been dull to the gospel. People are ready to hear the gospel.

Tell your congregation of the great need to advance the kingdom of God. The Cooperative Program is not merely "fund-raising" for denominational programs. It is a lifeline for the most important enterprise in the world. The Cooperative Program is worthy of the attention and support of the church because its aim is the fulfillment of the Great Commission. A church that is serious about seeking first the kingdom of God will find an unparalleled ally in the Cooperative Program.

TELL THEM OF THE GREAT STRATEGY

Jesus said, "The laborers are few." Even as he prayed for more laborers, he envisioned a plan for carrying out his mission. In Acts 1:8, as Jesus was approaching his ascension to heaven, he gave the church a battle strategy. The church would move out in concentric circles starting in Jerusalem and then into Judea and Samaria and then to the uttermost parts of the earth. Jesus saw his church as an ever-moving, ever-expanding, relentless, marching army of evangelists intending to reach the ends of the earth. That is how he envisioned his kingdom's work.

The Cooperative Program embodies this same strategy. While Baptists are ministering in their local "Jerusalems," the Cooperative Program allows them to engage the rest of the world, outside Jerusalem, and into Judea and into Samaria and the uttermost parts of the earth. It is the local church's vehicle for implementing the Great Commission.

We have identified four characteristics (the four Cs) that make the Cooperative Program a thoroughly biblical, unusually efficient, and superbly effective plan for reaching the world with the gospel.

The Cooperative Program is *coherent* rather than chaotic. There is a plan. The Cooperative Program is intentional and purposeful. It utilizes a thoughtful, prayerful strategy. Have you ever watched five-year-olds play soccer? The action in these games often consists of one player for each team sitting in opposite goals while the other twenty players from both teams move in a little mass of arms and legs wherever the ball is. It isn't very artful or effective although it is usually quite energetic and cute. As the children grow older, they are taught a more successful strategy for playing soccer, which covers the whole field and involves a thoughtful plan for actually getting the ball in the goal.

Some mission endeavors, while enthusiastic and well-intended, do not have a coherent plan for accomplishing their aims. They may not lack for enthusiasm, but they are not given to strategic planning or reliable reporting. The Cooperative Program undergirds a thoughtful, coherent, intentional strategy for systematically reaching the goal. It has the advantage of ministries based on sound, baptistic theological premises with oversight by committed leaders who are accountable to the churches for the resources utilized, the goals attempted, and the results achieved.

Second, the Cooperative Program is *constant* rather than spasmodic. As mentioned earlier, when the Southern Baptist Convention was founded, the dream was that it would be a way to "elicit and combine and direct the energies" of the Baptist denomination in America to reach the world with the gospel. The problem is that while it was a great dream, there was no mechanism to make that dream a reality. So, as we have noted, every Baptist ministry pursued its own aims and solicited its own support.

It was an inefficient system then. Those who depend on this "societal" or independent system of support today know it still is inefficient. The leaders of our SBC mission boards often meet with peers in other evangelical missions groups to pray for one another and share what is going on. Those other groups often bemoan the fact that swings in the economy are causing their missionaries to have to come home because they do not have the stream of support they need. They must raise new financial support, and only when it is secured are they able to return to the field. Many times they cannot. Their missionary forces are shrinking at a time when the population is burgeoning.

Southern Baptists can be thankful to God for the Cooperative Program because it is a constant stream of support. Year in, year out, the missionaries are supported. They don't have to come home and spend months of their time trying to get commitments. Our seminarians can finish school and begin their ministries without an undue burden of "education" debt because the Cooperative Program has paid a great portion of the cost of seminary preparation. All over the nation church planters, college ministers, church growth strategists, and other denominational workers give their full time and attention to their tasks without having to take time out to solicit financial support. Southern Baptists as a group partner together and provide that constant support for missions and ministry through the Cooperative Program.

The Cooperative Program is also *comprehensive* rather than isolated. The strategy reaches all across the United States and its territories as well as around the globe. Southern Baptist missiologists have the task of strategizing on how to reach into the parts of the world that have not yet been reached. They understand the goal is the "ends of the earth." They will settle for nothing less. Southern Baptists do not intend to follow a truncated version of the Great Commission. When a congregation—even the tiniest congregation—gives through the Cooperative Program, it is participating in a comprehensive approach that reaches everywhere, everyday, every year.

Recent decades have seen the growing popularity among Baptists of short-term mission trips. Mission trips are useful ministries for Baptist work. I have been involved in several myself. They allow church members to see firsthand the needs of people in different places. They provide opportunities for personal ministry and witness. Participants return home inspired and committed to missions. Many eventually commit their lives to full-time mission service.

As useful as short-term mission trips are, a caution is in order. Congregations must remember that the local church partnership mission trip is not a substitute for the Cooperative Program. It's a supplement to it. If churches are not careful, they will allow their interest in one particular isolated mission field to consume all their time and resources to the neglect of the rest of the world. A comprehensive strategy, made possible by the Cooperative Program, is crucial. It is the foundation that makes mission trips successful. Without the ongoing mission strategy supported by the Cooperative Program, the short-term trips would not be effective or, in many cases, even possible.

The Cooperative Program is *cooperative* rather than competitive. In the early days, the name was spelled and pronounced "Co-operative" Program. It literally means to "work together." It reminds us that we can do more together than we can do separately. It generates synergy. Synergy means the whole is greater than the sum of the parts. The Cooperative Program allows congregations of all sizes and strengths to make a difference in a common task. It reduces duplication and redundancy in mission endeavors. It maximizes resources, planning, personnel, and results. We get more done when we work together than when we work independently or competitively and try to do it by ourselves. The Cooperative Program sets us free from the temptation to control, to be concerned about getting credit, and the limitations of personal preferences and interests. It allows for the unleashing of a myriad of contributors marshaled into a mighty force for achieving great results.

The Cooperative Program is not the only plan for reaching the entire world for Christ, but it could be the most effective, efficient, far-reaching, consistent, missionary funding enterprise in the history of Christian denominations. Tell your church about the great strategy.

TELL THEM OF THE GREAT RESULTS

Only our Lord knows all the eternal good that has been done because of Cooperative Program missions and ministries. Too many Baptists are not hearing about the great results flowing directly from Cooperative

Program-supported endeavors. We need to tell our stories better. You can help by telling your congregation about the results.

Tell them about IMB missionaries Keith and Lisa Wagner who minister to the more than one million urban poor of Santo Domingo. What began as evangelistic worship services on an old stump in an urban slum of Santo Domingo, the Dominican Republic, has transformed into a vital, New Testament work called Los Rios Baptist Church. The church grows in faith and reaches others with the gospel. The church meets twice on Sunday under a tarp in a common area in the barrio. During the week, the members receive leadership training in evangelism and discipleship. The church would not be a reality without your faithful participation in Cooperative Program missions.

Tell them about a Yezidi Kurd we will call Milo (not his real name). Soviet schools taught him, growing up in Armenia, that God was not real. But as an adult, Milo grew desperate. Milo knew that Yezidi priests teach Yezidis to kill other Yezidis who embrace a different faith. For two months Milo went to church, listening to preaching about Jesus Christ. Milo also thought about killing the Yezidi Christians. After a personal encounter with Jesus, Milo became a believer. Despite persecutions, he is a light among Yezidis. He heads a church of Armenian and Yezidi believers. He wrote and compiled a Kurmanji Christian songbook. And because Yezidis love stories, he has written and published parables that flow from biblical principles. Your love for the Lord and commitment to reaching people through Cooperative Program missions supports churches such as the one where Milo met Christ.

Tell them about Carlos and Cristina De La Barra who, fourteen years ago, sold their computer business and left a financially secure life in their native Santiago, Chile, to help start Spanish-speaking churches in Hispanic areas in South Carolina, Indiana, and now Kentucky.

"I am a product of Southern Baptist missions," says Carlos. "I am a Christian and a missionary because a missionary couple answered God's call to Chile many years ago."

Tell them of my young friend Rob who serves in such a dangerous place that we cannot identify it; and about my young friends Brad and Tiffany Morrow who have gone with their small children to serve in Tanzania; and about the thousands of others like them who are serving the Lord, and serving us, to the ends of the earth.

Tell them about disaster relief work. Words can't describe the earth-quake that leveled the city of Bam, Iran, on December 26, 2003. Southern Baptists were able to begin responding within eight days, as teams from Alabama, Texas, and Georgia went to Iran to provide food, clothing, and medical help. The people of Bam attempted to pull survivors from the rubble and mourned the loss of 45,000 friends and family. The Baptist disaster relief volunteers fed about 3,300 people daily in two camps. In 28 days, 102,000 meals were served! Disaster relief helps open doors to minis-try and evangelism that normally are closed. God used these volunteers to touch the hearts of the Iranian people. The same kind of response is also taking place in those areas devastated by the 2004 Christmas tsunami.

Tell them about the university students and campuses that are being reached by the nearly seven hundred collegiate ministers supported by Baptist state conventions. Student ministry researcher Steve Shadrach identified Southern Baptist collegiate ministry as one of the top ten in the nation and the one that reached the most students.

Formerly known as "Baptist Student Union," they are now called "BCM" or "Christian Challenge" across the U.S. They are the campus arm of all the Southern Baptist churches in each state. Nationwide, there are over 880 campuses that have a BCM on it; they touch almost 250,000 very diverse students each year, with about 85,000+ actively involved.

Maybe you've been to a noon luncheon (free food!) or an evening worship service or plugged into their Metro ministry trying to reach all the commuter students in many major cities. Besides the weekly large group meetings and the small group Bible studies, they host weekend conferences, summer mis-sion trips, and an annual Beach Reach each spring break. Many BCM's are tied into Louie Giglio's excellent Passion ministry that sponsors the ONE DAY and THIRSTY conferences for students and campus workers.[2]

The next largest ministry, the very fine Campus Crusade for Christ orga-nization, has many more campus ministers (2,500+) but reaches only about 43,000 students.[3]

Recently, one Baptist collegiate ministry in Louisiana purchased "cricket" equipment and organized a cricket outing in order to attract the more than one hundred international students from India, mostly Hindu, who attend their university. The Indian students are now interacting with the BCM. College ministry is working all across our land.

Tell them of revival taking place in the Louisiana Penitentiary at Angola because of the New Orleans Baptist Theological Seminary extension courses being taught there and the scores of Baptist volunteers coordinated by the evangelism division of the state convention who conduct Bible studies and evangelistic events. In May of 2005, ninety-four inmates and thirty prison employees' family members prayed to receive Christ, and nearly fifty Christian inmates received Bible degrees from New Orleans Seminary. These graduates are leading the "church" inside the prison walls. One inmate named Greg crafted an acrylic plaque, thanking Baptists for their witness. This young man entered Angola as a satanist; he has come to Christ and is enrolled in the seminary program. The Cooperative Program is changing lives.

The Cooperative Program supports thousands of missionaries, thousands of seminary students, and hundreds of workers in children's homes and other helping ministries. All of them have inspirational stories of how God is changing lives. Thousands of volunteers serve every year in Southern Baptist missions endeavors and return rejoicing, bringing in the sheaves. We could interview the scores of professors who teach in seminaries and colleges and discover rich testimonies of fruitful ministry from their work. Tell your congregation of the voices that address the social and moral concerns in our culture through Baptist entities such as the SBC Ethics and Religious Liberty Commission and its state convention counterparts.

All the ministries and entities highlighted in this book are taking the truth of the gospel to a world in need of Jesus. By God's grace, Southern Baptists are caring people partnering together to touch the world. Tell your church that their gifts though the Cooperative Program are producing great results.

Tell Them of the Great Obligation

Jesus said, "Pray the Lord of the harvest to send forth workers into the harvest" (see Matt. 9:38). Those who first heard this plea ended up going themselves, and they went to their deaths serving the Lord. Peter was crucified. Andrew was crucified. James was beheaded. John was exiled. All the apostles were spreading the gospel at the cost of their lives to the far reaches of the known world.

The call comes to us to pray that God will send more into the harvest field. It comes down to that, doesn't it? It finally gets personal. What are you going to do about it? What is your response going to be? We suggest these:

- Pray. Jesus said, "Ask the Lord." Pray that God will mobilize a whole new generation. Pray that God will unleash the call of the gospel on to the world. It may be you who will answer the call.
- Go. There are no remote places anymore. You can get there, and you can communicate, and you can share the gospel. Get ready to go.
- Give. What a shame it would be if Southern Baptists locked up God's resources or frittered them away in an indiscriminate way rather than focusing them and directing them to the task that is on his heart and ought to be on our hearts. Let's make it so.

An official of the Canadian railroad got lost while hunting in Canada in the winter. He was just about to freeze to death. He happened upon some of his company's tracks and followed them until he came to the station house. He anticipated a warm welcome, but when he went inside, there was no fire in the stove in the waiting room. It was nearly as cold inside as it was outdoors. So he marched up to the lone telegrapher behind the window and said, "How come there's not a fire out here in this waiting room?" The telegrapher didn't know that he was an official of the railroad. He said, "Look, mister, I am too busy sending telegrams to build fires."

So the official grabbed a pad and wrote out an order to the home office to fire this telegrapher and send his replacement immediately. He affixed his official signature and said, "Here send this." In just a few minutes, the telegrapher came from behind his cage, with an armful of coal and kindling. As he started a fire, the railroad official asked him, "Did you send my telegram?" He replied, "Look, mister, I'm too busy building fires to send telegrams."

F. D. Bruner suggests the phrase "thrust out" laborers into the harvest, in Jesus' plea in Matthew 9, refers to God's workers who need "to have a fire lit under them."[4] Many Southern Baptist churches need a fire built under them. Congregations must set aside whatever else they are doing and become consumed with a passion for the gospel. Tell them one of the best ways they can do that is through the Cooperative Program.

Mrs. W. C. James was national WMU president in 1925 and served on the Future Program Commission that recommended the adoption of the Cooperative Program by the Southern Baptist Convention in Memphis, Tennessee. Over thirty years later, as she resided in a nursing home, she was asked about that momentous decision. She commented that it was the best thing she ever did, and then she added, "Tell Southern Baptists to keep it going!" Tell your Southern Baptist congregation to keep the Cooperative Program going. It could be the best thing we ever do.

Give of thy sons to bear the message glorious.
Give of thy wealth to speed them on their way.
Pour out thy soul for them in prayer victorious,
And all that thou spendest, Jesus will repay.[5]

Endnotes

Introduction

1. Franklin D. Roosevelt's Dedication Day Speech, 30 September 1935, http://xroads.virginia.edu/~MA98/haven/hoover/fdr.html.

2. Ibid.

3. Ibid.

4. *1845 SBC Annual*, Preamble and Constitution of the Southern Baptist Convention (H. K. Ellyson, 1945), 3.

5. *1925 SBC Annual*, First Annual Report of Future Program Commission to Southern Baptist Convention (Nashville: Marshall & Bruce Co., 1925), 27.

6. Cecil and Susan Ray, *Cooperation: The Baptist Way to a Lost World* (Nashville: The Stewardship Commission of the Southern Baptist Convention, 1985), 54.

Chapter One

1. There are changes taking place within some Mormon circles. For an assessment of these changes and critical challenges to Mormon scholarship, see the summer 2005 issue of *The Southern Baptist Journal of Theology*.

2. Various concessions have been made by Popes since Vatican II concluded in 1965. Other Christians are now often seen as "saved" but still only by virtue of the Roman Catholic Church's dispensation to make it so.

3. There were both General (Arminian) and Particular (Calvinistic) Baptists in England in the 1600s, but by the end of the century, the Particular Baptists made up the larger group, a situation that prevailed until the groups merged in the late nineteenth century.

4. Though I have singled out one group, Presbyterians, for the sake of simplicity, I could make similar comments about Baptist comparisons with Lutherans, Methodists, and so on.

5. On Baptist distinctives, see R. Stanton Norman, *The Baptist Way: Distinctives of a Baptist Church* (Nashville: Broadman & Holman, 2005); Tom Nettles, *Baptist Profiles* (Christian Focus, 2005); James L. Sullivan, *Baptist Polity As I See It*, rev. ed. (Nashville: Broadman & Holman, 1998); W. R. White, *Baptist Distinctives* (Nashville: The Baptist Sunday School Board, 1946).

6. See, for instance, the discussion in Grady C. Cothen and James M. Dunn, *Soul Freedom: Baptist Battle Cry* (Macon, Ga.: Smyth and Helwys, 2000), 9–20.

7. Millard Erickson, *Christian Theology*, 2nd ed. (Grand Rapids: Baker, 1998); James Leo Garrett, *Systematic Theology: Biblical, Historical, Evangelical*, 2 vols. (Grand Rapids: Eerdmans, 1990, 1995); Wayne Grudem, *Systematic Theology* (Grand Rapids: Zondervan, 1994); Dale Moody, *The Word of Truth* (Grand Rapids: Eerdmans, 1980).

8. J. L. Dagg, *Manual of Theology* (Harrisburg, Va.: Gano, 1990); James P. Boyce, *Abstract of Systematic Theology* (Pompano Beach, Fla.: Christian Gospel Foundation, n.d.); W. T. Conner, *Christian Doctrine* (Nashville: Broadman, 1937); E. Y. Mullins, *The Christian Religion in Its Doctrinal Expression* (Philadelphia: Judson, 1917); John Gill, *Body of Divinity* (Grand Rapids: Baker, 1978). I make the comment about Gill's premodern approach due to the fact that some postmodern thinkers have alleged that the recent concern to place Scripture first methodologically in systematic theology is a result of the rise of modernism, specifically the modern liberalism of the nineteenth century. Gill's work predates all of that.

9. Stanley Grenz, *Theology for the Community of God* (Nashville: Broadman & Holman, 1994), 494.

10. Stanley Grenz, *Revisioning Evangelical Theology* (Downers Grove, Ill.: InterVarsity, 2001).

11. By "unusual" we do not mean that Grenz is the only Baptist theologian to take this route. Northern Baptist theologians Shailer Mathews and William Newton Clarke from the early twentieth century and Molly Truman Marshall today have appealed to sources such as experience or to the "Spirit" leading the church today into new "truths," truths that often have no support in Scripture. William Newton Clarke, *An Outline of Christian Theology* (New York: Scribner's, 1906); Shailer Mathews, *The Faith of Modernism* (New York: Macmillan, 1924); Molly Truman Marshall, *Joining the Dance: A Theology of the Spirit* (Valley Forge: Judson, 2003). Timothy Weber refers to Clarke's *Outline* as "America's first systematic theology from a liberal perspective." T. P. Weber, "Clarke, William Newton (1841–1912)," *Dictionary of Baptists in America*, ed. Bill J. Leonard (Downers Grove: InterVarsity, 1994), 85.

12. Gordon Kaufman, *Systematic Theology* (New York: Scribner's, 1968), 69.

13. Morris Ashcraft, "Revelation and Biblical Authority in Eclipse," *Faith and Mission* 4 (Spring 1987), 2:9. Placing the church alongside Scripture as authority is not a historic Baptist principle.

14. *Annual*, Southern Baptist Convention, 1923.

15. B. B. Warfield, *The Inspiration and Authority of the Bible* (Nutley, N.J.: Presbyterian and Reformed, 1948), 133.

16. For such an attempt, see Charles H. Talbert, "The Bible's Truth Is Relational," in *The Unfettered Word: Southern Baptists Confront the Authority-Inerrancy Question*, ed. Robison B. James (Waco, Tex.: Word, 1987), 39–46.

17. Peter Jensen, *The Revelation of God* (Downers Grove: InterVarsity, 2002), 90.

18. Robison B. James, "Authority, Criticism, and the Word of God," in *The*

Unfettered Word: Southern Baptists Confront the Authority-Inerrancy Question, ed. Robison B. James (Waco, Tex.: Word, 1987), 84.

19. L. Russ Bush and Tom J. Nettles, *Baptists and the Bible: Revised and Expanded* (Nashville: Broadman & Holman, 1999), 271.

20. Ralph Elliott, *The Message of Genesis* (Nashville: Broadman, 1961), 14.

21. Ralph Elliott, *The "Genesis Controversy"* (Macon, Ga.: Mercer University Press, 1992), 34.

22. Though this is primarily a reference to the book of Revelation, the fact that it is placed "here at the very end of the only book that could come last in the New Testament canon can hardly be accidental. Thus, a secondary application of this verse to the entire canon does not seem inappropriate." Grudem, *Systematic Theology*, 130, n. 2.

23. I recognize that most in the Pentecostal/charismatic renewal do not believe modern "revelations" or "words of knowledge" are on a par with Scripture, but there have been some notable examples in practice in which that distinction has been somewhat blurred.

24. Timothy George, *Theology of the Reformers* (Nashville: Broadman, 1988), 98.

25. Franklin H. Littel, *The Anabaptist View of the Church: A Study in the Origins of Sectarian Protestantism*, 2nd ed. (Boston: Starr King Press, 1958), 118. I am indebted to James Leo Garrett for this citation (see below).

26. E. Glenn Hinson, "Baptists and 'Evangelicals'—There Is a Difference," in James Leo Garrett Jr., E. Glenn Hinson, and James E. Tull, *Are Southern Baptists Evangelicals?* (Macon, Ga.: Mercer University Press, 1983), 142. It is also questionable whether Mullins would have equated these two concepts.

27. James Leo Garrett "A Response to Professor Hinson," in *Are Southern Baptists Evangelicals?* 197.

28. Cothen and Dunn, *Soul Freedom*, 7.

29. Garrett, "A Response to Glenn Hinson," 198.

30. Timothy George, "The Priesthood of All Believers," in *The People of God: Essays on the Believers' Church*, ed. Paul Basden and David S. Dockery (Nashville: Broadman, 1991), 86.

31. B. H. Carroll, *Baptists and Their Doctrines* (New York: Fleming Revell, 1913), 16.

32. Quoted in R. Stanton Norman, *More Than Just a Name: Preserving Our Baptist Identity* (Nashville: Broadman & Holman, 2001), 139.

33. Quoted in J. M. Dawson, *Baptists and the American Republic* (Nashville: Broadman, 1956), 221.

34. Fisher Humphreys, *The Way We Were: How Southern Baptist Theology Has Changed and What It Means to Us All* (Macon, Ga.: Smyth & Helwys, 2002), 32–34.

35. George, "The Priesthood of All Believers," 86.

36. Ibid., 87.

37. Ibid., 88.

38. James P. Boyce, *Three Changes in Theological Institutions* (Greenville, S.C.: Elford and Job's, 1856), 44.

39. George, "The Priesthood of All Believers," 92.

40. W. R. White, quoted in Norman, *More Than Just a Name*, 152.

41. Curtis Lee Laws, "The Fiery Furnace and Soul Liberty," in *Baptist Roots: A Reader in the Theology of a Christian People*, ed. Curtis W. Freeman, James William McClendon Jr., C. Rosalee Velloso da Silva (Valley Forge: Judson, 1999), 257–62.

42. Philip Hamburger, *Separation of Church and State* (Cambridge: Harvard University Press, 2003).

43. We will examine the biblical evidence in the next chapter. In this segment we will simply take note of historical developments.

44. For an overview of the history of these developments, see Chad Owen Brand and R. Stanton Norman, "Introduction: Is Polity That Important?" in *Perspectives on Church Government: Five Views of Church Polity*, ed. Chad Owen Brand and R. Stanton Norman (Nashville: Broadman & Holman, 2004), 1–23.

45. Andrew Fuller, *Works*, 2:387.

46. Benjamin Keach, *Display of Glorious Grace* (London, 1698), 141, quoted in Tom J. Nettles, "Benjamin Keach (1640–1704)," in *The British Particular Baptists 1638–1910*, ed. Michael Haykin (Springfield, Mo.: Particular Baptist Press), 1:123.

47. Basil Manly, D.D., "Divine Efficiency Consistent with Human Activity," preached at Pleasant Grove Church, Fayette County, Alabama, quoted in Thomas J. Nettles, *By His Grace and for His Glory* (Grand Rapids: Baker, 1986), 192.

48. A. James Fuller, *Chaplain to the Confederacy: Basil Manly and Baptist Life in the Old South* (Baton Rouge, La.: Louisiana State University Press, 2000), 51. The internal quotes are from Basil Manly's "Sermon Notebook."

Chapter 2

1. Gerald F. Hawthorne, *The Presence and the Power: The Significance of the Holy Spirit in the Life and Ministry of Jesus* (Dallas: Word, 1991), 11–96.

2. Ibid., 113–98.

3. Frederick Dale Bruner, *A Theology of the Holy Spirit: The Pentecostal Experience and the New Testament Witness* (Grand Rapids: Eerdmans, 1970), 155–64.

4. Eckhard J. Schnabel, *Early Christian Mission, Volume 1: Jesus and the Twelve* (Downers Grove: InterVarsity, 2004), 401.

5. For a thorough discussion of Spirit baptism, see Chad Owen Brand, ed., *Perspectives on Spirit Baptism: Five Views* (Nashville: Broadman & Holman, 2004).

6. M. M. B. Turner, "The Spirit of Christ and Christology," in *Christ the Lord*, ed. H. H. Rowden (Leicester: InterVarsity, 1982), 413–36.

7. The Gospel of John especially places emphasis on the Spirit as *"inhering in* Jesus and *flowing from* him." Alasdair I. C. Heron, *The Holy Spirit* (Philadelphia: Westminster, 1983), 52, italics in original.

8. An excellent treatment of these historical details can be found in Vinson Synan, *The Holiness-Pentecostal Tradition: Charismatic Movements in the Twentieth Century* (Grand Rapids: Eerdmans, 1997).

9. Howard M. Ervin, *Spirit Baptism: A Biblical Investigation* (Peabody, Mass.: Hendrickson, 1987), 49–61. See also the various essays in Gary B. McGee, ed.,

Initial Evidence: Historical and Biblical Perspectives on the Pentecostal Doctrine of Spirit Baptism (Peabody, Mass.: Hendrickson, 1991).

10. There may be more to the prediction of fire than simply the "tongues of fire resting on them," but this is at least part of it.

11. Geerhardus Vos, "The Eschatological Aspect of the Pauline Conception of the Spirit," in *Redemptive History and Biblical Interpretation: The Shorter Writings of Geerhardus Vos* (Phillipsburg, N.J.: Presbyterian and Reformed, 1980), 91–125.

12. For an excellent, though dated, treatment of the relationship between the work of the Spirit in the Old and in the New Testaments, see Leon J. Wood, *The Holy Spirit in the Old Testament* (Grand Rapids: Zondervan, 1976), 64–89.

13. John Stott notes that there are four parts to baptism, whether it be water baptism or Spirit baptism: subject, object, element, and purpose or goal. John R. W. Stott, *The Baptism and Fullness of the Holy Spirit* (Chicago: InterVarsity, 1964), 15.

14. Some recent Pentecostal/charismatic interpreters have argued that Paul's theology of Spirit baptism is different from that of Luke. See Roger Stronstad, *The Charismatic Theology of St. Luke* (Peabody, Mass.: Hendrickson, 1984), 75–84; William W. Menzies and Robert P. Menzies, *Spirit and Power: Foundations of Pentecostal Experience* (Grand Rapids: Zondervan, 2000), 47–62.

15. If Paul wanted to say that we were baptized "by" the Holy Spirit, he would have used the Greek preposition *hypo* plus the genitive, not *en* plus the dative. Murray J. Harris, "Prepositions and Theology in the Greek New Testament," in *New International Dictionary of New Testament Theology*, ed. Colin Brown (Grand Rapids: Zondervan, 1981), 3:12:10.

16. James D. G. Dunn, "Baptism and the Unity of the Church in the New Testament," in *Baptism and the Unity of the Church*, ed. Michael Root and Risto Saarinen (Grand Rapids: Eerdmans, 1998), 83.

17. Along with the essays in the book edited by Gary McGee mentioned in a previous footnote, one might consult this volume for an analysis of the basic theological program of early Pentecostalism: Donald W. Dayton, *The Theological Roots of Pentecostalism* (Metuchen, N.J.: Scarecrow Press, 1987). On this issue see pages 87–114. See also Stanley M. Horton, "Spirit Baptism: A Pentecostal Perspective," in *Perspectives on Spirit Baptism: Five Views*, ed. Chad Owen Brand (Nashville: Broadman & Holman, 2004), 47–94.

18. Gordon Fee is a Pentecostal scholar who has rejected this traditional approach and opts for the view that Spirit baptism happens at conversion. Gordon D. Fee, *The First Epistle to the Corinthians*, New International Commentary on the New Testament (Grand Rapids: Eerdmans, 1987), 603–6.

19. For a brief analysis and critique, see Walter C. Kaiser Jr., "The Baptism of the Holy Spirit as the Promise of the Father: A Reformed Perspective," in *Perspectives on Spirit Baptism*, ed. Chad Owen Brand (Nashville: Broadman & Holman, 2004), 29–31.

20. John Calvin, *Institutes of the Christian Religion*, trans. Ford Lewis Battles (Philadelphia: Westminster, 1960), 3.1.4.

21. Donald G. Bloesch, *The Holy Spirit: Works and Gifts* (Downers Grove: InterVarsity, 2000), 103. Bloesch also notes that for Karlstadt, "the individual conscience becomes the sole criterion of faith." Ibid., 358, n. 20.

22. Gary D. Badcock, *Light of Truth and Fire of Love: A Theology of the Holy Spirit* (Grand Rapids: Eerdmans, 1997), 92.

23. Synan, *The Holiness-Pentecostal Tradition*, 146.

24. Ibid.

25. Frank S. Mead, *Handbook of Denominations in the United States*, tenth edition (Nashville: Abingdon, 1995), 242.

26. Robert Mapes Anderson, *Vision of the Disinherited: The Making of American Pentecostalism* (New York: Oxford University Press, 1979), 102, 104.

27. W. E. Warner, "Bell, Eudorus N.," *Dictionary of Pentecostal and Charismatic Movements*, ed. Stanley M. Burgess and Gary B. McGee (Grand Rapids: Zondervan, 1988), 53.

28. J. R. Flower to E. T. Clark, quoted in Anderson, *Vision of the Disinherited*, 172.

29. Vinson Synan, "Baptists Ride the Third Wave," *Charisma* (December 1986): 52.

30. Claude L. Howe, "The Charismatic Movement in Southern Baptist Life," *Baptist History and Heritage* 13 (1978): 3:21.

31. Ibid.

32. I suggest that those who disagree read Jonathan Edwards's two books, *A Faithful Narrative of the Surprising Work of God*, and *Treatise on Religious Affections*.

33. One Kentucky pastor from the period told of how he was disgusted at hearing a group of Baptists on their way to a revival meeting "barking like a flock of spaniels." Robert Baker, *Baptist Source Book* (Nashville: Broadman, 1966), 46. He continued, "These people would take the position of a canine beast, move about on all-fours, growl, snap the teeth, and bark in so personating a manner, as to set the eyes and ears of the spectator at the variance. . . . They would start up, suddenly in a fit of barking, rush out, roam around, and in a short time come barking and foaming back." These things did happen, and it is hard to imagine that the Spirit prompted such happenings, but that does not detract from the possibility that around such events true revivals and true conversions were taking place.

34. It seems that Paul uses the term to refer to the aggregate of churches or of believers in Ephesians and Colossians, but those are the exceptions that prove the rule. There are a few other specialized uses of the term as well in the New Testament. James Leo Garrett, *Systematic Theology: Biblical, Historical, and Evangelical*, vol. 2 (Grand Rapids: Eerdmans, 1995), 460–61.

35. Daniel L. Akin, "The Single-Elder-Led Church: The Bible's Witness to a Congregational/Single Elder-Led Polity," in *Perspectives on Church Government: Five Views of Polity*, ed. Chad Owen Brand and R. Stanton Norman (Nashville: Broadman & Holman, 2004), 27.

36. Fritz Rienecker and Cleon Rogers, *Linguistic Key to the Greek New Testament* (Grand Rapids: Zondervan, 1980), 299–300.

37. Ibid., 31.

38. Richard N. Longenecker, "Acts," *The Expositors' Bible Commentary*, vol. 9, ed. Frank E. Gaebelein (Grand Rapids: Zondervan, 1981), 451.

39. Charles Hodge, *An Exposition of the First Epistle to the Corinthians* (Grand Rapids: Eerdmans, 1956), 83.

40. Akin, "The Single-Elder-Led Church," 33.

41. See James Leo Garrett, "The Congregation-Led Church: Congregational Polity," in *Perspectives on Church Government: Five Views of Polity*, ed. Chad Owen Brand and R. Stanton Norman (Nashville: Broadman & Holman, 2004), 158–72.

42. Stanley Grenz discusses the calling of an ordination council from among other churches in a region and encourages this as a regular practice for churches but also emphasizes that this is at "the discretion of the local church" and should not be mandated by a denominational body. Stanley J. Grenz, *The Baptist Congregation* (Valley Forge, Pa.: Judson, 1985), 69.

43. Augustus H. Strong, *Systematic Theology* (Old Tappan, N.J.: Revell, 1907), 898.

44. As we will discuss in a later chapter, associations also have the right to determine just what their confessional documents will be.

45. We might also ask whether this argument for autonomy of local churches does not also negate the possibility of cooperative association. We will take that question up in a later chapter.

46. Alexander Strauch, *Biblical Eldership: An Urgent Call to Restore Biblical Church Leadership* (Littleton, Colo.: Lewis and Roth, 1995), 239–52.

47. Akin, "The Single-Elder-Led Church," 54–57.

48. James R. White, "The Plural-Elder-Led Church: Sufficient as Established— The Plurality of Elders as Christ's Ordained Means of Church Governance," in *Perspectives on Church Government: Five Views of Polity*, ed. Chad Owen Brand and R. Stanton Norman (Nashville: Broadman & Holman, 2004), 269.

49. R. C. H. Lenski, *The Interpretation of St. John's Revelation* (Minneapolis: Augsburg, 1943), 83.

50. Strong, *Systematic Theology*, 915–16.

51. Akin, "The Single-Elder-Led Church," 65.

52. James M. Renihan, "The Practical Ecclesiology of the English Particular Baptists, 1675–1705: The Doctrine of the Church in the Second London Baptist Confession as Implemented in the Subscribing Churches" (Ph.D. diss., Trinity Evangelical Divinity School, 1997), 196.

53. Mark Dever, ed., *Polity: Biblical Arguments on How to Conduct Church Life* (Washington, D.C.: Center for Church Reform, 2001), 98.

54. Strong, *Systematic Theology*, 915.

55. Akin, "The Single-Elder-Led Church," 65–69.

56. Mark Dever, *A Display of God's Glory* (Washington, D.C.: Center for Church Reform, 2001), 23; White, "The Plural-Elder-Led Church," 269–79.

57. Strong, *Systematic Theology*, 899.

Chapter Three

1. See the next chapter for a delineation of some of those efforts.

2. Specifically, today, this would refer to churches that are part of the Churches of Christ, though Disciples of Christ and the Christian Church are also descendants of Alexander Campbell. Campbell adhered to a very strict understanding of and enforcement of the Regulative Principle.

3. J. I. Packer, "The Puritan Approach to Worship," *The Evangelical* (1964): 4–5.

4. For a discussion of the evolution of this movement, see Sydney Ahlstrom, *A Religious History of the American People*, 2nd ed. (New Haven: Yale University Press, 2004), 449–52, 822–23.

5. Everett Ferguson, *The Church of Christ: A Biblical Ecclesiology for Today* (Grand Rapids: Eerdmans, 1996), 272. Ferguson is a theologian in the Churches of Christ.

6. Robert L. Reymond, *A New Systematic Theology of the Christian Faith* (Nashville: Thomas Nelson, 1998), 896.

7. The imprecatory Psalms are the psalms that call for judgment from God to be meted out to some individual, group, or nation.

8. William L. Lumpkin, *Baptist Confessions of Faith* (Valley Forge: Judson, 1959), 158.

9. Ibid., 280.

10. William A. Mueller, *A History of Southern Baptist Theological Seminary* (Nashville: Broadman, 1959), 240.

11. John Gill, *Collections of Sermons and Tracts* (London: George Keith, 1773), 2:371.

12. Ibid.

13. "Keach, Rev. Benjamin," in *The Baptist Encyclopedia*, ed. William Cathcart (Philadelphia: Louis H. Everts, 1881), 638.

14. Tom J. Nettles, "Benjamin Keach (1640–1704)," in *The British Particular Baptists, 1638–1910*, vol. 1, ed. Michael A. G. Haykin (Springfield, Mo.: Particular Baptist Press, 1998), 96.

15. Hugh Martin, "The Baptist Contribution to Early English Hymnody," *Baptist Quarterly* 19 (1962): 199.

16. H. Leon McBeth, *The Baptist Heritage: Four Centuries of Baptist Witness* (Nashville: Broadman, 1987), 94.

17. Austin Walker, *The Excellent Benjamin Keach* (Dundas, Ontario: Joshua Press, 2004), 280–97.

18. Michael A. G. Haykin, *Kiffin, Knollys and Keach* (Leeds: Carey Publications, 1996), 92–96.

19. Walker, *The Excellent Benjamin Keach*, 294.

20. Ernest A. Payne, *The Fellowship of Believers: Baptist Thought and Practice Yesterday and Today* (London: Carey Kingsgate Press, 1952), 92–94.

21. See, for instance, J. R. Graves, *The Trilemma, or, Death by Three Horns* (Nashville: Southwestern Publishing House, 1860), 80.

22. J. R. Graves, *The Great Iron Wheel, or, Republicanism Backwards and Christianity Reversed* (Nashville: Southwestern Publishing House, 1853), 559.

23. James E. Tull, *High Church Baptists in the South: The Origin, Nature, and Influence of Landmarkism* (Macon, Ga.: Mercer University Press, 2000), 48.

24. J. L. Dagg, *A Manual of Church Order* (Charleston: The Southern Baptist Publication Society, 1858), 301.

25. Ibid., 301.

26. Ibid., 12.

27. "Pedobaptist" is simply a term referring to churches that baptize infants.

28. Dagg, *A Manual of Church Order*, 97.

29. Walter B. Shurden, "Associationalism among Baptists in America, 1707–1814" (Ph.D. diss., New Orleans Baptist Theological Seminary, 1967), 1–58.

30. Robert G. Torbet, *A History of the Baptists*, 3rd ed. (Valley Forge: Judson, 1963), 66.

31. Lumpkin, *Baptist Confessions of Faith*, 349.

32. George W. Purefoy, *A History of the Sandy Creek Baptist Association, from Its Organization in AD 1758, to AD 1858* (New York: Sheldon & Co., 1859), 42–73.

33. J. R. Graves, *Old Landmarkism: What Is It?* (Texarkana: Baptist Sunday School Committee, 1928), 38.

34. McBeth, *The Baptist Heritage*, 750.

35. Dagg, *A Manual of Church Polity*, 279.

36. Barry Hankins, *God's Rascal: J. Frank Norris and the Beginnings of Southern Fundamentalism* (Lexington: University Press of Kentucky, 1996), 27–45.

37. Ibid., 27. We will discuss that campaign in chapter 5.

38. I. K. Cross, *The Truth about Conventionism* (Texarkana: Baptist Sunday School Committee, 1966), 10.

39. Ibid., 12. Anyone familiar with the presbyterial nature of the Congregationalist denomination will recognize the faultiness of this argument.

40. Joseph M. Stowell, *Background and History of the General Association of Regular Baptist Churches* (Hayward, Calif.: General Tracts Unlimited, 1949), 23, 33.

41. Of course, in 1950 the BBU broke apart, and many left to form the Baptist Bible Fellowship, primarily because of Norris's autocratic and domineering ways.

42. John B. Polhill, *Acts*, The New American Commentary, ed. Ray Clendenen (Nashville: Broadman & Holman, 1992), 218.

43. F. F. Bruce, *The Book of Acts*, The New International Commentary on the New Testament, ed. Gordon Fee (Grand Rapids: Eerdmans, 1954), 240.

44. Polhill, *Acts*, 271.

45. Richard N. Longenecker, "Acts," *The Expositor's Bible Commentary*, vol. 9, ed. Frank E. Gaebelein (Grand Rapids: Zondervan, 1981), 402.

46. Daniel Akin, "The Single-Elder-Led Church: The Bible's Witness to a Congregational, Single-Elder-Led Polity," in *Perspectives on Church Government: Five Views of Polity*, ed. Chad Owen Brand and R. Stanton Norman (Nashville: Broadman & Holman, 2004), 31.

47. Robert L. Reymond, "The Presbytery-Led Church: Presbyterian Church Government," in *Perspectives on Church Government: Five Views of Polity*, ed. Chad Owen Brand and R. Stanton Norman (Nashville: Broadman & Holman, 2004), 95–109.

48. Akin, "The Single-Elder-Led Church," 31.

49. Longenecker, "Acts," 405.

50. Douglas Moo, *The Epistle to the Romans*, The New International Commentary on the New Testament, ed. Gordon Fee (Grand Rapids: Eerdmans, 1996), 903.

51. Moo takes the word to mean that she was a deaconess but adds that the structure of such "offices" was not well developed at this time. Moo, *The Epistle to the Romans*, 917. Harrison demurs, noting that the word *deaconess* is not used here. Everett F. Harrison, "Romans," *The Expositor's Bible Commentary*, vol. 10, ed. Frank E. Gaebelein (Grand Rapids: Zondervan, 1976), 161.

52. Thomas R. Schreiner, *Romans*, Baker Exegetical Commentary on the New Testament, ed. Moises Silva (Grand Rapids: Baker, 1998), 988.

53. Polhill, *Acts*, 342.

54. Longenecker, "Acts," 458.

55. A. T. Robertson, *Word Pictures in the New Testament, Volume 4: The Epistles of Paul* (Nashville: The Sunday School Board, 1931), 616. On teaching as the essential role of pastors, see Wayne Grudem, "Prophecy—Yes, but Teaching—No: Paul's Consistent Advocacy of Women's Participation Without Governing Authority," *Journal of the Evangelical Theological Society* 30 (March 1987):11–23.

56. Donald Guthrie, *The Pastoral Epistles: An Introduction and Commentary*, Tyndale New Testament Commentaries (Grand Rapids: Eerdmans, 1957), 138.

57. Eckhard J. Schnabel, *Early Christian Mission, Volume 2: Paul and the Early Church* (Downers Grove: InterVarsity, 2004), 1228–29.

58. Bradley Blue, "Acts and the House Church," in *The Book of Acts in Its First Century Setting, Volume 2: Greco-Roman Setting*, ed. David W. J. Gill and Conrad Gempf (Grand Rapids: Eerdmans, 1994), 119–89; see also Roger W. Gehring, *House Church and Mission: The Importance of Household Structures in Early Christianity* (Peabody, Mass.: Hendrickson, 2004), 117–228.

59. Torbet, *A History of the Baptists*, 75.

60. McBeth, *The Baptist Heritage*, 501.

61. Ibid., 581.

62. Hugh Wamble, "The Concept and Practice of Christian Fellowship: The Connectional and Inter-Denominational Aspects Thereof, Among Seventeenth Century English Baptists" (Ph.D. diss., The Southern Baptist Theological Seminary, Louisville, Ky.: 1955), 255–74.

63. D. A. Carson, *Becoming Conversant with the Emerging Church: Understanding a Movement and Its Implications* (Grand Rapids: Zondervan, 2005), 41–42.

64. Bill J. Leonard, "Southern Baptist Confessions: Dogmatic Ambiguity," in *Southern Baptists and American Evangelicals: The Conversation Continues* (Nashville: Broadman & Holman, 1993), 167.

65. Robison B. James, "Authority, Criticism, and the Word of God," in *The Unfettered Word: Southern Baptists Confront the Inerrancy Question*, ed. Robison B. James (Waco, Tex.: Word, 1987), 73.

66. E. Glenn Hinson, *Jesus Christ* (New York: Consortium, 1977), 56.

67. Ibid., 57.

68. Henlee Barnette, "The Heresy of Inerrancy Continues to Plague Southern Baptists," *Baptists Today* 21 (September 1995): 16.

69. C. W. Christian, *Shaping Your Faith* (Waco: Word, 1973), 62.

70. *Baptist Press*, 14 December 1977.

71. Jeff Pool, *Against Returning to Egypt: Exposing and Resisting Credalism in the Southern Baptist Convention* (Macon, Ga.: Mercer University Press, 1998), 179.

72. Neither Wenham nor Durham even consider this possible interpretation. Gordon J. Wenham, *Genesis 16–50*, Word Biblical Commentary, ed. David A. Hubbard (Dallas: Word, 1994), 20; John I. Durham, *Exodus*, Word Biblical Commentary, ed. David A. Hubbard (Dallas: Word, 1987), 76.

73. Claus Westermann considers the suggestion of translating the term as "mother's breast," along with several other novel recommendations but concludes, "None of these etymological explanations accords accurately with any group of O. T. passages." Claus Westermann, *Genesis 12–36: A Commentary*, trans. John J. Sculion (Minneapolis: Augsburg, 1985), 258.

74. Kandy Queen-Sutherland, "Sticks and Stones = Broken Bones, but Words . . ." *Perspectives in Religious Studies* 24 (Summer 1997) 2:144.

75. Kirby Godsey, *When We Talk about God . . . Let's Be Honest* (Macon, Ga.: Smyth and Helwys, 1996).

76. Keith Hinson, "Dilday's View of Godsey Book Entails Strengths, Weaknesses," *Baptist Press*, 1 November 1996.

77. Quoted in Jerry Sutton, *The Baptist Reformation: The Conservative Resurgence in the Southern Baptist Convention* (Nashville: Broadman & Holman, 2000), 239.

78. James, "Authority, Criticism, and the Word of God," 88. I would also make the point that not all biblical criticism is inappropriate and, in fact, that at certain levels, it is necessary. But as we argued earlier, Baptists have historically begun their critical investigation with a hermeneutic of faith rather than suspicion. And so, some of the greatest scholars in the SBC tradition, such as A. T. Robertson, maintained their confidence in the trustworthiness of the text down to the end.

79. "One More of the Same," *Religious Herald*, 27 November 1884, 1, quoted in Gregory A. Wills, "Who Are the Baptists? The Conservative Resurgence and the Influence of Moderate Views of Baptist Identity," *The Southern Baptist Journal of Theology* 9 (Spring 2005):24.

Chapter Four

1. *The Didache* 13, *Apostolic Fathers*, Loeb Classical Library, ed. Kirsopp Lake (Cambridge: Harvard University Press, 1960).

2. *Constitutions of the Holy Apostles* 2.24–35, *The Ante-Nicene Fathers*, vol. 7, ed. Phillip Schaff (Grand Rapids: Eerdmans, n.d.).

3. *Constitutions* 2.26.

4. Cyprian *Letters*, 1, *The Fathers of the Church*, vol. 52, trans. Rose Bernard Donna (Washington: Catholic University Press, 1964).

5. Thomas Jefferson Powers, "An Historical Study of the Tithe in the Christian Church to 1648" (Th.D. diss., The Southern Baptist Theological Seminary, 1948), 41.

6. W. E. H. Lecky, *History of European Morals from Augustine to Charlemagne* (New York: Appleton, 1870), 385.

7. Powers, "An Historical Study of the Tithe," 48.

8. In *Homily 48*, quoted in Powers, "An Historical Study of the Tithe," 50.

9. Augustine *Psalm 148*, *Nicene and Post Nicene Fathers*, First Series, vol. 8, ed. Phillip Schaff (Grand Rapids: Eerdmans, n.d.).

10. Henry Lansdell, *The Sacred Tenth* (London: S.P.C.K., 1906), 1:251.

11. From the *Vita S. Severini*, quoted in Giles Constable, *Monastic Tithes: From Their Origins to the Twelfth Century* (Cambridge: Cambridge University Press, 1964), 21.

12. Ibid., 32.

13. Ibid., 37.

14. "Annates," *The Oxford Dictionary of the Christian Church*, 3rd ed., ed. F. L. Cross and E. A. Livingstone (Oxford: Oxford University Press, 1997), 71.

15. Constable, *Monastic Tithes*, 46.

16. Williston Walker, et al, *A History of the Christian Church*, 4th ed. (New York: Scribner's, 1985), 375.

17. Ibid., 397.

18. Barbara W. Tuchman, *The March of Folly: From Troy to Vietnam* (New York: Alfred A. Knopf, 1984), 51–126.

19. W. E. Shiels, *King and Church: The Rise and Fall of the Patronato Real* (Chicago: University of Chicago Press, 1961), 24–62.

20. Albert J. Nevins, "Patronato Real," in *Concise Dictionary of the Christian World Mission*, ed. Stephen Neill, Gerald H. Anderson, John Goodwin (Nashville: Abingdon, 1971), 474.

21. Timothy George, *Theology of the Reformers* (Nashville: Broadman, 1988), 101.

22. Ibid., 102.

23. Martin Luther, *Works of Martin Luther* (Philadelphia: Holman, 1931), 4:239–40, cited in Powers, "An Historical Study of the Tithe," 129.

24. E. Schling, "Tithes," *The New Schaff-Herzog Encyclopedia of Religious Knowledge* (New York: Funk and Wagnalls, 1911), 11:455.

25. Luther, *Works*, 4:69.

26. David W. Jones, *Reforming the Morality of Usury: A Study of the Differences That Separated the Protestant Reformers* (Lanham, Md.: University Press of America, 2004), 78–86.

27. John Calvin, *Commentary on a Harmony of the Evangelists, Matthew, Mark, and Luke* (Edinburgh: Edinburgh Printing Co., 1845), 3:92.

28. Alister E. McGrath, *A Life of John Calvin* (Oxford: Basil Blackwell, 1990), 111–14.

29. Andrew C. Ross, "Missionary Expansion," *Encyclopedia of the Reformed Faith*, ed. Donald K. McKim (Louisville: Westminster/John Knox, 1992), 242.

30. William L. Lumpkin, ed., *Baptist Confessions of Faith*, rev. ed. (Valley Forge: Judson, 1969), 119, spelling updated.

31. H. Leon McBeth, *The Baptist Heritage: Four Centuries of Baptist Witness* (Nashville: Broadman, 1987), 76.

32. Ibid.

33. Later he was quoted as adding "from God" at the end of each phrase, but those in attendance were clear that he did not do so. Timothy George, "William Carey," in *The British Particular Baptists 1638–1910*, vol. 2, ed. Michael Haykin (Springfield, Mo.: Particular Baptist Press, 2000), 147.

34. Albert McClellan, "Denominational Allocation and Distribution of Cooperative Program Money," *Baptist History and Heritage* 20 (April 1985):14.

35. Robert A. Baker, *The Southern Baptist Convention and Its People, 1607–1972* (Nashville: Broadman, 1974), 97.

36. McBeth, *The Baptist Heritage*, 239–43.

37. Baker, *Southern Baptist Convention*, 98.

38. Ibid., 98.

39. Robert Baker lists five differences between the society and associational methods. The associational method was geographically based while the society method was financially based. The association depended on an identification with the geographical area of the missionaries in question. Second, the association method usually involved some kind of denominational structure which sponsored several benevolences, while the society method was devoted to a single benevolence, that which was identified with that society. Third, the associational plan concerned persons who were members of churches related to the association so that giving was then channeled through the churches. The society method assumed no intrinsic connection between the society and churches. The fourth difference is that the associational approach is denominational in orientation, while the society approach is benevolence oriented. Fifth, the associational approach is "interdependent and connectional," while the society approach is voluntary and independent. Baker, *Southern Baptist Convention*, 100.

40. Minutes of the Charleston Association, 1802, quoted in James A. Rogers, *Richard Furman: Life and Legacy* (Macon, Ga.: Mercer University Press, 2001), 135–36.

41. Robert Baker and Paul Craven, *Adventure in Faith: The First 300 Years of the First Baptist Church of Charleston, S. C.* (Nashville: Broadman, 1982), 401.

42. W. W. Barnes, *The Southern Baptist Convention, 1845–1953* (Nashville: Broadman, 1954), 32. Wayland even urged the elimination of state conventions, calling for them to be replaced with missionary societies. Baker, *Southern Baptist Convention*, 164.

43. Albert L. Vail, *The Morning Hour of American Baptist Missions* (Philadelphia: American Baptist Publication Society, 1907), 100.

44. William R. Estep, "William Bullein Johnson (1782–1862)," *Dictionary of Baptists in America*, ed. Bill J. Leonard (Downers Grove: InterVarsity, 1994), 197.

45. Baker, *Southern Baptist Convention*, 309.

46. Jesse C. Fletcher, *The Southern Baptist Convention: A Sesquicentennial History* (Nashville: Broadman & Holman, 1994), 49.

47. Robert A. Baker, ed., *A Baptist Source Book* (Nashville: Broadman, 1966), 114.

48. Ibid., 117.

49. Baker, *Southern Baptist Convention*, 173.

Chapter Five

1. William R. Estep, *Whole Gospel—Whole World: The Foreign Mission Board of the Southern Baptist Convention, 1845–1995* (Nashville: Broadman & Holman, 1994), 63.

2. Ibid.

3. Robert A. Baker, *Southern Baptist Convention* (Nashville: Broadman, 1974), 247.

4. Joe Burton, *Epochs of Home Missions* (Atlanta: Home Mission Board, 1945), 77–84.

5. Baker, *Southern Baptist Convention*, 228.

6. *Proceedings*, Baptist General Association of Kentucky (Lexington, 1851), 8–9.

7. Albert McClellan, "Denominational Allocation and Distribution of Cooperative Program Money," *Baptist History and Heritage* 20 (April 1985):14. Still, agents were the mainstay of the Foreign Mission Board's revenue-raising.

8. Quoted in Timothy George, "The Southern Baptist Cooperative Program: Heritage and Challenge," *Baptist History and Heritage* 20 (January 1985):5.

9. Albert McClellan, *The Executive Committee of the Southern Baptist Convention, 1917–1984* (Nashville: Broadman, 1985), 43.

10. *SBC Annual*, 1913, 316.

11. Robert A. Baker, "The Cooperative Program in Historical Perspective," *Baptist History and Heritage* 10 (1975) 3:172.

12. Powell, "Opinions and Understandings Regarding the Cooperative Program," 26.

13. McClellan, *The Executive Committee*, 56–70.

14. *SBC Annual*, 1919, 23.

15. *SBC Annual*, 1919, 77–79.

16. Frank E. Burkhalter, "Southern Baptist's [sic] Tobacco Bill Would Pay Their Campaign Pledges," *Baptist Record* 26 n.s. (January 3, 1924) 1:2.

17. L. R. Scarborough, "The One Vital Need Now: A Southwide Revival," *Baptist Courier* 55 (June 19, 1924) 24:1.

18. Ibid.

19. George E. David, "What Would Failure Mean?" *Baptist Courier* 55 (October 16, 1924) 42:4.

20. "It is to be the year [1924] of destiny, the day of judgment, the day of a crown of victory or the day of a denominational defeat." L. R. Scarborough, "What 1924 Holds for Southern Baptists," *Baptist Courier* 55 (June 10, 1924) 2:4. "It will embalm our futures or crown our triumphs." Ibid. "It is to be Southern Baptist conscience year." Ibid. "What a dark foreboding rests over the hearts of those Boards waiting the issues of 1924." Ibid.

21. One pastor from Missouri gave his savings to help meet the obligation of the Seventy-five Million Campaign. "Missouri Baptist Pastor and Wife Give Their Savings as Special Offering to Campaign," *Baptist Record* 26 n.s. (May 20, 1924) 12:5. A Memphis woman borrowed money to pay her pledge. Thomas J. Watts, "75 Million and Future Program," *Baptist Courier* 55 (October 2, 1924) 40:2.

22. "The Seventy-five Million Campaign and the New Program," *Baptist Messenger* 12 (August 6, 1924) 30:4.

23. "Who Is to Blame for the Debts of the Boards?" *Baptist Courier* 55 (June 5, 1924) 23:1.

24. Frank E. Burkhalter, "Nearly 100 Young Missionaries to Remain at Home Because Foreign Board Is Unable to Send Them Out," *Baptist Record* 26 n.s. (July 3, 1924) 27:2.

25. Catherine Allen, *A Century to Celebrate: History of the Woman's Missionary Union* (Birmingham, Ala.: WMU, 1987), 128–29.

26. The failure of the Seventy-five Million Campaign was very significant for the SBC. It would take over a decade for the SBC to pull out of its malaise. But that is not to say that the campaign was a total failure. McClellan listed eight ways in which it made a positive contribution to the work of the SBC:

"(1) It demonstrated that Southern Baptists could work together cooperatively in a great organized money-raising plan. (2) It brought together for the first time the organized forces of the local Southern Baptist Convention, the state conventions, and the local associations into an effective partnership in cooperative promotion. (3) It led Southern Baptists to begin an intensive use of three modern and efficient tools for local church finance—the church budget, the every-member canvass, and weekly giving. (4) It pinpointed state leadership as the group most responsible for leading the churches to adopt better stewardship programs. (5) It proved that Southern Baptists, if forced into debt, could come through with banners flying. (6) It combined all the conventions and their agencies into one gigantic program of cooperation and proved that the Southern Baptist denominational program is the good Baptists do for each other and for the world in working together for Jesus Christ. (7) It reinforced the already existing feeling in the churches that the Southern Baptist Convention provided a worthy channel through which they can witness to the world. (8) It erected a solid base of cooperation and responsibility on which the Cooperative Program could be established. Indeed, it may have been the beginning of the Cooperative Program." McClellan, *The Executive Committee*, 64–65.

27. "A Challenging Call to Southern Baptists by the Commissions of Old and New Programs," *Baptist Record* 25, n.s. (July 10, 1924) 28:4.

28. M. E. Dodd, "The 1925 Program of Southern Baptists," *Baptist Courier* 55 (September 11, 1924) 37:1.

29. C. E. Burts, "The Right Approach to the 1925 Program," *Baptist Courier* 55 (October 16, 1924) 42:1. Burts was even more bold: "We are obeying the Great Commission in the only way possible in this modern world." Ibid.

30. "It is quite evident that there is wide-spread dissatisfaction in our brotherhood over the older methods of an annual high-pressure, 'whoop-'em-up' campaign." M. E. Dodd, "The 1925 Program of Southern Baptists," *Baptist Courier* 55 (September 18, 1924) 38:1.

31. In actuality, this even split has been rarely achieved, as state conventions have generally retained more than 50 percent for their own programs.

32. Albert McClellan, "Cooperative Program," *Encyclopedia of Southern Baptists*, ed. Howard Paul Colson, et al (Nashville: Broadman, 1971), 3:1666.

33. "What the unified budget would become to each church, the Cooperative Program would be to each state convention and the Southern Baptist Convention." W. E. Grindstaff, *Our Cooperative Program* (Nashville: Convention Press, 1965), 5.

34. N. T. Tull, "The Budget Idea Growing," *Baptist Record* 26 n.s. (May 29, 1924) 22:4.

35. M. E. Dodd, "The 1925 Program of Southern Baptists," *Baptist Courier* 55 (October 9, 1924) 41:1.

36. Baker enumerates three such weaknesses: the need for better support of the benevolences promoted by the Convention, the loss of several agencies (such as the first Sunday School Board) due to lack of funds, and the haphazard means of collecting funds for support. Baker, *Southern Baptist Convention*, 402.

37. This is a way for all Baptists to give to "all causes." James L. Sullivan, *Baptist Polity—as I See It*, rev. ed. (Nashville: Broadman & Holman, 1998), 120.

38. Dodd claimed that the new program was "Simple, Sensible, Scriptural, and Sublime." M. E. Dodd, "The 1925 Program of Southern Baptists," *Baptist Courier* 55 (October 16, 1924):4.

39. See the eleven "Recommendations" proposed by the committee. *SBC Annual*, 1924, 68–69.

40. Paying off the debts incurred by the shortfall of the Seventy-five Million Campaign, coupled with the arrival of the Great Depression, compounded by a scandal at the Home Mission Board in which the treasurer embezzled nearly a million dollars, all added to SBC money troubles for the next decade.

41. The Future Program Commission in 1925 recommended to the SBC that "from the adoption of this report by the Convention our co-operative work be known as 'Cooperative Program of Southern Baptists.'" Quoted in Austin Crouch, "Cooperative Program," *Encyclopedia of Southern Baptists*, ed. Clifton Judson Allen, et al (Nashville: Broadman, 1958), 1:323.

42. Barnes, *Southern Baptist Convention*, 230.

43. In 1920 the Convention met in Washington D.C., where it had met in 1895. In 1895 there were 870 messengers at the meeting, while in 1920 there were 8,359.

44. On the importance of and recommendations by the Business Efficiency Committee, see Austin Crouch, "Business Efficiency Committee," *Encyclopedia of Southern Baptists*, ed. Clifton Judson Allen, et al (Nashville: Broadman, 1958), 1:214.

45. Albert McClellan, "The Origin and Development of the SBC Cooperative Program," *Baptist History and Heritage* 10 (April 1975) 2:76.

46. McClellan, *The Executive Committee*, 124–29.

47. Ibid., 127.

48. Ibid., 128.

Chapter Six

1. *2004 SBC Annual*, SBC Bylaws, 7.

2. *SBC Executive Committee Minutes*, February 16–17, 1998, 45–46C.

3. *2004 SBC Annual*, SBC Bylaws, 9.

4. Robert A. Baker, *The Southern Baptist Convention and Its People 1607–1972* (Nashville: Broadman, 1974), 315–16.

5. *2004 SBC Annual*, SBC Bylaws, 5.

6. James L. Sullivan, *Baptist Polity as I See It* (Nashville: Broadman, 1983), 27.

Chapter Seven

1. James Leo Garrett, *Systematic Theology: Biblical, Historical, & Evangelical*, vol. 2 (Grand Rapids: Eerdmans, 1995), 373–92. This is the only recent systematic theology text with a separate chapter on stewardship.

2. *2004 SBC Annual*, Business and Financial Plan, IV. The Disbursing Entity, 23.

3. *1928 SBC Annual*, VI. Relation of Southern Baptist Convention to Other Baptist Bodies, 32–33.

4. *SBC Executive Committee Minutes*, Report of the Budget Process Study Committee, September 21–22, 1998, 14.

5. Cecil and Susan Ray, *Cooperation: The Baptist Way to a Lost World* (Nashville: The Stewardship Commission of the Southern Baptist Convention, 1985), 84.

Chapter Eight

1. Cecil and Susan Ray, *Cooperation: The Baptist Way to a Lost World* (Nashville: Stewardship Commission of the Southern Baptist Convention, 1985), 65.

2. Southern Baptist Convention Associational Directors of Missions Web site, www.sbcadom.net.

3. James L. Sullivan, *Baptist Polity As I See It* (Nashville: Broadman, 1983), 28.

4. Cecil and Susan Ray, *Cooperation: The Baptist Way to a Lost World*, 112.

5. North American Mission Board, Cooperative Strategies Division, 2004.

6. *1995 SBC Annual*, Covenant for a New Century, 153.

7. Ibid., 151.

8. Ibid., 154.

9. Implementation Task Force final report to the SBC Executive Committee, June 16, 1997, 8.

Chapter Nine

1. William Warren Sweet, *Religion on the American Frontier: The Baptists, 1783–1830* (New York: Holt, 1931), 79.

2. Earle E. Cairns, *Christianity Through the Centuries: A History of the Christian Church*, 3rd ed. (Grand Rapids: Zondervan, 1996), 365.

3. Sydney E. Ahlstrom, *A Religious History of the American People*, 2nd ed. (New Haven: Yale University Press, 2004), 189–90.

4. Ibid., 162.

5. David B. Calhoun, *Princeton Seminary: Faith and Learning, 1812–1868* (Edinburgh: Banner of Truth Trust, 1994), xxi.

6. Cairns, *Christianity Through the Centuries*, 365.

7. "Brown University," *The Baptist Encyclopedia*, ed. William Cathcart (Philadelphia: Louis A. Everts, 1881), 152.

8. Blanchard, *Sermons and Addresses*, quoted in George M. Marsden, *Fundamentalism and American Culture* (Oxford: Oxford University Press, 1980), 28.

9. Donald W. Dayton, *Discovering an Evangelical Heritage* (New York: Harper and Row, 1976), 7–14; Marsden, *Fundamentalism and American Culture*, 28–32.

10. Finney's approach to revivals was very different from that of Edwards, the primary student of and theologian of revival from the previous century. Whereas Edwards believed that one ought always to be prepared for revival, the coming of revivals was a sovereign act of God. Finney believed revivals could be engineered in the way a farmer engineers the harvest of a crop by the machines he uses and the techniques he applies. (The farming analogy is Finney's.) So Finney employed a variety of new measures, including female exhorters in the services, harsh denunciatory preaching against specific sins, the anxious bench, and protracted services. See the discussion in Iain H. Murray, *Revival and Revivalism: The Making and Marring of American Evangelicalism, 1750–1858* (Edinburgh: Banner of Truth Trust, 1994), 223–52.

11. Ralph McDanel, "University of Richmond," in *Encyclopedia of Southern Baptists*, ed. Clifton Judson Allen et al (Nashville: Broadman, 1958), 2:1438.

12. James A. Rogers, *Richard Furman: Life and Legacy* (Macon, Ga.: Mercer University Press, 2001), 260.

13. Classes began in 1827.

14. "Mercer, Jesse," *The Baptist Encyclopedia*, ed. William Cathcart (Philadelphia: Louis A. Everts, 1881), 780.

15. Edwin Wilbur Rice, *The Sunday-School Movement and the American Sunday-School Union* (Philadelphia: Union Press, 1917), 18.

16. C. G. Thorne Jr., "Raikes, Robert," *The New International Dictionary of the Christian Church*, rev. ed., ed. J. D. Douglas (Grand Rapids: Zondervan, 1978), 823.

17. Frank E. Gaebelein, "Education, Christian," *The New International Dictionary of the Christian Church*, rev. ed., ed. J. D. Douglas (Grand Rapids: Zondervan, 1978), 332.

18. Dean Kelley, *Why Conservative Churches Are Growing* (Macon, Ga.: Mercer University Press, 1995).

19. Gaebelein, "Education, Christian," 333.

20. H. Leon McBeth, *The Baptist Heritage: Four Centuries of Baptist Witness* (Nashville: Broadman, 1987), 370.

21. Jesse C. Fletcher, *The Southern Baptist Convention: A Sesquicentennial History* (Nashville: Broadman & Holman, 1994), 54.

22. Robert A. Baker, *The Southern Baptist Convention and Its People: 1607–1972* (Nashville: Broadman, 1974), 205.

23. McBeth, *The Baptist Heritage*, 415.

24. Ibid., 633.

25. Fletcher, *The Southern Baptist Convention*, 56.

26. McBeth, *The Baptist Heritage*, 639.

27. Arthur B. Rutledge, *Mission to America: A Century and a Quarter of Southern Baptist Home Missions* (Nashville: Broadman, 1969), 31.

28. Ibid., 32.

29. McBeth, *The Baptist Heritage*, 639.

30. Fletcher, *The Southern Baptist Convention*, 92.

31. Rutledge, *Mission to America*, 212–23.

32. Fletcher, *The Southern Baptist Convention*, 97.

33. Ibid., 99.

34. Clifton J. Allen, "Sunday School Board," *Encyclopedia of Southern Baptists*, ed. Clifton Judson Allen et al (Nashville: Broadman, 1958), 2:1318.

35. Quoted in Ibid., 1318–19.

36. McBeth, *The Baptist Heritage*, 650.

37. Walter B. Shurden, *The Sunday School Board: Ninety Years of Service* (Nashville: Broadman, 1981), 95–96.

38. Retta O'Bannon, "Relief and Annuity Board," *Encyclopedia of Southern Baptists*, ed. Clifton Judson Allen, et al (Nashville: Broadman, 1958), 2:1140.

39. McBeth, *The Baptist Heritage*, 651.

40. O'Bannon, "Relief and Annuity Board," 1141.

41. McBeth, *The Baptist Heritage*, 652.

42. Ibid.

43. A. C. Miller, "Christian Life Commission, The," *Encyclopedia of Southern Baptists*, ed., Clifton Judson Allen et al (Nashville: Broadman, 1958), 1:260.

44. Floyd A. Craig and Foy C. Valentine, "Christian Life Commission," *Encyclopedia of Southern Baptists*, ed. Howard Paul Colson et al (Nashville: Broadman, 1971), 3:1646.

45. Gary Dorrien, *The Making of American Liberal Theology: Imaging Progressive Religion, 1805–1900* (Louisville: Westminster, 2001), 18.

46. William A. Mueller, *A History of the Southern Baptist Theological Seminary* (Nashville: Broadman, 1959), 1–51.

47. Ibid., 22.

48. This was written into the charter of the seminary as affirmed April 30, 1858. Mueller, *A History of the Southern Baptist Seminary*, 238.

49. McBeth, *The Baptist Heritage*, 446.

50. Mueller, *A History of the Southern Baptist Theological Seminary*, 37.

51. Robert A. Baker, *Tell the Generations Following: A History of Southwestern Baptist Theological Seminary, 1908–1983* (Nashville: Broadman, 1983), 111–96.

52. Edwin E. Sylvest, "Practical Work of the Baptist Bible Institute," *Louisiana Baptist Message* (May 14, 1925): 4–5.

53. Roland Q. Leavell, "New Orleans Baptist Theological Seminary," *Encyclopedia of Southern Baptists*, ed. Clifton Judson Allen et al (Nashville: Broadman, 1958), 2:968.

54. B. H. DeMent, "Baptist Bible Institute," *Baptist Standard* (May 9, 1918): 11.

55. Leavell, "New Orleans Baptist Theological Seminary," 969.

56. McBeth, *The Baptist Heritage*, 627.

57. William A. Carleton, "Golden Gate Baptist Theological Seminary," *Encyclopedia of Southern Baptists*, ed. Clifton Judson Allen et al (Nashville: Broadman, 1958), 1:568.

58. "Are Four Seminaries Enough?" *Baptist Standard* (March 2, 1950): 4.

59. "Southern Baptists Gather in the 'Windy City' for Convention," *Western Recorder* (June 5, 1950): 4.

60. John J. Hurt, "Sixth Seminary, New Churches Get Approval," *The Christian Index* (June 6, 1957): 2.

61. www.wmu.com. For more information about WMU, see Catherine Allen, *A Century to Celebrate: History of the Woman's Missionary Union* (Birmingham, Ala.: WMU, 1987).

62. www.wmu.com.

63. Ministry Report to the Executive Committee, 2005.

64. FTE is not a head count but a number arrived at by dividing the total number of hours taken at a seminary in a single year by twenty-four. That is based on the idea that an average full-time load will be twelve hours per semester, or twenty-four per year. The actual nonduplicating head count for each seminary in a year is somewhat, and at times significantly, higher than the FTE. The FTE does not include extension students.

65. *SBC Book of Reports*, 2005.

66. Ibid.

67. www.wmu.com.

Chapter Ten

1. Robert A. Baker, *The Southern Baptist Convention and Its People 1607–1972* (Nashville: Broadman, 1974), 174.

2. Albert McClellan, *The Executive Committee of the Southern Baptist Convention 1917–1984* (Nashville: Broadman, 1985), 79.

3. *2004 SBC Annual*, SBC Bylaws, 14.

4. *SBC Annual*, 1958, 430. See also McClellan, *The Executive Committee of the Southern Baptist Convention*, 202–3.

Chapter Eleven

1. SBC Pastor's Survey Conducted for the SBC Executive Committee, May 27, 2004.

2. The following books contain information on the conservative resurgence: James Carl Hefley, *The Conservative Resurgence* (Hannibal, Mo.: Hannibal Books, 1991); James Carl Hefley, *The Truth in Crisis*, Volumes 1–5 (Hannibal, Mo.: Hannibal Books, 1987); Bill J. Leonard, *God's Last and Only Hope* (Grand Rapids: Eerdmans, 1990); Paul Pressler, *A Hill on Which to Die: One Southern Baptist's Journey* (Nashville: Broadman & Holman, 1999); Jerry Sutton, *The Baptist Reformation* (Nashville: Broadman & Holman, 2000); and Nancy Tatom Ammerman, *Baptist Battles* (New Brunswick: Rutgers University Press, 1990).

3. James L. Sullivan, *Baptist Polity* (Nashville: Broadman, 1983), 174.

4. For a full discussion of Baptists' historic commitment to and reliance on a high view of Scripture for their beliefs, see L. Russ Bush and Tom J. Nettles, *Baptists and the Bible* (Chicago: Moody, 1980).

5. William R. Estep, *Baptists and Christian Unity* (Nashville: Broadman, 1966), 176.

6. Karin Miller, *Crisis Possible If Baptists Keep Giving Less*, AP, September 27, 2003, quoted in the Nashville *Tennessean*.

7. *1928 SBC Annual*, Relation of Southern Baptist Convention to Other Bodies, 32–33.

8. Cecil and Susan Ray, *Cooperation: The Baptist Way to a Lost World* (Nashville: The Stewardship Commission of the Southern Baptist Convention, 1985), 60.

9. Ibid.

10. *1925 SBC Annual*, First Annual Report of Future Program Commission to Southern Baptist Convention (Nashville: Marshall & Bruce Co., 1925), 37.

11. Ibid., 34.

12. *1983 SBC Annual*, Recommendation (3), 46.

13. Ibid.

14. Cecil and Susan Ray, *Cooperation: The Baptist Way to a Lost World*, 123–24.

15. John L. and Sylvia Ronsvalle, *The State of Church Giving Through 2001* (Champaign, Ill.: empty tomb, 2003), 7.

Chapter Twelve

1. James T. Draper Jr., *Authority: The Critical Issue for Southern Baptists* (Old Tappan, N.J.: Fleming H. Revell, 1984), 105–6.

2. Morris H. Chapman, *Southern Baptist Tradition: What Is It?* Response to the Welcome at the Southern Baptist Convention, St. Louis, Mo., 1980.

3. *1925 SBC Annual*, First Annual Report of the Future Program Commission to Southern Baptist Convention (Nashville: Marshall & Bruce Co. 1925), 26.

4. Nate Adams, vice president, Mobilization and Media, North American Mission Board, 2004.

5. "Partners in the Harvest," sermon by David E. Hankins, 1998.

6. Cecil and Susan Ray, *Cooperation: The Baptist Way to a Lost World* (Nashville: The Stewardship Commission of the Southern Baptist Convention, 1985), 33.

7. *1928 SBC Annual*, VI. Relation of Southern Baptist Convention to Other Baptist Bodies, 32.

8. Cecil and Susan Ray, *Cooperation: The Baptist Way to a Lost World*, 33.

9. Ibid., 131–35.

10. *1925 SBC Annual*, First Annual Report of Future Program Commission to Southern Baptist Convention (Nashville: Marshall & Bruce Co., 1925), 35–36.

11. Cecil and Susan Ray, *Cooperation: The Baptist Way to a Lost World*, 65.

12. George Barna Research Group, http://www.barna.org/.

13. *SBC Executive Committee Minutes*, "The State of Giving in the Southern Baptist Convention," report of the SBC Funding Study Committee, September 23, 2003, 108–9.

14. Ibid., 109.

15. Harold S. Songer, "The Doctrine of the Church and Support of Missions," in *Mission Unlimited*, ed. Morris Ashcraft (Nashville: Stewardship Commission of the Southern Baptist Convention, 1976), 305.

16. *1925 SBC Annual*, First Annual Report of Future Program Commission to Southern Baptist Convention (Nashville: Marshall & Bruce Co., 1925), 25.

17. National Cooperative Program Promotion Campaign Meeting, Minutes, September 8, 2004, 2–3.

Conclusion

1. Jim Collins, *Good to Great* (New York: HarperBusiness, 2001).

2. Boundless Webzine, 2004, www.boundless.org, Steve Shadrach, "10 Top College Ministries in the U.S."

3. Ibid.

4. Frederick Dale Bruner, *Matthew, A Commentary: The Christbook*, vol. 1, rev. ed. (Grand Rapids: Eerdmans, 2004), 451.

5. From the hymn "O Zion Haste!"

Index